Lecture Notes
in Economics and
Mathematical Systems

Managing Editors: M. Beckmann and W. Krelle

253

Cees Withagen

Economic Theory and International Trade in Natural Exhaustible Resources

Springer-Verlag
Berlin Heidelberg New York Tokyo

Managing Editors

Prof. Dr. M. Beckmann
Brown University
Providence, RI 02912, USA

Prof. Dr. W. Krelle
Institut für Gesellschafts- und Wirtschaftswissenschaften
der Universität Bonn
Adenauerallee 24–42, D-5300 Bonn, FRG

Author

Dr. Cees Withagen
Department of Philosophy and Social Sciences
Eindhoven University of Technology
P.O. Box 513, 5600 MB Eindhoven, The Netherlands

ISBN-13: 978-3-540-15970-4 e-ISBN-13: 978-3-642-46558-1
DOI: 10.1007/978-3-642-46558-1

2142/3140-543210

PREFACE

This study is concerned with the economic theory of exhaustible resources. My interest in exhaustible resources dates back several years when prof.dr. J. Cramer and prof.dr. C. von Weizsäcker stimulated me to direct my research, at the Faculty of Actuarial Science and Econometrics of the University of Amsterdam, to the exploitation of Dutch natural gas. This issue raised many theoretical problems, in which I got gradually more and more involved. I was lucky to find in prof.dr. H. Weddepohl a person prepared to listen patiently and to read and critisize my numerous attempts to solve these problems.

The actual work on the present monograph started in 1982 at the Faculty of Philosophy and Social Sciences of the Eindhoven University of Technology, in the context of the program "Equilibrium and Disequilibrium" of the "voorwaardelijke financiering" (universitary financing system). I wish to thank here my supervisors prof.dr. P. Ruys and prof.dr. H. Weddepohl for their comments on earlier drafts of this monograph. When looking back, I realize that their remarks and our discussions have led to notable improvements. Also the International Institute for Applied Systems Analysis (Laxenburg, Austria) has made a valuable contribution by offering me the opportunity to spend three months in its serene academic environment in the summer of 1983. Thanks also to the energy group of I.I.A.S.A. and the I.I.A.S.A. foundation Netherlands. The Faculty of Social Sciences of the Hebrew University and, in particular, prof.dr. D. Levhari should be mentioned here for enabling me in the spring of 1984 to discuss parts of my thesis with the staff of the Faculty.

Many others have directly or indirectly contributed to the present result: prof.dr. J. Aarrestad (University of Bergen), drs. Ch. Elbers (Free University, Amsterdam), prof.dr. G. Heal (Columbia University, New York), prof.dr.ir. M. Hautus and dr. J. van Geldrop (Eindhoven University of Technology).

I would also like to thank ing. D. Zwama who has put much effort in arranging secretarial facilities and Mrs. E. Baselmans, Mrs. F. duBuisson and Mrs. T. Pellegrino who have typed out the manuscript. The financial support of the "Samenwerkingsorgaan K.H.T.-T.H.E."is gratefully acknowledged.

CONTENTS

1. *INTRODUCTION*

The present monograph deals with exhaustible natural resources, as the title suggests. It seems therefore self-evident to start by providing a definition of this concept. This is not an easy task. The problem is not in classifying resources of an economic system as being natural resources or not, but in the description of exhaustibility. Among economists there is some agreement that an exhaustible resource is a resource which is not producible, in the sense that no human activity can add to the existing size of it. This classification is not restrictive enough, since land would then in principle be an exhaustible resource, which is counterintuitive.

For this reason, Dasgupta and Heal (1979) add the condition that "the intertemporal flow of the services provided by a given stock of an exhaustible resource is finite". This description seems to be operational and to apply to resources which are generally considered as exhaustible, such as oil, bauxite, copper, iron, etc. However, if the horizon taken is infinity, as is generally done, then one should recognize that, in a proper environment, these resources are in some sense renewable. One way out of this rather embarassing dilemma is given by the following argument.

The problem would be solved if the economic system under consideration had a finite horizon, small enough such that the assumption of a finite flow of services is appropriate. Obviously, then, the horizon could be rather large. It has been discovered by Koopmans (1965) that, in the well-known neoclassical one sector growth model, optimal programs are not very sensitive for the choice of the horizon, if it is far enough away. This turns out to be the case in many resource models as well. And Arrow (1968) remarks that "As elsewhere in mathematical approximation to the real world, it is frequently more convenient and more revealing to proceed to the limit to make a mathematical infinity in the model correspond to the vast futurity of the real world".

We conclude, therefore, that the mathematical convenience of working with infinite horizon models may justify a definition of classes of commodities, not as rigorous as one would in general wish.

Bearing this in mind, we turn to the motivation behind the present study. Economists have intermittently paid attention to exhaustible resources. W. Jevons predicted the end of the industrial revolution in the United Kingdom as a consequence of the physical limits of coal production. Ricardo and Taussig have studied rents in mining. In the first decades of the 20th century economic theory showed almost no interest in exhaustible resources. This could be explained by pointing at the fact that for the western world the availability of such resources did not constitute a problem since the reserves owned by the industrialized countries were considered sufficient or they could dispose of resources in (ex-) colonies at low prices. Even the long-run economic growth literature of the 50's and the 60's has not dealt with the phenomenon of exhaustible resources. It should be remarked here that there are a few notable exceptions. Gray (1914) was the first to formulate a theory of the mine and Hotelling (1931) in fact founded the contemporary theory of exhaustible resources: almost all the issues which nowadays are considered relevant in this field, such as optimal exploitation and free competition versus monopoly, are dealt with. Also Herfindahl (1955) should be mentioned. Not surprisingly, economists's interest in resource problems experienced an enormous upswing as a consequence of Forrester's (1971) book on World Dynamics, and especially by the oil crisis of the beginning of the 70's. Nowadays it is hard to find an economic textbook not referring to exhaustible resources.

A large number of questions has been raised and (partly) answered. These questions have a rather broad range as can be seen from the following examples: when are resources essential; what is, in some sense, the optimal depletion rate of a given reserve of an exhaustible resource in a closed economic system; how should research and development towards close substitutes of an exhaustible resource be directed; what price system could sustain optimal exploitation; what price-paths can be expected when a resource is owned by a monopolist or when the market is supplied by an oligopoly; what influence is to be expected from extraction costs?

Some of these questions refer to resource problems on a world scale or within closed economies; others take into account that exhaustible resources, or at least the withdrawal from these resources, are traded

between economies. In view of the origins of the recent interest in exhaustible resources it is legitimate to make this distinction.
In the present monograph emphasis is put on the international trade aspect, since it seems to be important and since we recognize that global resource problems cannot be dealt with when one ignores international trade. In the subsequent chapter a review is given of the economic literature existing on this subject. From this survey it is concluded that relatively minor attention has been paid to "small", resource-owning, open economies. What particular problems do they encounter? When thinking of Norway, the Netherlands, Mexico and others, several problems are self-evident. These countries possess a relatively large reserve of an exhaustible resource (oil, natural gas) which is, at prices taken as given on the world market, traded and which has, in several ways, an important impact on their economy.
The first question, then, we address to is how the revenues of selling the withdrawal from the resources should be used in order to obtain maximal welfare (yet to be defined), what exploitation pattern should be followed and how sensitive the optimal policy is with respect to variations in expected prices, the non-resource technology and balance of payments conditions. This problem will be dealt with in chapter 3. It is found that the role of the balance of payments is crucial. To be more specific: the results are drastically different according to whether or not there exists a perfect world market for lending and borrowing. Also with regard to the recent financial crises in some resource-owning countries (especially in Latin-America) it seems interesting to examine more closely the role of balance of payments conditions. In a simple model we shall describe the differences in optimal extraction policies according to three alternative régimes with respect to international borrowing facilities. Chapter 4 is devoted to this issue.
A common feature of almost all the models described in the survey of the literature in chapter 2 is that each participant in trade in the withdrawal from exhaustible resources takes the world market prices or, at least, the demand schedules of the resource commodities as given. Hence a partial equilibrium approach is pursued. This line of study is also followed in chapters 3 and 4. It turns out, however, that for several reasons a general equilibrium approach is in some

cases more appropriate. This is clearly so when one is interested in explaining the internationally ruling rate of interest. Other advantages of such an analysis will be given in due course. Interest in general equilibrium models of international trade in exhaustible resources is rather recent. In our opinion we face an unexplored field of important research. The intention of chapter 5 is to make a contribution in this area.

The summing-up of the issues dealt with subsequently, may suggest that definite solutions of the problems mentioned will be obtained. Not so. The models employed are in several respects more general than those used before in economic theory. In this sense some progress is made. But still many questions remain unsettled. To mention a few of them: our analysis is on a high level of aggregation, with respect to technological postulates as well as with respect to preferences; our models do not incorporate uncertainty, which is pertinent to all aspects of planning for the future; finally, relatively few attention is paid to designing mechanisms capable of implementing policy recommendations in a decentralized way. As a modest defense we recall to mind the notable words of Koopmans (1957): "The study of the simpler models is protected from the reproach of unreality by the consideration that these models may be prototypes of more realistic, but also more complicated, subsequent models".

Finally some remarks are in order, concerning the rigor of the analysis given below. Exhaustible resource problems are by their nature dynamic, they have a time dimension. This observation, together with the fact that we shall deal with optimizing behaviour, calls for the use of techniques such as dynamic programming or optimal control. Although these tools of analysis are becoming more and more familiar to economists, it seemed to be useful to add an appendix providing the major theorems involved in the main text of this monograph. This appendix will be frequently referred to. Notwithstanding this, the main text contains quite a lot of mathematics. It is hoped that the attempt to give a formal treatment has not removed the flavour economists seem to appreciate.

2. *EXHAUSTIBLE RESOURCES AND INTERNATIONAL TRADE, A SURVEY*

2.1. *Introduction*

It has been pointed out in the preceding chapter that the public's interest in exhaustible resources experienced an enormous upswing at the beginning of the seventies when the world suffered from the oil crisis and when the Report of the Club of Rome was broadly disseminated. Since that time economic theory has been enriched by an abundant literature. We refer to Peterson and Fisher (1977) and Withagen (1981 a) for surveys and to Dasgupta and Heal (1978) for a standard introduction. In view of the origins of the recent interest it is remarkable that, at least in economic theory, the international trade aspect has only received minor attention. Admittedly the Club of Rome put special emphasis on the global resource problem and if one is interested in the problem of how the world as an entity can meet for example the energy scarcity, international markets do not necessarily enter into the analysis. However, the oil crisis revealed the vulnerability of some parts of the world through international trade problems. Nevertheless some work has been done here and it is the objective of this chapter to survey this. Apart from the merits such a survey has on its own by systematically arranging the results obtained thus far, it also provides an opportunity to point at some important questions that are not yet settled, and hence serves as a starting point for further research.

Two preliminary remarks are in order.

First, the uneven distribution of resources over the world and its implications for international trade have been studied by economists ever since the profession came into existence. Classical papers on this subject have been written by Singer (1950) and Prebisch (1959). The results obtained have elegantly been extended by Kemp and Ohyama (1978). Although not explicitly mentioned, it is clear that the analysis often refers to exhaustible resources. However the exhaustibility is not taken into account. Since we wish to concentrate on the implications of exhaustibility, this type of work will not be reviewed.

Hence also the contributions made by Chichilnisky (1982), Lawrence and Levy (1980) and others, however interesting, will not be discussed. Second, some of the studies discussed below refer to firms trading in exhaustible resources. It will be shown in the next section that in those particular cases firm's optimal behaviour will result in an exploitation pattern that coincides with the policy pursued by a welfare maximizing economy. This observation justifies the convention followed in the sequel to talk about economies only.

The plan of this chapter is as follows. In the analysis a distinction can be made between partial equilibrium models and general equilibrium models. Broadly speaking, the former category deals with exploitation of natural resources in a single economy facing a given world demand schedule. Section 2.2 is devoted to such models. Section 2.2.1 sketches a rather general model into which the subsequent models fit. Section 2.2.2 deals with perfect competition in one- and two-sector models. Imperfect competition is considered in 2.2.3. In section 2.3 general equilibrium models are reviewed. Here demand for the commodities involved is derived within the models and the question is what prices will constitute a general equilibrium in a world with a given number of countries. Finally section 2.4 summarizes and concludes.

2.2. *Partial equilibrium*

2.2.1. A general model

In this section a unifying framework is presented into which the theoretical contributions to be discussed in the sequel will fit. An economy can be characterized by its:

1) preferences,
2) endowments,
3) technology,
4) external relations.

ad 1. The economy is a welfare maximizer in the utilitarian sense. Utility is derived from the consumption of certain commodities. Welfare maximization does not take place in a time-less world but is instead carried out taking into account the dynamic environment in which the economy finds itself.

ad 2. The endowments of the economy consist of a stock of capital goods, a (homogeneous) labour force, and of natural resources.

ad 3. The economy's technical constraints can broadly be described as follows. Resource goods are goods withdrawn from the exhaustible resources. Labour and capital are inputs in the exploitation technology. The rate of exploitation might also be subject to other constraints. Labour, capital and resource goods are combined to produce non-resource commodities. The final two factors of production are perfectly mobile within the economy (i.e. between sectors) and labour is immobile between economies.

ad 4. The external relations refer to the existence of world markets and the conditions that prevail on these markets.

We now proceed to a more formal treatment and start by giving some notation. Time will be denoted by t and is considered continuous, except in some places where for expository purposes a two-period analysis is convenient. The time index is omitted when there is no danger of confusion. In the economy there are $n + m$ productive sectors. The first n sectors produce the non-resource commodities. There is no joint production, so each sector can be identified by the commodity it produces. The final m sectors are engaged in resource exploitation. We shall not make an explicit distinction between row vectors and column vectors; the distinction will be clear from the context. The further notation used is as follows.

$B(t)$ is the amount of numéraire commodities, held at t, to be delivered to the country under consideration at some future date; alternatively, the amount of bonds held at t.

C_i is the rate of consumption of commodity i $(i = 1,2,\ldots,n)$.

C $= (C_1, C_2, \ldots, C_n)$.

E_ℓ is the rate of exploitation of resource sector ℓ $(\ell = 1,2,\ldots,m)$.

E $= (E_1, E_2, \ldots, E_m)$.

F^i $: R_+^{n+m+2} \to R_+$, denotes the production function of sector i $(i = 1,2,\ldots,n)$.

G^ℓ $: R_+^{n+3} \to R_+$, denotes the exploitation function of resource sector ℓ $(\ell = 1,2,\ldots,m)$.

I_i is the rate of investments in commodity i $(i = 1,2,\ldots,n)$.

I $= (I_1,I_2,\ldots,I_n)$.

K_j^i is the stock of capital of type j $(j = 1,2,\ldots,n)$ employed in sector i $(i = 1,2,\ldots,n+m)$.

K^i $= (K_1^i,K_2^i,\ldots,K_n^i)$, $(i = 1,2,\ldots,n+m)$.

K_j $\sum_i K_j^i$, the total amount of capital of type j employed in the economy $(j = 1,2,\ldots,n)$.

K $= (K_1,K_2,\ldots,K_n)$.

L^i is the amount of labour employed in sector i $(i = 1,2,\ldots,n+m)$.

$\bar{L}$ is the supply of labour.

M_i denotes the import flow of commodity i $(i = 1,2,\ldots,n+m)$.

M $= (M_1,M_2,\ldots,M_{n+m})$.

M_g $= (M_1,M_2,\ldots,M_n)$.

M_e $= (M_{n+1},M_{n+2},\ldots,M_{n+m})$.

p_i is the world market price of commodity i $(i = 1,2,\ldots,n+m)$.

p $= (p_1,p_2,\ldots,p_{n+m})$.

p_g $= (p_1,p_2,\ldots,p_n)$.

p_e $= (p_{n+1},p_{n+2},\ldots,p_{n+m})$.

r is the rate of interest on the world market for financial capital.

R_ℓ^i is the rate of use of resource commodity ℓ $(\ell = 1,2,\ldots,m)$ in sector i $(i = 1,2,\ldots,n)$.

R^i $= (R_1^i,R_2^i,\ldots,R_m^i)$.

R_ℓ $= \sum_i R_\ell^i$, the total amount of resource commodity ℓ employed in the economy $(\ell = 1,2,\ldots,m)$.

R $= (R_1,R_2,\ldots,R_m)$.

$S_{\ell o}$ is the initial reserve of resource ℓ $(\ell = 1,2,\ldots,m)$.

$S_\ell(t)$ is the reserve of resource ℓ at time t $(\ell = 1,2,\ldots,m)$.

U $: R_+^n \to R$ is the instantaneous utility function.

W denotes the economy's non-resource wealth.

X_i denotes the export flow of commodity i $(i = 1,2,\ldots,n+m)$.

X $= (X_1,X_2,\ldots,X_{n+m})$.

X_g $= (X_1,X_2,\ldots,X_n)$.

X_e $= (X_{n+1},X_{n+2},\ldots,X_{n+m})$.

Y_i is the rate of production of non-resource sector i $(i = 1,2,\ldots,n)$.

Y $= (Y_1,Y_2,\ldots,Y_n)$.

ρ $\geqq 0$ denotes the rate of time preference.

The model can now be described as follows. The economy's objective is to maximize the social welfare function

$$J(C) = \int_0^\infty e^{-\rho t}\, U(C)dt. \tag{2.1}$$

Here a utilitarian postition is taken. Instantaneous utility is assumed only to depend on non-resource consumption. The utility function U is constant over time. Utility is discounted at the constant rate of time preference ρ. Welfare maximization takes place over an infinite horizon, reflecting the view that society as a whole should not be myopic. Obviously many modifications of this type of objective functional are possible. It is usual to make the following (more or less technical) assumptions about U. It is strictly quasi-concave and increasing and $\partial U/\partial C_i = \infty$ for $C_i = 0$.

The maximization of (2.1) takes place under a number of constraints, whose description is in order presently. Sector i $(i \leqq n)$ produces a non-resource commodity according to a production function F^i, having as inputs n capital goods (identified by the first n sectors), m resource goods (identified by the final m sectors) and labour, whereas disembodied technical progress may play a role:

$$Y_i = F^i(K^i,R^i,L^i,t), \quad i = 1,2,\ldots,n. \tag{2.2}$$

The argument t reflects the possibility of technical progress occurring. It is assumed that the exhaustible resources are not replenishable. Hence there is no combination of factors of production that can add to the existing resource stocks. This implies that the rate of exploitation is always nonnegative. It furthermore implies that total exploitation over time cannot exceed the amount the resources originally contain. Hence

$$\int_0^\infty E_\ell(t)dt \leq S_{\ell o}, \quad \ell = 1,2,\ldots,m. \tag{2.3}$$

$$E_\ell(t) \geq 0, \quad \ell = 1,2,\ldots,m. \tag{2.4}$$

With regard to the mode of resource exploitation several assumptions can be (and are) made. First, one could argue that exploitation requires the input of factors of production. Thus one postulates

$$E_\ell \leq G^\ell(K^{n+\ell}, L^{n+\ell}, S_\ell(t), t), \quad \ell = 1,2,\ldots,m. \tag{2.5}$$

$S_\ell(t)$ playing a role in the exploitation technology G^ℓ indicates that exploitation might become more difficult the smaller is the reserve remaining. In (2.5) the argument t allows for technical progress. It could be postulated that in order to exploit resource ℓ it is necessary to use some of the other resource goods. In the models to be discussed below this is not done, so this possibility is not incorporated here. For further details on the specification of G^ℓ see Heal (1976), Solow and Wan (1977) and Zimmerman (1977).
The set of inequalities (2.5) puts constraints on the rates of exploitation, depending on the efforts that are undertaken. Alternatively (or in addition) one could assume that there exist upper bounds on the rates of exploitation, irrespective of such efforts, due to, for example, geological conditions:

$$E_\ell \leq \bar{E}_\ell, \quad \ell = 1,2,\ldots,m. \tag{2.6}$$

Specification (2.6) (which formally can be incorporated into (2.5)) is widely used since it is easy to handle and for example excludes exploitation at an infinite rate.
Since labour can only be used at home, the fairly obvious constraint with respect to its employment is:

$$\sum_{i=1}^{n+m} L^i \leq \bar{L}(t), \tag{2.7}$$

where $\bar{L}(t)$ is the exogenously given supply of labour.
Next we introduce world markets. It turns out to be convenient to work in discrete time for the moment. Let's take one of the non-resource commodities as the numéraire and define $\bar{B}(t)$ as the amount of numéraire commodities, which in the past (i.e. before t) have been promised by foreign countries to be delivered to the country under consideration, during some future period. Two remarks are in order.

1) $\bar{B}(t)$ might be negative. In that case the economy has a debt.
2) For some applications it might be useful to make a distinction within the set of claims according to the date at which the debts will be redeemed and the different interest rates. We shall ignore this by assuming that if a market for lending and borrowing exists, arbitrage is always possible.

Define $\bar{K}(t)$ as the n-vector of stocks of capital the economy owns at the outset of period t. The value of these stocks is $p_g(t)\bar{K}(t)$. Define the economy's wealth as

$$\bar{W}(t) = \bar{B}(t) + p_g(t)\bar{K}(t). \tag{2.8}$$

Remark that the value of the exhaustible resources is not taken into account here. At the beginning of period t the economy makes a production/exploitation plan. This implies a choice with respect to the input of capital. We require that capital is in loco before production starts. By $K_{df}(t)$ we denote the stocks of capital sold abroad at the beginning of period t and $K_{fd}(t)$ is bought abroad. Hence denoting by B(t) the amount of claims after these transactions, we have:

$$B(t) = \bar{B}(t) + p_g(t)(K_{df}(t) - K_{fd}(t)). \tag{2.9}$$

Therefore the stocks of capital that are going to be used in period's t domestic production/exploitation equal

$$K(t) = \bar{K}(t) + K_{fd}(t) - K_{df}(t). \tag{2.10}$$

After production and exploitation during period t, trade takes place at prices p(t+1) and the economy receives interest on its claim. Hence

$$\bar{B}(t+1) = B(t) + p_g(t+1)(Y(t) - C(t) - I(t)) +$$

$$+ r(t)B(t) + p_e(t+1)(E(t) - R(t)), \qquad (2.11)$$

where the final term refers to the balance of resource exports. At the end of period t the stocks of capital are

$$\bar{K}(t+1) = K(t) + I(t). \qquad (2.12)$$

Then again trade takes place in capital goods:

$$B(t+1) = \bar{B}(t+1) + p_g(t+1)(K_{df}(t+1) - K_{fd}(t+1)). \qquad (2.13)$$

$$K(t+1) = \bar{K}(t+1) + K_{fd}(t+1) - K_{df}(t+1). \qquad (2.14)$$

The surplus on the current account equals B(t+1) - B(t), or, alternatively, $\bar{B}(t+1) - \bar{B}(t)$. The change in the economy's wealth (after trade in capital goods) is easily seen to equal

$$B(t+1) - B(t) + p_g(t+1)K(t+1) - p_g(t)K(t) =$$

$$= p_g(t+1)(Y(t) - C(t)) + r(t)(B(t) + p_g(t)K(t)) + p_e(t+1)$$

$$((E(t) - R(t)) + (p_g(t+1) - p_g(t))K(t) - r(t)p_g(t)K(t). \qquad (2.15)$$

For continuous time we arrive at

$$\dot{W} = p_g(Y-C) + r(W-p_gK) + p_e(E-R) + \dot{p}_g K. \qquad (2.16)$$

Now several possibilities arise with respect to the current account of the balance of payments.

A. One extreme position is that, for example for institutional reasons, the economy requires a permanent equilibrium on the current account: B(t) is constant over time. In the contributions discussed below this case is specified by requiring B(t) = 0. If there is only one type of capital good, then

$$\dot{K} = I, \tag{2.17}$$

and since this commodity is by definition the numéraire it follows from (2.15):

$$I = Y - C + p_e(E-R). \tag{2.18}$$

If there are more types of capital then (2.9) allows for discontinuities in the time-path of each individual type.
The case B(t) ≠ 0, but constant, is not found in the literature.

B. The other extreme position is that neither the economy nor the world needs to care about the economy's current account. As such this would in view of the objective functional obviously lead to borrowing at unbounded amounts. Therefore, in order to have an amenable model one is in need of some constraint that would prevent the economy from behaving in this way. In principle a large number of possibilities is open but we shall consider here only the constraint that is used in the literature almost everywhere. It says that the economy can lend and borrow as much as it wants provided it submits plans such that in the limit its wealth, defined above, is positive:

$$\lim_{t\to\infty} W(t) \geqq 0. \tag{2.19}$$

Alternatively one may require that in the limit discounted wealth is positive:

$$\lim_{t\to\infty} W(t)e^{-\int_0^t r(\tau)d\tau} \geqq 0. \tag{2.20}$$

To see how this works out, define q(t) as

$$q(t) = e^{-\int_0^t r(\tau)d\tau} \tag{2.21}$$

Premultiply (2.16) by q(t) and integrate. It then follows that:

$$W_0 + \int_0^\infty (q(t)p_g(Y-C-r(t)K) + q(t)p_e(E-R) + q(t)\dot{p}_g K)dt \geqq 0, \tag{2.22}$$

where W_0 is the initial value of wealth. Here it should be understood that in (2.22) the interest rate and the prices are primarily the interest rate and the prices the economy at hand expects to prevail in the future but that of course these expectations should not conflict with those held by the lenders.
Condition (2.22) is very convenient since it allows for the application of the separation theorem, at least for some likely cases. Assume that the economy's expectations with respect to the interest rate and the prices do not depend on the planned activities on the part of resource exploitation. This occurs for example when the world markets for resource commodities are competitive as well as the markets for capital goods used in exploitation, and when the numéraire market is competitive. Then a necessary condition for welfare maximization is profit maximizing from resource activities. This is easily seen as follows. Formula (2.22) can be rewritten as:

$$\int_0^\infty q(t)p_g\, C\, dt \leqq \int_0^\infty q(t)p_g(Y - rK_g - p_e R)dt +$$
$$+ \int_0^\infty q(t)(p_e E - rp_g K_e)dt + \int_0^\infty q(t)\dot{p}_g\, K\, dt + W_0, \tag{2.23}$$

where K_g is the n-vector of capital goods employed in the non-resource sectors and K_e is the n-vector of capital goods employed in the resource sectors. Now suppose the statement is false so that the welfare maximizing trajectory of the economy does not maximize the second term in the right hand side of (2.23). Then we obtain a contradiction since by increasing this term, which is possible by assumption, we can enlarge the region in which C lies and since U is increasing in C this is preferred. An immediate consequence of this theorem is that if one is only interested in optimal resource exploitation, one can restrict oneself to the problem of profit maximization from resource activities, knowing that optimal resource management does not depend on any of the parameters of the welfare functional.

This completes our description of the general model. When the initial stocks of capital and wealth are given as well as the economy's expectations with respect to prices and interest rate, the problem is clearly set and can, under appropriate assumptions with respect to the economy's technology, be tackled. Nevertheless a few final remarks are in order.

1) We have neglected depreciation. This might be looked upon as a serious omission. If however depreciation of capital goods is considered as an exponential process, as is usually done in this type of literature, the model needs only a slight modification.

2) It has been assumed that there exist world markets for all commodities involved, at least as far as commodity flows are considered. If a market for some commodity flow does not exist, this can, in the model presented above, easily be taken care of by putting imports and exports of such a commodity equal to zero by definition.

The question becomes more serious when we turn to markets for stocks. Chapter 3 will elaborate on this matter. It will be shown there that in the case of a perfect market for borrowing and lending no difficulties arise. When the current account of the balance of payments is required to equilibriate, then, in the presence of markets where property rights on capital stocks or resource stocks are traded, the models will give outcomes different from the case where such markets are absent. In this chapter the latter assumption is made throughout. Therefore the condition of equilibrium on the current account can be written as:

$$p(X - M) = 0, \tag{2.24}$$

where it should be recalled that X and M are flows.

For the alternative condition under B) we have

$$\int_0^\infty q(t)p(X-M)\,dt + \int_0^\infty q(t)\dot{p}_g K\,dt + W_o \geq 0. \tag{2.25}$$

2.2.2. Perfect competition

In this subsection a survey is given of partial equilibrium models of international trade involving exhaustible resources, where the economies under consideration act as price-takers. Attention is paid first to some contributions where there is at most one non-resource sector explicitly mentioned. Subsequently, two-sector models will be discussed. The models presented here describe the case of one exhaustible resource. Therefore in (2.2) - (2.6) n = m = 1 and we shall omit indices where there is no danger of confusion. Obvious conditions such as

$$\int_0^\infty E(t)dt \leqq S_o,$$

$$E(t) \geqq 0,$$

will hereafter not be mentioned. Also other nonnegativity constraints will be omitted.

The model studied by Vousden (1974) looks as follows:

$$\max_C J(C),$$

subject to

$$Y = F(L^1), \tag{2.26}$$

$$E = G(L^2), \tag{2.27}$$

$$L^1 + L^2 = \bar{L}(t) = \bar{L}, \tag{2.28}$$

$$C = Y + p_e E. \tag{2.29}$$

The only input in production is labour of which there is inelastic and constant supply $\bar{L}$, L^2 is devoted to exploitation and L^1 to non-resource production. Referring to our general model we have $p = (p_g, p_e) = (1, p_e)$. Here p_e is assumed to be constant. Equation (2.29) reflects the requirement that the current account of the balance of payments equilibriates at all instants of time:

$$p_g(X_g - M_g) = Y - C, \tag{2.30}$$

$$p_e(X_e - M_e) = p_e E, \tag{2.31}$$

$$p(X - M) = 0. \tag{2.32}$$

Before giving the results some *technical assumptions* should be listed. G and F are such that the transformation curve is strictly concave: G and F are strictly quasi-concave increasing functions for example. The outcomes can now be summarized as follows:

a) if $F'(\bar{L}) > p_e G'(0)$, then exploitation will never take place. This is obvious since in the case at hand marginal revenue in the non-resource sector is larger than in the resource industry for all possible allocations of labour.
b) if $F'(0) / G'(\bar{L}) > p_e > F'(\bar{L}) / G'(0)$, there will occur simultaneous non-resource production and exploitation initially. After finite time the economy specializes in non-resource production. The interpretation of this result is not straightforward. It is however easily seen that the second inequality implies that for some input of labour exploitation will be profitable. Hence during some interval of time exploitation takes place. The first inequality guarantees that the economy does not specialize in exploitation.

These results occur when the rate of time preference is positive. If it equals zero the optimal program is indeterminate. Finally, Vousden points at the fact that if the resource is competitively owned (i.e. there are many individuals each exploiting part of the resource), the exploitation pattern will in general differ from the socially optimal one. This might for example be due to discount rates different from the social rate of time preference. He then shows that imposing a tax per unit of extraction induces the competitive owners to exploit in the socially optimal way.
Two remarks should be made. Here (i.e. in our version of the model) it is assumed that the resource good does not directly attribute to

social welfare. By doing so, Vousden's contribution is not given full justice since in his set-up the resource good is incorporated in the instantaneous utility function U. However, we do not think that this refinement offers many new insights. For completeness it should also be mentioned that in Vousden's model the economy's horizon is finite. The results given here apply to the modified model with an infinite horizon.

Kemp and Suzuki (1975) generalize the previous model in two respects:

i) it is assumed that the resource good is an input in non-resource production. Hence:

$$Y = F(L^1, R). \tag{2.33}$$

ii) the efforts to be made to extract the resource depend on the remaining stock. This is specified by:

$$E = L^2\, G(S). \tag{2.34}$$

Also here the supply of labour is inelastic and constant so that (2.28) holds. In view of (2.33), (2.29) should be modified:

$$C = Y + p_e(E - R). \tag{2.35}$$

In first instance p_e is assumed to be constant. The *technical assumptions* are:
F is quasi-concave, exhibits constant returns to scale and satisfies the so-called Inada conditions: $F'(L^1/R,1) = 0$ for $L^1/R = \infty$, $F^1(L^1/R,1) = \infty$ for $L^1/R = 0$. G is concave, $G(0) = 0$, $G'(0) = \infty$, $G(\infty) = \infty$, $G'(\infty) = 0$. This merely means that exploitation becomes more difficult the more has already been extracted.
Under these conditions it is shown that if the initial size of the resource is 'small' no resource activities will be undertaken at all. This can easily be seen. First notice that C can be written as $wL^1 + p_e L^2 G(S)$, where w is a given constant. This is due to the constant returns to scale property of F. If $w > p_e G(S)$ it is optimal to

allocate all labour to the non-resource sector. This defines the critical value of the stock of the resource. It follows immediately that the resource will not be exhausted. If the initial stock is large ($w < p_e G(S_o)$) it will be extracted at the maximal rate until the critical value is reached. Hence production is always specialized. Again, this is due to the constant returns to scale property. The optimal exploitation trajectory is also rather sensitive to variations of the expected time path of world market prices of the resource commodity. A few remarks are devoted to the non-unrealistic case when prices grow exponentially. Then eventually both resource and non-resource activities will be carried out simultaneously and the resource stock approaches zero. This is what one would expect: exponential growth of the resource price lowers the critical value of the resource.

Long (1974) is the first to introduce capital. There is only one type of it, so indices can be omitted here. Capital is a necessary input in exploitation. No other inputs are required:

$$E = G(K). \tag{2.36}$$

Two types of exploitation functions are considered. They are described in the following *technical assumptions*:

i) the first type is strictly concave with $G(0) = 0$ (figure 2.1.a);

ii) the second type is strictly concave for all K larger than some $\bar{K}$ (> 0) and $G(K) = 0$ for $K \leq \bar{K}$. Here $\bar{K}$ reflects set-up costs. See figure 2.1.b.

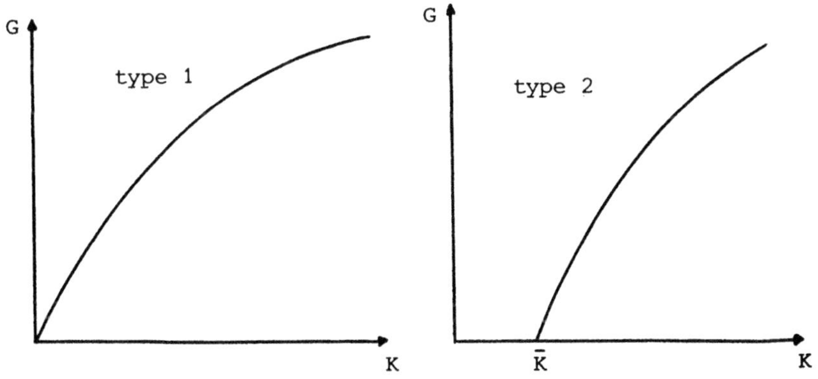

figure 2.1.a. figure 2.1.b.

For capital services there exists a world market. The economy owns a fixed stock of capital W, which at the world market earns a rental rate r_o. If the economy is a net borrower on the world market, the rental rate charged is non-decreasing as more capital is borrowed. Formally, let $r(K-W)$ be the rental rate when $K-W$ is borrowed. For $W > K$, $r(K-W) = r_o$; for $K > W$, $r'(K-W) > 0$. Then Long defines

$$\phi(K) = r_o W + r(K-W) * (K-W). \tag{2.37}$$

$\phi(K)$ is called the social cost of capital used. Subsequently Long formulates the economy's problem as follows:

$$\underset{T,C,K}{\text{maximize}}\ J(C) := \int_0^T e^{-\rho t}\, U(C)\,dt, \tag{2.38}$$

subject to

$$\int_0^T e^{-\delta t}\, p_g C\,dt \leqq \int_0^T e^{-\delta t}(G(K) - \phi(K))\,dt. \tag{2.39}$$

Here C is a vector of consumer goods to be bought on the world market at (constant) prices p_g. T is the time horizon, to be determined endogenously and δ is the 'market rate of discount'. Remark that the exploited commodity serves as the numéraire.

It seems to us that the problem is not well formulated and that the model is inconsistent in some respects . Suppose the economy never engages in exploitation. Then $G(K) = \phi(K) = 0$. From (2.39) this implies that the budget is nil. On the other hand, however, it is assumed that the economy owns a stock of capital W at the outset. Therefore to the right hand side of (2.39) should be added

$$\int_0^T e^{-\delta t}\, r_o W\,dt.$$

In the previous section we have seen that the solution of the problem posed is such that the right hand side of (2.39) is maximized, subject to the resource constraints: the economy will wish to consume from a budget as large as possible. Hence exclusive attention is paid to the problem of optimal exploitation. Assuming that there exists $K > 0$ with $G(K) > \phi(K)$ and that ϕ is convex, we can summarize the results as follows.

If the market rate of interest δ equals zero, then the original problem of utility maximization does not have a solution since the term that is to be added to (2.39) is unbounded (recall that T is to be determined endogenously), unless of course W = 0. So let's consider the case W = 0. Then for type 1 exploitation functions no optimum exists: the economy should choose the rate of exploitation as close to zero as possible. For type 2 exploitation functions however an optimum does exist. The rate of exploitation is either zero or such that the average costs of extraction equal the marginal costs of extraction. The time profile of exploitation is indeterminate.
When the market rate of interest is positive, an optimum exists for both types of exploitation functions. For both cases the rate of exploitation decreases, towards zero for type 1 functions and to E* (> 0) for type 2 functions, where E* is the rate of exploitation minimizing average costs of exploitation. The resource is exhausted in finite time. The larger the market rate of interest the sooner exhaustion takes place.

Withagen (1981 b) studies a similar problem. But now the world market for capital services is perfect, implying that the price the economy has to pay does not depend on the amount of services demanded. Special attention is paid to the sensitivity of optimal exploitation patterns to the expected growth rates of world market prices. This, together with the assumption of the perfection of the capital market, justifies to consider the following problem:

$$\underset{K}{\text{maximize}} \int_0^\infty e^{-rt}(p_e(t)G(K) - p_k(t)K)dt, \tag{2.40}$$

subject to the usual constraints with respect to the finiteness of the resource. Here r is the constant rate of interest. It is assumed that the economy has firm and fixed expectations of the growth rates of the world market prices:

$$\dot{p}_e/p_e = \gamma, \quad \dot{p}_k/p_k = \psi \tag{2.41}$$

where γ and ψ are given constants. *Technical assumptions* on G are: G(0) = 0 and G is strictly concave. The analysis is rather tedious and lengthy. Let's therefore restrict ourselves here and suppose that in addition to the existence of a perfect world market for lending and borrowing there exists a perfect world market for the type of capital goods used in exploitation. Arbitrage is possible now. Hence $r = \psi$, otherwise this market would not equilibriate. Obviously, no optimal program exists when $\gamma > r$ since under this condition the economy will find it profitable to postpone exploitation forever. If $\gamma = r$ (and supposing $p_e(0)G(K) > p_k(0)K$ for some $K > 0$) no optimum exists either: the economy will wish to exploit at a level as low as possible. Finally, if $\gamma < r$ exploitation will come to an end within finite time. Possibly something is left in the ground. It follows from the analysis that in considering models of open economies with exhaustible resources and perfect world markets, one should be careful in choosing price expectations of the relevant variables.

The problem of international borrowing is also tackled by Aarrestad (1979). Physical capital is absent from the model, so the economy's wealth only consists of bonds (B) yielding a constant rate of interest r. The resource good is exported at the price p_e and the consumer good is imported at the price p_g. Hence (see (2.16)):

$$\dot{B} = p_e E + rB - p_g C. \tag{2.40}$$

It is convenient to present the rest of the model in its original form:

$$\underset{C,E}{\text{maximize}}\ J = \int_0^T e^{-\rho t}\, U(C/\bar{L})dt, \tag{2.41}$$

subject to

$$E \leqq \bar{E}e^{nt}, \tag{2.42}$$

$$\dot{B} \geqq -\bar{z}e^{nt} + nBe^{nt}, \quad \text{if } B \leqq 0, \tag{2.43}$$

$$B(T) \geqq 0, \quad B(0) = 0, \tag{2.44}$$

$$\dot{p}_e/p_e = \gamma, \quad \dot{p}_g/p_g = \psi, \tag{2.45}$$

$$\bar{L} = L_o e^{nt}. \tag{2.46}$$

The most notable feature of the model is given by inequality (2.43). It says that if the economy has a debt (i.e. when the amount of bonds held is negative) the per capita debt may increase but for institutional reasons this increase is bounded by some positive number $\bar{z}$. Aarrestad is taking a position here between requiring permanent equilibrium on the current account and assuming a perfect world market for lending and borrowing.

Some remarkable aspects of this model should be mentioned. First consider (2.42). The upper bound on E is motivated by technical reasons. Why then should the upper bound grow at the rate of population growth n? One possible explanation is that this growth rate coincides with the rate of technical progress. Such an explanation is however highly artificial (and is not given by the author). Fortunately the qualitative results do not require n to be positive. Second, crucial in the formulation of the model is the fixed finite horizon (T). It is straightforward to see that an optimal strategy gives B(T) = 0. After T the economy is left with nothing. Aarrestad 'solves' this problem by introducing a constant exogenous stream of consumer goods which the economy has costlessly at its disposal. Such a solution is not entirely satisfactory. For a general discussion on horizon problems see Takayama (1974).

The results are summarized as follows (for n = 0, $T > S_o/\bar{E}$ and U with constant elasticity of marginal utility).

a) When the expected growth rate of the resource price (γ) is larger than the interest rate, it is optimal to extract at the maximal rate at the end of the planning period. In the first part of the planning period the economy is borrowing abroad and under plausible assumptions (e.g. $\psi \geq 0$) borrowing is increasing, possibly at the maximal rate. Repayment takes place at the end of the planning period. If the rate of time preference is relatively large (small), consumption is decreasing (increasing) during the planning period.

b) When the growth rate of the resource price is smaller than the rate of interest, extraction takes place at the beginning of the planning period, at the maximal rate. During this period the economy lends abroad. Afterwards the bonds and the returns on them are used for consumption purposes. Consumption is increasing over time if and only if $\rho > r-\psi$.

In the articles described so far, the accumulation of physical capital is neglected. It seems however very unrealistic to make such a simplification. A second contribution by Aarrestad (1978) is to be considered very important: its main objective is to argue that there is a 'need for an integrated model of the economy where optimal savings and resource extraction can be determined simultaneously'. Defining net revenues from exploitation by Q and denoting the rate of depreciation by μ we represent the model by

$$\underset{C,s,E}{\text{maximize}}\ J := \int_0^\infty e^{-\rho t}\, U(C/\bar{L})dt, \tag{2.47}$$

subject to

$$Y = F(K,L), \tag{2.48}$$

$$C = (1-s)(Y+Q) + \bar{C}e^{nt}, \tag{2.49}$$

$$\dot{K} = s(Y+Q) - \mu K, \tag{2.50}$$

$$0 \leqq s \leqq 1, \tag{2.51}$$

$$E \leqq \bar{E}e^{nt}, \tag{2.52}$$

$$L = \bar{L} = L_o\, e^{nt}, \tag{2.53}$$

Unfortunately we must again start by pointing at some peculiar features of the model. With respect to the *rate of population growth*, we already commented on specification (2.52). In this particular model there are two additional reasons for rejecting a positive growth rate of the population. The first reason refers to the formulation of the problem as an infinite horizon problem. This obviously does not allow for a constant positive growth rate. The second reason has to do with the specification of extraction costs. Aarrestad defines per capita costs as $b(E/\bar{L})$. Here b does not have t as an argument. This is highly implausible. What should be understood by costs of exploitation? Within the present model perhaps the only way to interprete costs is to assume that, in order to exploit, some factor of production should be imported in return for which one has to offer V(E) units of consumer goods when E is extracted. But since the per capita costs, b, are a function of $E/\bar{L}$ only, V(E) must have been of the type $V(E) = aE$, where a is a constant. Then the case $b''(\cdot) < 0$, which is relevant in Aarrestad's article, does not occur. Alternatively one may assume that V depends not only on E but on time as well: $V = V(E,t)$. But then the question arises what the costs should have to do with the growth rate of the population. We conclude that for several reasons the model is unacceptable for $n > 0$. A second remarkable feature of the model is the specification of (2.49) - (2.51). Using the notation of the previous section we have (assuming $n = 0$)

$$p_e(X_e - M_e) = p_e E,$$

$$p_g(X_g - M_g) = Y + \bar{C} - C - I - V(E,t),$$

where I denotes gross domestic investments out of current production. It can be seen from (2.50) and (2.48) that the economy is not investing abroad. Hence the current account is in equilibrium at all instants of time. Now, our second objection concerns the savings ratio s. Why should s a priori be restricted to the unit interval (2.51)? Since there is an exogenous stream of consumer goods ($\bar{C}$) social welfare might be increased when s is allowed to exceed unity. In principle the optimal s might also be negative, which would actually be so if the economy's initial stock of capital is very large. But Aarrestad goes even further and remarks that regimes with $s = 0$ 'are of limited economic relevance and will not be referred to'. We conclude that the analysis is not entirely satisfactory.
How can the results be described? They are of a partial nature. Define the possible policy regimes as follows:

	I	II	III	IV	V	VI
s	1	1	1	$0 < s < 1$	$0 < s < 1$	$0 < s < 1$
E	$\bar{E}$	$0 < E < \bar{E}$	0	$\bar{E}$	$0 < E < \bar{E}$	0

Suppose that for a given (K_o, S_o) constellation the optimal sequence is V → VI. This will be the case when K_o is not too large, say for $K_o < K^1$. Now, under the *technical assumptions* that F exhibits constant returns to scale and $\partial Q/\partial E > 0$, $\partial^2 Q/\partial E^2 < 0$, there exist K^i $(i = 1,2,3,4)$ such that the optimal policy sequences are

$$
\begin{aligned}
K^2 < K_o < K^1 &: \quad \text{IV} \rightarrow \text{V} \rightarrow \text{VI},\\
K^3 < K_o < K^2 &: \quad \text{I} \rightarrow \text{IV} \rightarrow \text{V} \rightarrow \text{VI},\\
K_o = K^3 &: \quad \text{I} \rightarrow \text{V} \rightarrow \text{VI},\\
K^4 < K_o < K^3 &: \quad \text{I} \rightarrow \text{II} \rightarrow \text{V} \rightarrow \text{VI},\\
K_o = K^4 &: \quad \text{I} \rightarrow \text{II} \rightarrow \text{VI},\\
K_o < K^4 &: \quad \text{I} \rightarrow \text{II} \rightarrow \text{III} \rightarrow \text{VI}.
\end{aligned}
$$

It should be mentioned that regime V cannot occur when exploitation costs are linear. Finally, Aarrestad remarks that 'the higher the capital intensity of the economy, the lower (is) the price rise needed to make a rising extraction path optimal'.
These results are rather appealing. However, nothing is said about the characteristics of the critical values of the initial stock of capital. In spite of our objections, we think that Aarrestad's work is very valuable.

The extension to two-sector models has been given independently by Harris (1981) and Kemp and Long (1979). In the economy under consideration there are two non-resource sectors. Each sector produces one output by means of the resource good and capital. Capital and the resource good are not tradeable on world markets. Capital is mobile within the economy and it is available in a constant amount $\bar{K}$. On the world market the economy can lend and borrow as much as it wants at the constant rate of interest r, of course under the kind of proviso discussed in the previous subsection. Hence the separation theorem can be applied and the maximization of social welfare implies the maximization of the discounted returns from activities involving exploitation. Then the model reads:

$$\text{maximize} \int_0^\infty e^{-rt}(p_1 Y_1 + p_2 Y_2)dt,$$

subject to

$$Y_1 = F^1(K^1, R^1),$$

$$Y_2 = F^2(K^2, R^2),$$

$$K^1 + K^2 \leqq \bar{K},$$

$$R^1 + R^2 \leqq E.$$

This problem can to a large extent be analysed with the aid of the results of the well-known neoclassical two-sector growth models (see e.g. Uzawa (1961), Inada (1964) and Shell (1967)). The *technical assumptions* are: F^i is neoclassical and exhibits constant returns to scale and the technology does not allow for factor reversals, i.e. one sector will be more capital intensive than the other for any $(\bar{K},E)$ constellation.

Now the following can be proved:

a) the economy will for any $(\bar{K},S_o)$ constellation specialize;

b) if the relatively resource intensive commodity is ever produced, this lasts for a finite period. This period is followed by a period with production of the relatively capital intensive commodity. If the marginal revenues with respect to the resource input are bounded from above in this sector, when the resource input becomes small, the resource will be exhausted within finite time. Otherwise the capital intensive sector will produce forever.

Some comparative dynamic results are:

c) when the price of the resource intensive good increases, the length of the period during which this good is produced increases, but if the resource was initially depleted within finite time, then it takes a shorter time now to exhaust the resource.

d) when the initial reserve of the resource increases, the time to depletion (if exhaustion takes place within finite time) increases as well as the duration of the production of the resource intensive good. It has no effect on the length of the period the economy produces the capital intensive good.

Kemp and Long show that the result with respect to specialization remains valid when technological progress is incorporated and/or extraction is costly in the sense that the amount of capital needed to extract is in fixed proportion with the number of units extracted.

In an earlier paper Harris (1978) allows for capital accumulation. He assumes that all new capital is bought on the world market and that capital, once imported, cannot be exported anymore. Hence, to the previous model are added

$$\dot{K} = I - \mu K, \tag{2.54}$$

$$I \geqq 0. \tag{2.55}$$

The maximand should read now

$$\int_0^\infty e^{-rt}(p_1Y_1 + p_2Y_2 - I)dt.$$

The optimal policy is 'characterized with an initial jump in the capital stock and then no subsequent investments until possibly resource depletion occurs'. Furthermore 'the comparative static results and the optimal path are similar' to those given in Harris (1981).

For completeness we refer to Kemp and Long (1980a, 1980b). The models presented there are highly specialized and not of general interest. Therefore we restrict ourselves to mentioning them.

2.2.3. Imperfect competition

2.2.3.1. Introduction

It is not far-going to assert that the economists's interest in imperfect competition on resource markets is based on real world evidence. The questions that can be raised are large in number: how does imperfect competition influence the world market prices of natural resources compared with perfect competition; what order of exploitation can one expect when the market is supplied by a large cartel together with many competitive suppliers; do small competitive resource holders benefit from cartelization; what (partial) equilibrium concepts are appropriate; etc.? Many of these questions are indeed posed in the literature discussed in the sequel of this section.

The analysis can be thought of as to refer to firms within a single economy. It is however clear that the questions raised are primarily relevant in an international context. We shall therefore not make an explicit distinction between firms and countries. Common to all contributions is that they consider the situation where each economy involved maximizes the present value of profits from resource activities. Although not explicitly mentioned (except in Dasgupta, Eastwood and Heal (1978)) the underlying assumption is that there exists a perfect world market for lending and borrowing (bonds) and that the world market prices of the commodities that appear in each economy's welfare function are not influenced by the economy's activities on the resource market. Hence the separation theorem applies (see section 2.2.1). Furthermore, attention is restricted to the case of one homogeneous resource commodity. World demand for the commodity is given bv $p_e = p_e(E)$, where E is de amount demanded. Observe that this demand function is stationary, i.e. demand does not shift over time.

In this section we shall first pay attention to Dasgupta's, Eastwood's and Heal's (1978) work who merely prove that the separation theorem applies to their model of a monopoly. Second, we study some work by Salant (1976), Ulph and Folie (1980a) and Lewis and Schmalensee (1980a, 1980b). They have in common that Nash-Cournot equilibrium is considered in a world with oligopoly or with one dominant firm and many competitive firms. It has been recognized by Gilbert (1978) that this equilibrium concept might not be suitable and that the Von Stackelberg equilibrium notion is in many cases more appropriate. Ulph and Folie (1980b), Newbery (1981) and Ulph (1982) elaborate on this observation. Their results are described in the fourth subsection. Several of these authors have put forward that when use is made of the Von Stackelberg equilibrium concept the problem of so-called dynamic inconsistency might arise. The final subsection will be devoted to this phenomenon. It should be remarked that the discussion of the papers just mentioned does not cover the entire literature on imperfect competition in exhaustible resources. However, in our opinion the most relevant issues are being dealt with in this survey.

2.2.3.2. Monopoly

Dasgupta, Eastwood and Heal (1978) consider the following model:

$$\text{maximize } J(C) := \int_0^\infty e^{-\rho t}\, U(C)dt,$$

subject to

$$\int_0^\infty E(t)dt \leqq S_o, \tag{2.56}$$

$$E(t) \geqq 0, \tag{2.57}$$

$$Y = F(K,R,t), \tag{2.58}$$

$$\dot{W} = Y + r(W-K) + p_e(E)(E-R) - C. \tag{2.59}$$

Equations (2.56)-(2.58) should be familiar to the reader by now. (2.59) is the same as (2.16) if there we take $\dot{p}_g = 0$. In the model at hand there is only one non-resource commodity, which serves as the numéraire. Hence its price is constant. Equation (2.59) describes the motion of the economy's wealth. $p_e(E)(E-R)$ is the balance of resource exports. $Y-C$ becomes available for investments from current production. $r(W-K)$ gives the revenues from net investments. It is assumed that the world market rental rate is constant. We remark that one would expect an additional constraint such as

$$\lim_{t\to\infty} W(t) \geqq 0.$$

This constraint is absent from the model, hence the economy might increase its debt beyond any bound. Since the authors assume in the sequel of their article that an optimal program exists, we suppose that they have overlooked this problem.

It is shown in the article that for given specification of U $(= (\frac{1}{1+\eta})C^{1+\eta},\ \eta < 0)$, F $(= e^{\beta t} K^{\alpha_1} R^{\alpha_2},\ \alpha_1 + \alpha_2 < 1)$ and $p_e(E)$ $(= \gamma E^{\gamma-1},$ $0 < \gamma < 1)$ the optimal rate of exploitation is independent of the parameters of the welfare function (ρ and η). Hence an example is provided of how the separation theorem works. The growth rate of resource exports is $(r/(\gamma - 1))$ and the growth rate of resource input in domestic production is $(\beta - (1-\alpha_1)r) / (1 - \alpha_1 - \alpha_2)$. Therefore it is required that $\beta - (1-\alpha_1)r < 0$. The separation result is 'proved' to remain valid when the international rental rate exhibits an exponential trend. If however the return on capital depends on the amount of capital supplied, this does no longer hold. It should be mentioned that the separation theorem has been used before Dasgupta c.s. did, by Long (1977) in a renewable resource model for an open economy.

2.2.3.3. Cartel versus fringe; Nash-Cournot equilibrium

The work of Salant (1976) is evidently inspired by the actual industrial organization of the world oil market. But it applies to many other resource markets such as for bauxite and copper, where cartels are in existence (see Pindyck (1978) for an empirical analysis). It seems worthwhile to cite from his introduction (p. 1079) since it states very clearly the motivation of much of the work to be discussed in the sequel: 'The current structure of the world's oil industry bears little resemblance to the extremes assumed in the theoretical literature on exhaustible resources. There is neither a single cartel (or firm) which owns all the world's oil ...., nor is there an abundance of measureless 'Mom-and-Pop' oil extractors dotting the globe. Instead the industry contains one cartel with more power than any other extractor; but other extractors do exist and have enough importance .... to restrain the full exercise of monopoly power'. The purpose of Salant's article is to take this structure into account.

With regard to demand conditions the following assumptions are made:

i) there exists a 'choke price' $\bar{p}_e$. This means that if the price of the resource good is larger than $\bar{p}_e$, demand is zero.
ii) there exists p_e^* such that the price elasticity of demand equals -1 at p_e^*.
iii) the price elasticity of demand increases in absolute value as p_e increases.

These final two conditions are satisfied when the demand function is linear or concave. They are also satisfied for many convex demand functions. Subsequently Salant assumes that demand is met by a given number of plants, not necessarily firms or countries. Initially, i.e. when no cartel is present, each plant is owned by one firm. An important assumption is furthermore that each plant is endowed with the same amount of the resource and that all plants have identical cost structures. A cartel is defined as a firm owning more than one plant. The equilibrium concept used is Nash-Cournot: the cartel takes the supply of the fringe (the set of suppliers not belonging to the cartel) as given and sets a price so as to maximize its discounted profits and, given this price path, each member of the fringe maximizes its discounted total profits. The discount rate is equal for all firms and constant. It is denoted by r.
First the case of constant and equal marginal extraction costs is considered. It is shown that an equilibrium exists, characterized as follows. Initially marginal profits rise at the rate r. During this period the fringe is exhausting its resource and there is some simultaneous exploitation. After finite time the cartel takes over. It then becomes the sole supplier. Marginal profits now rise at a rate less than r. Cartel's resource will be exhausted at some date T, where the price path reaches the choke price. Figure 2.2 summarizes the results.

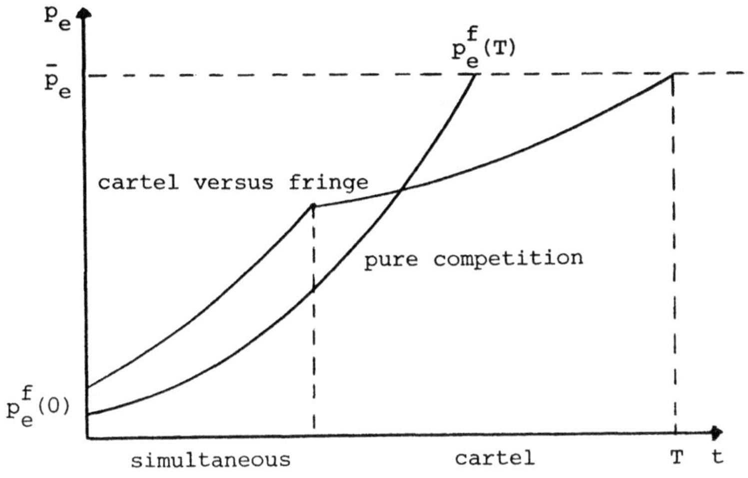

figure 2.2.

If the cartel were not in existence the price path would look like $p_e^f(0) \rightarrow p_e^f(T)$. Marginal profits are increasing at the rate r. The conclusion is that, in terms of the present value of profits, both the cartel and the fringe benefit from cartelization: the consumers are the only losers. This is seen as follows. Discounted profits of fringe members are $(p_e(0) - C)S_o^f$, where C denotes extraction costs. Since in pure competition as well as in a cartel-fringe structure all resources will be exhausted, the price trajectories have a point of intersection. This implies that the initial price when pure competition rules, is smaller than in the presence of a cartel. It is furthermore shown that the fringe benefits more from cartelization than the cartel.
Second, Salant analyses the case of increasing marginal costs per plant. Then the relative advantage of the cartel is not only due to a larger stock of the resource but also to the fact that it can produce cheaper than any individual plant. It is shown that qualitatively the same results hold. The order of exploitation remains unchanged and the benefits from cartelization for the fringe members are greater than for the cartel members.

Ulph and Folie (1980a) argue that these results crucially depend on the assumption that all plants have identical reserves and cost structures. To illustrate their point they adopt a linear demand schedule:

$$p_e = \bar{p}_e - aE. \tag{2.60}$$

First the case of constant marginal costs is considered. c^c and c^f denote marginal cost of each member of the cartel and the fringe respectively. It is then shown that 7 cases can occur. Sufficient conditions for each of these cases can be found in Ulph and Folie (1977) and in the more accessible Ulph (1982) contribution. They are listed in table 2.1. C, F and S stand for cartel production, fringe production and simultaneous production, respectively.

Table 2.1. Equilibrium policy sequences

costs	endowment cartel	exploitation sequence
$c^f > \frac{1}{2}(\bar{p}_e + c^c)$	large	C → S → F
$c^f > \frac{1}{2}(\bar{p}_e + c^c)$	small	S → F
$c^f = \frac{1}{2}(\bar{p}_e + c^c)$	irrelevant	S → F
$c^c < c^f < \frac{1}{2}(\bar{p}_e + c^c)$	large	S → F
$c^c < c^f < \frac{1}{2}(\bar{p}_e + c^c)$	border case	S
$c^c < c^f < \frac{1}{2}(\bar{p}_e + c^c)$	small	S → C
$c^c = c^f$	irrelevant	S → C
$c^c > c^f$	large	S → C
$c^c > c^f$	small	F → S → C

It is concluded from this table that the cases where the fringe is the sole supplier eventually, occur when the cartel is relatively powerful. It is shown that under this condition the fringe will lose under cartelization. Although the mathematics behind this result are not straightforward, there is some simple economic intuition making it plausible. Since the resources are not replenishable, aggregate supply over time cannot exceed initial endowments. This holds true irrespective of the structure of the market for the resource good. The assumptions with respect to exploitation costs guarantee that in finite time the resources will be exhausted. If the cartel succeeds in raising the price at the moment it comes into existence, then the price cannot remain larger than the competitive one. Therefore, at some future date the two price trajectories will intersect. When the costs of the cartel

equal the costs of the fringe, this is an incentive for the fringe to exploit during the interval of time where price is higher than the competitive price and therefore the fringe will gain from cartelization (provided cartel's reserves are small). But if the cartel has considerable advantage over the fringe, fringe production might not even be profitable at the outset. Hence the fringe is urged to sell at prices lower than the competitive ones. One important proviso should be made, namely that the fringe is not producing when the cartel comes into existence.
Subsequently, Ulph and Folie argue that if cost curves are convex and if the cartel's resources are large compared with the fringe's, it is likely that the results obtained will continue to hold.

Lewis and Schmalensee (1980a, 1980b) generalize the model in several respects. They provide a proof of the existence of Nash-Cournot equilibrium in a world with N suppliers, possibly differing in endowments and (constant) marginal extraction costs. It is furthermore shown that if all suppliers are identical, increasing the number of firms (while holding total endowments fixed) leads to a more competitive-like equilibrium.

2.2.3.4. Cartel versus fringe: Von Stackelberg equilibrium

The Nash-Cournot equilibrium concept attributes equal power to the suppliers in the sense that each participant in the non-cooperative game takes the others's actions as given. Hence the cartel does not behave strategically by taking into account the fringe's reactions.
It can be argued that when a cartel is really strong, meaning that it owns a relatively large stock and/or has a relatively large advantage in costs, the Von Stackelberg equilibrium concept is more appropriate. To see how the introduction of this concept works out, is the motivation behind the contribution of Gilbert (1978).
With respect to the world demand schedule Gilbert's postulates differ drastically from those made by Salant. Gilbert focuses on the world market for oil and reports some figures regarding price elasticities (estimated by Nordhaus (1975), Pindyck (1978) and Cremer and Weitzman (1976)) indicating that oil demand is inelastic. But following the contributions already mentioned, he also assumes that there exists a

choke price ($\bar{p}_e$). Therefore the demand schedule looks as follows: for $p_e < \bar{p}_e$ demand has constant elasticity smaller than unity (in absolute value). For $p_e > \bar{p}_e$ demand is zero.
Equilibrium in this model is a price trajectory $p_e(t)$ and exploitation patterns $E^c(t)$ and $E^f(t)$ for the cartel and the fringe respectively, such that demand is always met, such that total discounted profits of the fringe are maximized given the price trajectory and such that cartel's total discounted profits are maximized, taking into account fringe's supply schedule.
The results are not extremely striking. If marginal costs are constant, fringe's resources will be exhausted within finite time. This occurs not later than the moment the price reaches the choke price. As an example the case of no costs is solved. It is shown that the growth rate of the price equals the interest rate. The Von Stackelberg solution coincides with the Nash-Cournot solution in this case.

Newbery (1981), Ulph and Folie (1977, 1980b) and Ulph (1982) elaborate on the Von Stackelberg equilibrium concept. We restrict ourselves here to the case of linear demand functions first.
It turns out that, provided marginal costs differ between cartel and fringe, no simultaneous exploitation will occur. This is easily seen. If the fringe exploits, the world market price minus its marginal cost increases at the rate of interest and the fringe is indifferent between allocating exploitation at the end or at the beginning of an interval where prices develop according to this rule. However, the cartel is not indifferent because marginal costs are not equal. The results are summarized in table 2.2.

Table 2.2. Equilibrium policy sequences

marginal costs	relative endowments cartel	exploitation sequence
$c^f > \frac{1}{2}(\bar{p}_e + c^c)$	irrelevant	C → F
$c^c \leqq c^f \leqq \frac{1}{2}(\bar{p}_e + c^c)$	large	C → F → C
$c^c \leqq c^f \leqq \frac{1}{2}(\bar{p}_e + c^c)$	small	C → F
$c^c > c^f$	irrelevant	F → C

Given that no simultaneous exploitation occurs, these results do not differ much from the exploitation sequences in Nash-Cournot equilibria. However, there is one important qualitative difference. This will have our attention in the next subsection.

Newbery (1981) considers the case of different discount rates. He puts forward that 'one of the main sources of inefficiency in the world energy market is the inability of the 'Low Absorbing' O.P.E.C. producers to earn a satisfactory real rate of return on their overseas assets'. Following Gilbert (o.c.) he postulates the existence of a backstop technology at some $\bar{p}_e$, and assumes that for $p_e < \bar{p}_e$ demand is inelastic:

$$E = b(a - p_e), \quad p_e \leqq \bar{p}_e \leqq 2a,$$
$$E = 0, \qquad p_e > \bar{p}_e, \tag{2.61}$$

where a and b are of course positive constants. One possible outcome is depicted in figure 2.3.

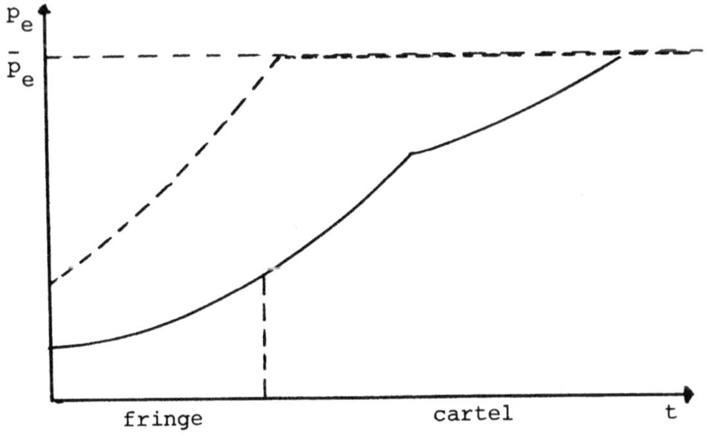

figure 2.3.

The Nash-Cournot trajectory is the dotted line. We shall come back to Newbery's results below.

One final remark is in order. It seems that the demand functions used are rather specific. However, the results obtained by Ulph remain qualitatively the same when a demand function is postulated for which the elasticity increases in absolute value when prices increase.

2.2.3.5. Dynamic Inconsistency

Above we have studied Nash-Cournot and Von Stackelberg equilibria when the market is supplied by a cartel and a fringe. Here we shall concentrate on a conceptual problem that might arise. In first instance we shall restrict ourselves to the case where demand is linear and discount rates are equal.
What institutional framework is necessary for either equilibrium concept to be plausible? For Nash-Cournot all participants must assume ex ante that their behaviour does not affect any other participant's actions. In a Von Stackelberg concept the fringe recognizes the market power of the cartel and takes the supply schedule of the cartel as given. The cartel is capable of using this information. Now suppose that the market power of each participant is agreed upon. Then, at the outset of the period under consideration, the cartel sets prices for the entire period. A crucial assumption made in the tables presented above is that each supplier will in the future act in accordance with the *announced* price trajectory. In other words: the equilibrium outcomes presented are the outcomes that would occur when the contracts are binding. This does not cause any conceptual problem in Nash-Cournot equilibrium since at all future dates no supplier has an incentive to deviate from the contract. However, in a Von Stackelberg equilibrium the problem of dynamic inconsistency might arise. This in fact will happen in two cases.

a) When $c^c > c^f$ the Von Stackelberg price trajectory looks as follows (see figure 2.4).

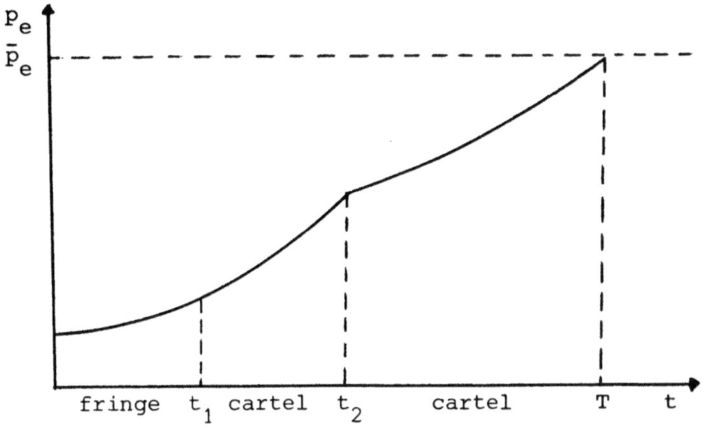

figure 2.4.

For an initial period of time ($0 \leqq t \leqq t_1$), $p_e(t) = e^{rt} \lambda^f + c^f$, where λ^f is some constant. This is necessary for the fringe to exploit. Along the Von Stackelberg binding contracts equilibrium, price will continue to move according to the given formula, even after the fringe's resources have been exhausted. There is a final phase ($t_2 < t \leqq T$) where the cartel produces alone and where the price trajectory is less steep. But what happens as soon as time actually arrives at t_1? Then the cartel has an incentive to break the contract and to start acting as a monopolist, since it has become the only holder of resources. Hence the price will jump at t_1. Thus the Von Stackelberg equilibrium is dynamically inconsistent if contracts are not binding.

b) When $c^c < c^f \leqq \frac{1}{2}(\bar{p}_e + c^c)$ and the reserves of the cartel are relatively large, the binding contract equilibrium looks as in figure 2.5.

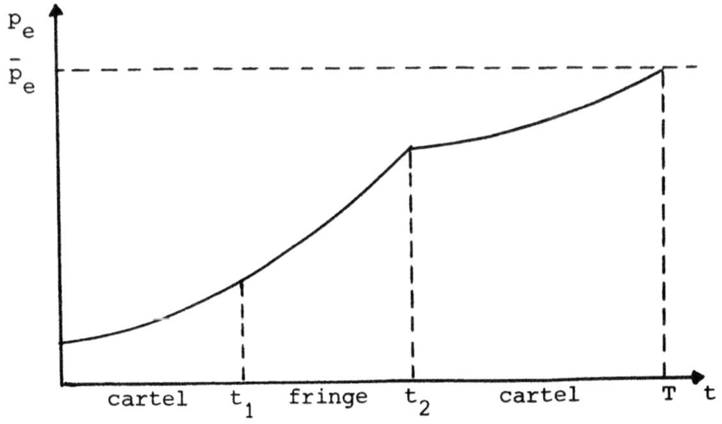

figure 2.5.

Here the cartel starts exploitation. This phase is followed by a period where the fringe exploits alone. In both phases the price trajectory is $p_e(t) = e^{rt} \lambda^f + c^f$, where λ^f is a constant. Now suppose that the first phase has actually come to an end. It is then profitable for the cartel to undercut the fringe; in other words to transfer sales from (t_2,T) to (t_1,t_2). Hence again the cartel will break the contract.

It will be clear by now that the example given by Newbery, involving different discount rates, presents also the problem of dynamic inconsistency.

Finally, Newbery and Ulph suggest that the first two cases of dynamic inconsistency can occur also when the elasticity of demand is constant or is increasing (in absolute value) with price. Also introduction of a backstop technology does not change the results.

Therefore, we conclude that the problem of dynamic inconsistency will arise when cartel's marginal costs exceed fringe's marginal costs and when cartel's cost advantage is not very large but the cartel owns relatively much of the resource. It might also arise when the discount rates differ. What is then in these cases an appropriate equilibrium concept? Newbery defines it as an 'extraction plan for each agent and an implied price-path which maximizes the present discounted profit for each agent at each successive date, *and not just at time zero*'. It turns out that it is very difficult to calculate such so-called rational expectations Von Stackelberg equilibria. They must satisfy two conditions: 'the fringe must not exhaust before reaching the unconstrained monopoly price trajectory if it is to remove the risk of a price jump, and the leader must have no power to deviate from the price path before it reaches the unconstrained monopoly path - after this the monopolist will not wish to deviate from the predicted trajectory' (Newbery, o.c. p. 632, Ulph (1982) p. 218). These conditions are met in Nash-Cournot equilibrium (the second by definition) and Newbery suggests that indeed Nash-Cournot might be a good approximation but will in general not coincide with the rational expectations equilibrium. A formal proof of the latter statement is given by Ulph (1982). These rather vague and negative conclusions indicate that the problem of finding rational expectations equilibria is not yet solved. It is subject to further research.

2.3. *General equilibrium*

Only rather recently attention has been paid to general equilibrium models of open economies trading in natural resources. The number of contributions in this field is very small. There is no clear explanation of these facts. The relevance of a general equilibrium approach seems to be indisputable since it not only covers the partial equilibrium line of work but it might in addition provide conditions to be taken into account when dealing with partial equilibrium models. These conditions may concern price trajectories of the resource or of other commodities, the interest rate or the demand schedule.

In this section four models will be described which, to our knowledge, give an exhaustive account of what has been done in this field so far. The first model is due to Kemp and Long (1980c). There are two countries. One of the countries (indexed 1) owns a natural resource, of given size S_o. Exploitation is costless. This country is unable to produce consumer goods and, since utility is derived only from these goods, it exports all that is exploited. Hence the first country seeks to maximize

$$\int_0^\infty e^{-\rho_1 t} U_1(C_1)dt, \tag{2.62}$$

subject to

$$C_1 = p_e E, \tag{2.63}$$

$$\int_0^\infty E(t)dt \leqq S_o, \tag{2.64}$$

where p_e is the relative world market price of the resource. For the time being it is taken as given. C_1 is the rate of consumption. The second country is not in the possession of a natural resource but instead has the disposal of a technology to convert the raw material into the consumer good. The second country's problem is to maximize

$$\int_0^\infty e^{-\rho_2 t} U_2(C_2)dt, \tag{2.65}$$

subject to

$$Y = F(E), \tag{2.66}$$

$$C_2 = Y - p_e E, \tag{2.67}$$

where F is the conversion technology, strictly concave with $F'(0) = \infty$. It is seen from the equations that the current accounts of the balances of payments are equilibriating at all instants of time. It now follows that in equilibrium $F'(E) = p_e$. No other general conclusion can be drawn: the signs of $\dot{C}_i$, $\dot{p}_e$ and $\hat{E}$ depend on the elasticity of marginal utility and the elasticity of production of country 1. If these quantities are bounded from below by -1, then the rate of exploitation is steadily decreasing. An example is provided by means of the 'Cobb-Douglas' case.

$$U_i(C_i) = C_i^{\nu_i}, \quad 0 < \nu_i < 1, \quad i = 1,2, \tag{2.68}$$

$$F(E) = E^{\alpha}, \quad 0 < \alpha < 1. \tag{2.69}$$

In this special case, which can be solved explicitly, exploitation is decreasing exponentially at a rate $-\rho_1/(1 - \alpha\nu_1)$ and the world market price increases at a rate $\rho_1(1-\alpha)/(1-\alpha\nu_1)$.
Subsequently it is assumed that the resource-rich country starts behaving as a monopolist, while the resource-poor country keeps behaving passively. In general nothing more can be said than that the solution pattern differs from the competitive one. If however the production function exhibits constant elasticity of production the two solution paths coincide, that is: the resource-rich country has no effective monopoly power. This conclusion crucially depends on the specification of the technology and has been reached before by Stiglitz (1976) for a closed economy (see also Withagen (1981c)). If, on the other hand, the resource-poor country becomes aggressive, it is offering an arbitrarily low price for the resource good, which must be accepted by the resource-rich country in order to survive.

Chiarella (1980) works along the same lines as Kemp and Long. The differences compared with the previous model are:

i) in both countries the population (L_i) grows exponentially at an exogenously given rate n_i;
ii) the utility functions U_i are $L_i \ln C_i/L_i$;
iii) the model allows for capital accumulation and technical progress (λ) in the resource-poor country in the following way:

$$Y = e^{\lambda t} K^{\alpha_1} E^{\alpha_2} L_2^{\alpha_3}, \quad \alpha_i > 0 \quad \Sigma\alpha_i = 1, \tag{2.70}$$

$$\dot{K} = Y - p_e E - C_2. \tag{2.71}$$

Both countries behave as price takers. A rather complicated and tedious analysis yields the following results:

a) Due to the particular utility function of the resource-rich country the supply of the resource good is inelastic.
b) For the share of each country in total consumption there exists a value which is monotonically approached as an asymptote. Whether or not the optimal path tends to this value from above depends on the initial values S_o, K_o and L_{io}.
c) The asymptotic growth rate of the price of the resource good is

$$\{\alpha_3(n_2 - n_1 + \rho_1) + \lambda\} / (1 - \alpha_1).$$

The formulation above describes economies with permanent equilibrium on the current accounts. The possibility of lending and borrowing is introduced in the second part of Chiarella's article. This is done as follows. Let B_i denote the amount of bonds held by country i (i = 1,2). In the context of the model this means that country 1, not disposing of productive uses of capital at home, lends B_1 units of capital to country 2. Denoting by r the rate of interest we have:

$$\dot{B}_1 = p_e E + rB_1 - C_1. \tag{2.72}$$

Capital actually used as an input in country 2 (K) shows the following time path:

$$\dot{K} = Y - p_e E - rB_1 - C_2 + \dot{B}_1. \tag{2.73}$$

In equilibrium (characterized by $B_1 + B_2 = 0$) we have:

a) the growth rate of the price of the resource equals the rental rate r;

b) the asymptotic growth rate of the price of the resource is the same as in the previous model;

c) the consumption share always moves in favour of the country with the smallest ρ_i^* $(= \rho_i - n_i)$.

Undoubtedly Chiarella's work is very important, for example to the extent that it is shown that resource price and rental rate heavily depend on almost all parameters of the model.

A rather peculiar general equilibrium model is presented by Suzuki and Ogawa (1979). They also postulate a resource-poor and a resource-rich country, but now each country disposes of the same non-resource technology:

$$Y_i = e^{\lambda t} K_i^{\alpha_1} R_i^{\alpha_2} L_i^{\alpha_3}, \quad (i = 1,2). \tag{2.74}$$

The labour force is assumed to grow at an exponential rate n in both countries. The resource-rich country exports X_1 of the resource at price p_e. The current account of each country is assumed to equilibriate. Out of national income a fraction s_i is saved and invested:

$$\dot{K}_1 = s_1(Y_1 + pX_1), \tag{2.75}$$

$$\dot{K}_2 = s_2(Y_2 - pX_1). \tag{2.76}$$

Capital is assumed not to depreciate. In equilibrium:

$$p_e = \partial Y_i/\partial R_i, \quad i = 1,2. \tag{2.77}$$

Then it is assumed that the asset market only exists in the resource-rich country and that it is in equilibrium. If the resource is competitively owned in country 1 this implies:

$$\dot{p}_e/p_e = \partial Y_1/\partial K_1. \tag{2.78}$$

Finally we have:

$$\dot{S} = -X_1 - R_1. \tag{2.79}$$

Suzuki and Ogawa are interested in steady state equilibria. They show that a sufficient and necessary condition for these to exist is that the savings share of the resource-rich country is smaller than the share of capital ($s_1 < \alpha_1$). It is furthermore shown that the shares of production and consumption for each country converge to positive constants, smaller than unity.

Finally some work by Elbers and Withagen (1984) is reviewed. They are concerned with general equilibrium too, but in a world where both countries are in the possession of a natural resource. The model is very simple in that the resource good is the only commodity in existence. Associated with exploitation there are costs, differing between the countries. If E_i is the amount exploited the consumable amount is $F_i(E_i)$. One can think here of transportation losses. It is assumed that F_i is increasing and strictly concave.
There exists a perfect world market for bonds, allowing each country to borrow and lend. By definition:

$$\dot{B}_i = F_i(E_i) + rB_i - C_i, \quad (i = 1,2), \tag{2.80}$$

where B_i is the amount of bonds (expressed in resource goods) held by country i. The constraint is that in the limit each economy's debt is nonnegative, implying that $B_i \to 0$ as $t \to \infty$ for both i. Hence

$$\int_0^\infty q(t)M_i(t)dt \leqq \int_0^\infty q(t)X_i(t)dt + B_0, \tag{2.81}$$

where

$$q(t) = e^{-\int_0^t r(\tau)d\tau},$$

and M_i and X_i denote imports and exports of the resource good respectively. Now for country i the problem is to maximize

$$J_i(C_i) = \int_0^{\infty} e^{-\rho_i t} U_i(C_i)dt, \qquad (2.82)$$

subject to (2.81) and the usual resource constraints.
General equilibrium is an allocation (i.e. $\hat{C}_i(t)$, $\hat{E}_i(t)$, $\hat{M}_i(t)$, $\hat{X}_i(t)$) for each country and an associated price pattern $\hat{r}(t)$ such that each country's objective function is maximized under the conditions given and such that for all t

$$\hat{M}_1 - \hat{X}_1 = \hat{X}_2 - \hat{M}_2. \qquad (2.84)$$

The results are the following. An equilibrium exists. Equilibrium price is continuous and decreasing. General equilibrium is Pareto efficient. An example with $F_i(E_i) = (E_i + a_i)^{\alpha_i} - a_i^{\alpha_i}$, $0 < \alpha_i < 1$, suggests that one of the resources is exhausted within finite time. This is interesting since it provides a very simple illustration of the problem of dynamic inconsistency in a general equilibrium model.

2.4. *Conclusions*

In this section we wish to evaluate the models presented in the preceding paragraphs and to suggest some further research. A broad (but practical) distinction can be made between the models primarily focused on optimal resource management at prices not endogenously determined within the model, and the models designed to explain resource price developments.
Large part of the analysis has been devoted to the former type of models, involving small, or at least price taking, economies in the possession of a natural resource. Such an economy has been characterized by its endowments (labour, capital, the reserves of the resource), its industrial structure (the set of technologies) and a balance of payments condition (specifying borrowing and lending facilities). World market prices are data. This type of model is important since many of the world's economies belong to the category just described. One can think of Norway, the Netherlands and resource-rich developing countries. The theories discussed above have led to the insight that, at least when the country under consideration is a welfare maximizer,

the outcomes are rather sensitive for altering the balance of payments condition and that, in relation with this condition, optimal resource management cannot be separated from optimal capital management. These observations are due to Aarrestad. Unfortunately they are illustrated by means of models that are not analysed in full detail and are subject to some criticism. With regard to the balance of payment conditions one could ask whether it is relevant to restrict the speed of borrowing rather than the amount of borrowing. Therefore one is in need of a further development of the theory into these directions.
In the first class of models it is generally assumed that world market prices are constant or grow exponentially. This kind of behaviour is not explained within the models. However, in order to develop an exploitation plan the economy under consideration must estimate price movements. On the conditions with respect to this estimation a very elegant literature has evolved. The cartel versus fringe case is extensively treated and has offered much new insights. Obviously, the problem of finding rational expectations Von Stackelberg equilibria is a starting point for further research. But also a second problem might be very interesting to study more closely. In the cartel versus fringe models the discount rates are exogenous. Some very preliminary attempts have been made in the general equilibrium literature on exhaustible resources and international trade to explain prices and interest rate simultaneously. It seems not far-going to conclude that this area too offers many opportunities for fruitful further research.

3. *OPTIMAL EXPLOITATION AND INVESTMENTS IN A SMALL OPEN ECONOMY*

3.1. *Introduction*

One of the conclusions drawn from the survey of the literature on exhaustible resources in open economies, was that a closer examination of the problem of simultaneous determination of optimal exploitation of the resource and the optimal savings rate was in order. This is the purpose of the present chapter. It will turn out that the results heavily depend on whether or not certain markets are in existence and on the expectations the economy under consideration holds with respect to the prices that come about on these markets. This observation gives rise to various models, to be dealt with subsequently. We shall outline here some of the characteristics the economy will always (i.e. in all models) be assumed to exhibit and we shall present a description of the environments in which the economy may find itself. Essentially the models are special cases of the general model presented in chapter 2 section 2.2.1.
We consider an economy in the possession of a single type of a natural resource. The initial size of this resource (denoted by S_o) is given. The resource is not replenishable and there exists an upper bound $\bar{E}$ on the rate of exploitation. The economy has furthermore the disposal of a technology, to produce one single commodity by means of capital. F(K) denotes the output when an amount K of capital is employed. F is assumed to be neoclassical and it fulfils

$$F(0) = 0, \; F'(0) = \infty, \; F'(\infty) = 0.$$

These assumptions are made for mathematical convenience. It is assumed that capital depreciates at a constant rate μ. The initial stock of capital (K(0)) is given. The models used would be more general if the resource commodity would enter into the production function. This would however seriously complicate the analysis in a number of models to be discussed below. Non-resource output consists of a commodity that can be used for consumption purposes and for investments. In this sense output is perfectly malleable. The economy's objective is to maximize

$$J := \int_0^{\infty} e^{-\rho t}\, U(C(t))dt, \tag{3.1}$$

where $\rho(> 0)$ is the rate of time preference, $C(t)$ is the rate of consumption at date t and U is the instantaneous utility function. It will be assumed that U is strictly increasing, concave and that $U'(0) = \infty$. By $\eta(C)$ we shall denote the elasticity of marginal utility $(U''C/U')$. It will sometimes be assumed that $\eta(C) = \eta$, a constant. Then $U(C) = \frac{1}{1+\eta} C^{1+\eta}$. Of course $\eta(C) < 0$.

For the consumer good and for the exploited commodity there exist perfect world markets. The price that comes about on the world market of the latter good at time t is denoted by $p(t)$. The small country assumption boils down to postulating that the economy takes $p(t)$ as given for all t. It will be convenient to write

$$\dot{p}/p = \gamma(t), \; p(0) \text{ given.}$$

The consumer good serves as the numéraire.

Several other markets may or may not be in existence. Three of them are particularly relevant since they are related to the commodities which are of importance to the economy at hand.

1) First, there is the world market for bonds. In this chapter it will be assumed that if this market exists, it is perfect, meaning that at the going interest rate $r(t)$ the economy can lend and borrow as much as it wants, provided that it submits plans such that the present discounted value of total expenditures is smaller than the present discounted value of total income.

2) The second and third market of relevance are the markets for capital stocks and resource stocks.

These possibilities give rise to three models that will be studied below. The first model describes the situation where there is no world market for bonds, nor world markets for capital and resource stocks. Section 3.2. is devoted to this model. In section 3.3. we introduce markets for capital stocks and resource reserves while maintaining the assumption that the world market for bonds is not in existence. In the third model, to which section 3.4. is devoted, the latter assumption is dropped. In the sequel optimal programs for the economy will be characterized. In section 3.5 these programs of the different models will be compared. There also the conclusions of this chapter are presented.

3.2. *No world market for bonds, no world markets for stocks*

3.2.1. The model and preliminary results

In the model presented in this section there is no world market for bonds nor markets for capital and resource stocks. Non-existence of the world market for bonds implies that the current account of the balance of payments of the economy under consideration must equilibriate at all instants of time. Furthermore, since there are no markets for stocks, the stock of capital and the reserve of the resource must be continuous. The state of the economy at time t is given by the stock of capital $K(t)$ and the remaining reserve of the resource $S(t)$. The instruments by which the economy tries to reach its goal are the rate of exploitation of the resource $E(t)$ and the rate of consumption $C(t)$. We shall a priori $E(t)$ and $C(t)$ require to be piece-wise continuous. This class of functions is quite large. Allowing for more general classes would make the use of the Pontryagin maximum principle, given in appendix B, impossible. A *feasible program* is a quadruple

$$z(t) = \{K(t),\ S(t),\ C(t),\ E(t)\},$$

defined for all $t \geqq 0$, with $K(t)$ and $S(t)$ continuous and $C(t)$ and $E(t)$ piece-wise continuous, such that for all t:

$$\dot{K}(t) = F(K(t)) + p(t)\ E(t) - \mu\ K(t) - C(t), \tag{3.2}$$

$$\dot{S}(t) = -E(t), \tag{3.3}$$

$$K(t) \geqq 0,\ S(t) \geqq 0, \tag{3.4}$$

$$K(0) \text{ is given},\ S(0) = S_o, \text{ given}, \tag{3.5}$$

$$C(t) \geqq 0, \; \bar{E} \geqq E(t) \geqq 0. \qquad (3.6)$$

A feasible program is called *optimal* if there is no other feasible program yielding a larger value for the objective functional (3.1). Ample use will be made of the results of the one-sector optimal growth model. These results are summarized in appendix A, which we recommend to the reader not familiar with this model. It will be assumed in this section that $\gamma(t)$ is a positive constant, denoted by γ. Before giving the Lagrangean of the problem some remarks are in order.

i) the specification of the instantaneous utility function U guarantees that in an optimal program the rate of consumption is positive at all instants of time.

ii) the assumptions with respect to the production function F guarantee that along an optimal program the stock of capital is positive.

iii) it follows from (3.3) that

$$S(t) = S_o - \int_0^t E(t)dt.$$

Since in view of (3.6) ($E \geqq 0$) the reserve of the resource is decreasing, we may write as a necessary condition

$$\int_0^\infty E(t)dt \leqq S_o,$$

or

$$\int_0^\infty (be^{-bt} S_o - E(t))dt \geqq 0,$$

where b is an arbitrary positive constant.

Now the Lagrangean of the problem is

$$L(K,C,E,\phi,\lambda,\alpha,\beta) = e^{-\rho t} U(C) + \phi(F(K) - \mu K + p(t)E - C) +$$

$$+ \lambda(be^{-bt} S_o - E) + \alpha E + \beta(\bar{E} - E).$$

Let $\hat{z}(t) = \{\hat{K}(t), \hat{S}(t), \hat{C}(t), \hat{E}(t)\}$ be an optimal program. Then, according to the maximum principle, there exist continuous $\hat{\phi}(t)$, a constant $\hat{\lambda}$ and piece-wise continuous $\hat{\alpha}(t)$ and $\hat{\beta}(t)$ (possibly discontinuous at points of discontinuity of $\hat{E}$) such that for all t:

$$\partial L/\partial C = 0 \qquad : e^{-\rho t}\, U'(\hat{C}(t)) = \hat{\phi}(t), \tag{3.7}$$

$$\partial L/\partial K = -\dot{\hat{\phi}}(t) \quad : \hat{\phi}(t)(F'(\hat{K}(t)) - \mu) = -\dot{\hat{\phi}}(t), \tag{3.8}$$

$$\partial L/\partial E = 0 \qquad : p(t)\ \hat{\phi}(t) + \hat{\alpha}(t) - \hat{\beta}(t) = \hat{\lambda}, \tag{3.9}$$

$$\hat{\alpha}(t)\ \hat{E}(t) = 0,\ \hat{\alpha}(t) \geqq 0, \tag{3.10}$$

$$\hat{\beta}(t)(\bar{E}-\hat{E}(t)) = 0,\ \hat{\beta}(t) \geqq 0. \tag{3.11}$$

In the sequel we shall omit time indices when there is no danger of confusion.

To interprete the necessary conditions let's assume that the economy is competitive and that the ruling interest rate r(t) is given to each agent in the economy. The consumer good serves as the numéraire. Define

$$q(t) = e^{-\int_0^t r(\tau)d\tau}\ . \tag{3.12}$$

q(t) represents the present market value of a consumer good: it is the number of consumer goods the *consumer* would have to pay at time zero in order to get one consumer good delivered at time t. Given a present discounted life-time income of, say, M, a rate of time preference ρ and instantaneous utility function U, the representative consumer will at each point of time demand consumer goods such that his marginal rate of substitution equals the discount factor:

$$e^{-\rho t}\ U'(\hat{C}(t)) = q(t)\ U'(\hat{C}(0))\ . \tag{3.13}$$

In economic terms (3.13) means that the intertemporal marginal rate of substitution equals the price ratio (q(t)). To see that (3.13) holds true, suppose

$$e^{-\rho t} U'(\hat{C}(t)) > q(t) U'(\hat{C}(0)).$$

Consider a discrete time two-period analogue. Construct an alternative consumption pattern with α units less in period 0 and augment period 1's consumption by $\alpha(1 + r)$. Hence, the budget constraint remains satisfied. Then, for α sufficiently small,

$$U(\hat{C}(0)-\alpha) + (1/(1+\rho))U(\hat{C}(1)+\alpha(1+r)) > U(\hat{C}(0)) + (1/(1+\rho))U(\hat{C}(1)).$$

Therefore the original consumption plan is not optimal: a contradiction. A contradiction would also be obtained when the marginal rate of substitution is smaller than the discount factor. Now consider a typical *non-resource producer* aiming at the maximization of the present discounted value of his profits. He is discounting at the rate $r(t)$ and in equilibrium the rental rate of capital coincides with r. So his problem is to maximize

$$\int_0^\infty q(t) \ (F(K) - (r+\mu)K)dt.$$

Hence the optimal choice of K is such that

$$F'(K) = r + \mu,$$

which is equivalent to

$$F'(K) - \mu = -\dot{q}/q. \tag{3.14}$$

Finally consider a *resource owner*, maximizing his present discounted profits from exploitation:

$$\int_0^\infty q(t) \ p(t) \ E(t)dt,$$

under constraints (3.4) and (3.6). Suppose that, during some interval of time, he decides to exploit at a level $0 < E < \bar{E}$. Then $q(t)p(t)$ must be constant during this interval. For if it were growing during some subinterval, it would be profitable to allocate sales to this subinterval. The same kind of contradiction can be obtained if $q(t)p(t)$ were decreasing during some subinterval. If, for an interval of time, it is optimal to exploit at a maximal level then obviously the level of present discounted profits per unit of extraction $(q(t)p(t))$ is larger than for the case of interior exploitation. For $E = 0$ the opposite holds.

Let us now return to the necessary conditions (3.7)-(3.11). It follows from the preceding analysis that $\hat{\phi}$ can be interpreted as the discount factor $q(t)$ times marginal utility of initial consumption. Suppose $\hat{\phi}(t)$ is given. Then the rate of consumption follows from (3.7). The rental rate $(-\dot{\hat{\phi}}/\hat{\phi})$ determines the supply of the non-resource good through (3.8). Exploitation is determined in (3.9)-(3.11). Therefore, we conclude that the necessary conditions can be given a nice economic interpretation. The problem is of course to find the optimal ϕ.

Before tackling this question we give some preliminary results. We introduce two definitions that will frequently be used. $K_{\gamma+\mu}$ is the solution of $F'(K) = \gamma + \mu$; $K_{\rho+\mu}$ is the solution of $F'(K) = \rho + \mu$. By virtue of the properties of F both solutions exist. For shortness of notation the following convention will be adopted. For a variable $x(t)$ we define:

$$x(t+) = \lim_{h \downarrow 0} x(t+h),$$

$$x(t-) = \lim_{h \uparrow 0} x(t+h).$$

We first show that, in order to have interior exploitation $(0 < \hat{E} < \bar{E})$, the stock of capital must equal $K_{\gamma+\mu}$.

<u>Lemma 1</u>

Let $t_1 < t_2$. If $0 < \hat{E}(t) < \bar{E}$ for all $t \in V := [t_1, t_2]$, then $\hat{K}(s) = K_{\gamma+\mu}$ for all $s \in V$.

<u>Proof</u>

It follows from (3.10) and (3.11) that in V $\hat{\alpha} = \hat{\beta} = 0$. Hence $\dot{\hat{\phi}}/\hat{\phi} = -\gamma$. Substitution into (3.8) gives the desired result. □

To interprete this lemma let us consider a discrete time analogue with two periods. Capital is installed at the beginning of each period. Let subscripts refer to the periods.

$$\hat{C}_1 = F(\hat{K}_1) - \mu\hat{K}_1 + p_1 \hat{E}_1 - (\hat{K}_2 - \hat{K}_1),$$

$$\hat{C}_2 = F(\hat{K}_2) - \mu\hat{K}_2 + p_2 \hat{E}_2 - (\hat{K}_3 - \hat{K}_2).$$

Now construct the following alternative trajectory

$$\tilde{C}_1 = F(\hat{K}_1) - \mu\hat{K}_1 + p_1 \tilde{E}_1 - (\tilde{K}_2 - \hat{K}_1),$$

$$\tilde{C}_2 = F(\tilde{K}_2) - \mu\tilde{K}_2 + p_2 \tilde{E}_2 - (\hat{K}_3 - \tilde{K}_2),$$

$$\tilde{C}_1 = \hat{C}_1,$$

$$\hat{E}_1 + \hat{E}_2 = \tilde{E}_1 + \tilde{E}_2.$$

Hence the alternative path uses the same amount of the resource and ends up with the same amount of capital. Straightforward calculations (using the concavity of F) yield:

$$\tilde{C}_2 - \hat{C}_2 \geqq (F'(\tilde{K}_2) - (\mu + \gamma))(\tilde{K}_2 - \hat{K}_2).$$

Hence if $\hat{K}_2 < K_{\gamma+\mu}$ the optimal program can be overtaken by investing (and exploiting) more in the first period. For then $\tilde{K}_2 - \hat{K}_2 > 0$ and $\tilde{K}_2$ can be chosen such that the first factor of the right hand side is positive. A similar conclusion is reached for $\hat{K}_2 > K_{\gamma+\mu}$. Therefore, if $\hat{E}_1$ and $\hat{E}_2$ are both interior and $\hat{K}_2 \neq K_{\gamma+\mu}$, then the program is not optimal. The lemma thus actually says that net returns on activities (non-resource production and exploitation) should be equalized.

Next a sufficiency theorem is provided.

<u>Theorem 1</u>

Let $\hat{z} = \{\hat{K}, \hat{S}, \hat{C}, \hat{E}\}$ be a feasible program, which, together with $\hat{\lambda}$, $\hat{\phi}$, $\hat{\alpha}$ and $\hat{\beta}$, satisfies the necessary conditions (3.7)-(3.10). Let

$$\lim_{t\to\infty} \hat{S}(t) = 0, \quad \lim_{t\to\infty} \hat{\phi}(t)\,\hat{K}(t) = 0.$$

Then $\hat{z}$ is the unique optimal program.

<u>Proof</u>

Let z be an alternative program with $z \neq \hat{z}$ for some interval of time. Then application of the concavity of U and F, (3.2), (3.6)-(3.11) and integration by parts yield:

$$\begin{aligned}
J_T := \int_0^T e^{-\rho t}(U(\hat{C})-U(C))dt &\geqq \int_0^T e^{-\rho t}\, U'(\hat{C})(\hat{C}-C)dt \\
&\geqq \int_0^T \hat{\phi}(F'(\hat{K}) - \mu)(\hat{K}-K)dt + \int_0^T \hat{\phi} d(K-\hat{K}) + \int_0^T p\,\hat{\phi}(\hat{E}-E)dt \\
&= \int_0^T -\hat{\phi}(F'(\hat{K}) - \mu)(\hat{K}-K)dt - \int_0^T \dot{\hat{\phi}}(K-\hat{K})dt + (K(T)-\hat{K}(T))\hat{\phi}(T) \\
&+ \int_0^T \hat{\lambda}(\hat{E}-E)dt - \int_0^T \hat{\alpha}(\hat{E}-E)dt + \int_0^T \hat{\beta}(\hat{E}-E)dt \\
&\geqq \hat{\phi}(T)(K(T)-\hat{K}(T)) + \hat{\lambda}(S(T)-\hat{S}(T))
\end{aligned}$$

$$\lim_{T\to\infty} J_T \geqq -\lim_{T\to\infty} \hat{\phi}(T)\hat{K}(T) - \hat{\lambda} \lim_{T\to\infty} \hat{S}(T) = 0 .$$

In fact the inequality will be strict since U and F are strictly concave and $z \neq \hat{z}$ for an interval of time. □

The following lemma shows that the necessary conditions impose some constraints on the ways jumps may occur in the rate of exploitation. It says that if during some interval of time the optimal stock of capital is smaller than $K_{\gamma+\mu}$ and if, for some instant of time in that interval, the rate of exploitation is zero, then exploitation will after that instant of time be zero, at least as long as the stock of capital is smaller than $K_{\gamma+\mu}$. Mutatis mutandis the same holds for the stock of capital larger than $K_{\gamma+\mu}$ and a rate of exploitation equal to $\bar{E}$.

<u>Lemma 2</u>

Let $\hat{z}$ be the optimal program. Then $\hat{z}$ has the following properties:

a) Let $t_1 < t_2$. Define V as $[t_1, t_2]$. If $\hat{K}(t) < K_{\gamma+\mu}$ for all $t \in V$ and $\hat{E}(s) = 0$ for some $s \in V$, then $\hat{E}(t) = 0$ for all $t \in [s, t_2]$.

b) Let $t_1 < t_2$. Define V as $[t_1, t_2]$. If $\hat{K}(t) > K_{\gamma+\mu}$ for all $t \in V$ and $\hat{E}(s) = \bar{E}$ for some $s \in V$, then $\hat{E}(t) = \bar{E}$ for all $t \in [s, t_2]$.

Proof

a) $\hat{K} < K_{\gamma+\mu} \Rightarrow F'(\hat{K}) > \gamma+\mu$ since F is strictly concave. Then from (3.6) $F'(\hat{K}) - \mu = -\dot{\hat{\phi}}/\hat{\phi} > \gamma$ and $\hat{\phi}p$ is decreasing in V. Since $\hat{E}(s) = 0$ we have $\hat{\beta}(s) = 0$. $\hat{\lambda}$ is constant, hence $\hat{\alpha}$ is increasing. An upward jump in $\hat{E}$ implies that $\hat{\alpha}$ jumps downwards. $\hat{\alpha} - \hat{\beta}$ is continuous and therefore $\hat{\beta}$ jumps to a negative value, which is not allowed in view of (3.11).

b. This proof runs along the same line as the proof under a. □

The sequel of this section will be organized as follows. In 3.2.2 the case $\rho > \gamma$ is considered, 3.2.3 is devoted to the case $\gamma > \rho$. 3.2.4 deals with $\rho = \gamma$. Finally in 3.2.5 we go into problems that may arise when the upper bound $\bar{E}$ is "small". The exact meaning of the expression "small" in this context will become clear below.

3.2.2. The case $\rho > \gamma$

Here the situation is analysed where the rate of time preference is larger than the expected growth rate of the price of the resource good. Our main objective is to prove existence of optimal programs and to give a characterization.

In the sequel some additional notation will be used. We define C^* as the optimal rate of consumption at time T when $K(T) = K_{\gamma+\mu}$, $S(T) = 0$. Hence C^* is the unique rate of consumption solving the problem of optimal economic growth in the neoclassical one-sector model. See Appendix A. The modified golden rule rate of consumption is denoted by $C_{\rho+\mu}$:

$$C_{\rho+\mu} := F(K_{\rho+\mu}) - \mu K_{\rho+\mu}.$$

In an analogous way we define

$$C_{\gamma+\mu} := F(K_{\gamma+\mu}) - \mu K_{\gamma+\mu}.$$

These concepts are illustrated in figure 3.1 for $\rho > \gamma$.

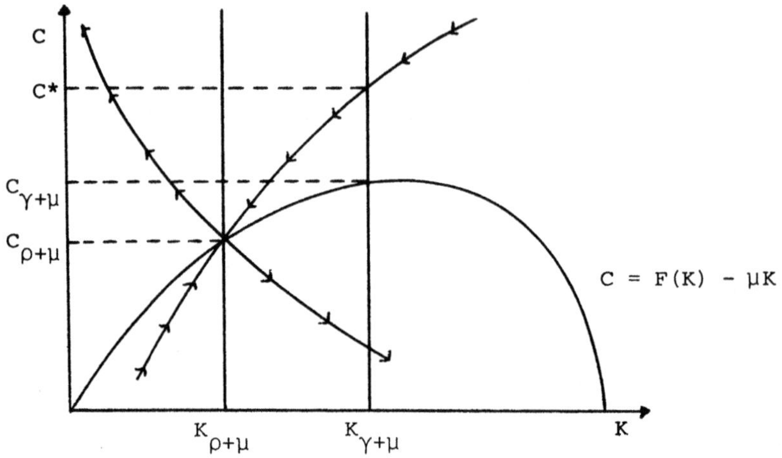

figure 3.1.

We first prove

Lemma 3

Suppose $\rho > \gamma$. Let $t_1 < t_2$. If $\hat{K}(t_1) = \hat{K}(t_2) = K_{\gamma+\mu}$, then $\hat{K}(t) \leqq K_{\gamma+\mu}$ for all $t \in [t_1, t_2]$.

Proof

If the lemma were not true, then the $\hat{K}$ trajectory depicted in figure 3.2. could be optimal.

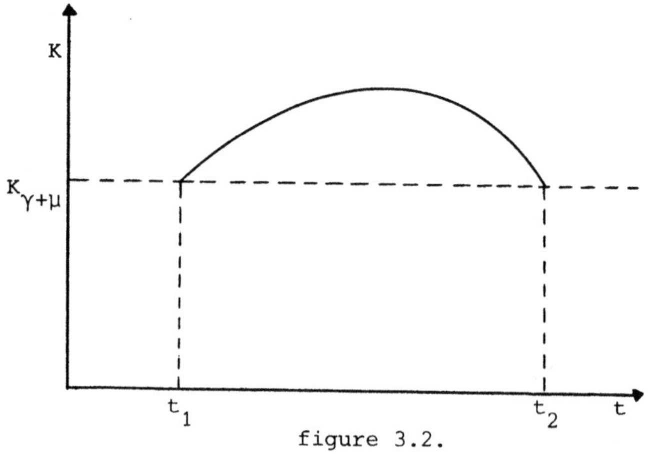

figure 3.2.

Since $\dot{\hat{K}}(t_1+) > 0$ and $\dot{\hat{K}}(t_2-) < 0$ we have (using (3.2))

$$\hat{C}(t_1) < C_{\gamma+\mu} + p(t_1)\ \hat{E}(t_1+),$$

$$\hat{C}(t_2) > C_{\gamma+\mu} + p(t_2)\ \hat{E}(t_2-).$$

Observe first, that neither $\hat{E}(t_1+)$ nor $\hat{E}(t_2-)$ is interior, since for $t \in (t_1, t_2)$ $K(t) \neq K_{\gamma+\mu}$ (lemma 1).
If $\hat{E}(t_1+) = 0$, $\hat{C}(t_1) < \hat{C}(t_2)$. If $\hat{E}(t_1+) = \bar{E}$, then, by virtue of lemma 2, $\hat{E}(t_2-) = \bar{E}$, and again $\hat{C}(t_1) < \hat{C}(t_2)$.
It follows from

$$-\dot{\hat{\phi}} = \hat{\phi}(F(\hat{K}) - \mu), \tag{3.8}$$

that $\dot{\hat{\phi}}/\hat{\phi} \geqq -\gamma$ for $\hat{K} \geqq K_{\gamma+\mu}$. Differentiation with respect to time of

$$e^{-\rho t}\ U'(\hat{C}) = \hat{\phi} \tag{3.7}$$

yields

$$\eta(\hat{C})\ \dot{\hat{C}}/\hat{C} = \rho + \dot{\hat{\phi}}/\hat{\phi} \geqq 0.$$

Hence, for $\hat{K} \geqq K_{\gamma+\mu}$, $\hat{C}$ is non-increasing, a contradiction. □

It will turn out to be useful to make a distinction between the cases $K(0) < K_{\gamma+\mu}$ and $K(0) > K_{\gamma+\mu}$. The case $K(0) < K_{\gamma+\mu}$ is analysed first.

Theorem 2

Suppose $\rho > \gamma$, $K(0) < K_{\gamma+\mu}$. If there is no upper bound on the rate of exploitation, then the optimization problem posed has no solution.

Proof

Suppose that the theorem does not hold true. It follows from lemma 1 that exploitation will take place only when $\hat{K} = K_{\gamma+\mu}$. Since exploitation is costless, it is optimal to exploit somewhere in the future. Until then $\hat{E} = 0$. $\hat{K}$ is required to be continuous. As long as $\hat{K} < K_{\gamma+\mu}$, $\hat{\phi}p$ is decreasing, hence $\hat{\alpha}$ must increase (see 3.9). Therefore as soon as $K_{\gamma+\mu}$ is reached exploitation cannot become positive for that would require that $\hat{\alpha}$ jumps downwards, contradicting the continuity of $\hat{\alpha}$. But at some point of time exploitation must start. Hence $\hat{K}$ can be depicted as follows:

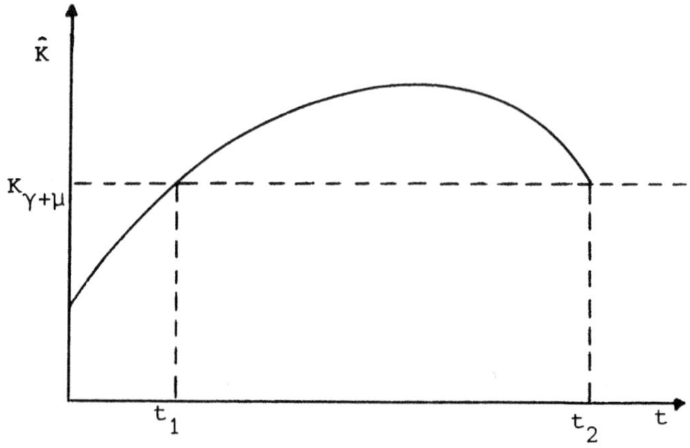

figure 3.3.

But such a K-trajectory has been excluded by the previous lemma. □

It will be clear that the non-existence of a solution is caused by the continuity requirements with respect to $\hat{S}$ and $\hat{K}$. What actually the economy would desire is to exploit at an infinite rate in order to enlarge its stock of capital as fast as possible. We shall return to this issue below.

Theorem 2 holds irrespective of the magnitudes of the initial stock of capital and the reserve of the exhaustible resource. It therefore implies that in the presence of an upper bound on the rate of extraction, this upper bound will be binding, at least for an initial period of time. Then two possibilities arise.

a) The resource is exhausted during the phase where $\hat{E} = \bar{E}$.

b) The phase with $\hat{E} = \bar{E}$ is followed by a phase with an interior solution for the rate of exploitation.

It is easily seen that there are no other possibilities. It follows from theorem 2 that $\hat{E} = \bar{E}$ for all t such that $\hat{K}(t) \leqq K_{\gamma+\mu}$, $\hat{S}(t) > 0$. Hence a jump to $\hat{E} = 0$ could occur only when the resource is exhausted, giving the type a program, or for $\hat{K} > K_{\gamma+\mu}$. But this possibility is ruled out by lemma 2 that says that jumps to $\hat{E} = 0$ can occur only for $\hat{K} < K_{\gamma+\mu}$. In order to present a more precise description of the optimal program we prove the following lemma.

<u>Lemma 4</u>

Suppose $\rho > \gamma$. Suppose that there exists an interval of time, starting at, say, t_1 such that, along this interval, the optimal rate of exploitation is interior. Then there exists $t_2 > t_1$ such that

i) $0 < \hat{E}(t) < \bar{E}$, $\dot{\hat{E}}(t) < 0$, $t_1 \leqq t \leqq t_2$,

ii) $\hat{S}(t_2) = 0$,

iii) $\hat{C}(t_2) = C^*$,

iv) $\hat{K}(t) = K_{\gamma+\mu}$, $t_1 \leqq t \leqq t_2$.

Proof

During an interval following t_1, $\hat{E}$ is interior. It follows from lemma 1 that there $\hat{K} = K_{\gamma+\mu}$ and from (3.2) and (3.7) - (3.11) that there exists $\hat{\lambda}$ with

$$U'(F(K_{\gamma+\mu}) - \mu K_{\gamma+\mu} + p\hat{E}) = e^{(\rho-\gamma)t}\,\hat{\lambda}/p(0). \tag{3.15}$$

Since $\rho > \gamma$, the solution $p\hat{E}$ of (3.15) is decreasing. $\gamma > 0$, hence $\hat{E}$ is decreasing. If the interval with interior exploitation would be followed by an interval with maximal exploitation, then $\dot{\hat{K}}$ would jump upwards (3.2). But the economy cannot maintain maximal exploitation forever. Hence, one should return to interior exploitation, with $\hat{K} = K_{\gamma+\mu}$ (lemma 1) or to zero exploitation, which, in view of lemma 2, can only occur after some instant of time with $\hat{K} = K_{\gamma+\mu}$. Both cases are excluded by lemma 3, however. Hence the interval with interior exploitation lasts until the resource has been exhausted or the interval is followed by a period where the resource is not exploited, although being positive. However, the latter possibility is ruled out by theorem 2, saying that exploitation is maximal for $\hat{K} < K_{\gamma+\mu}$. We conclude that interior exploitation lasts until the resource is exhausted.

It follows from (3.15) that, indeed, the resource will be exhausted within finite time. Since $\rho > \gamma$, the right-hand side goes to infinity, implying from the concavity of U that $\hat{E}$ goes to zero within finite time. From the moment of exhaustion on, the economy will pursue the program leading to the modified golden rule. Therefore t_2 can be derived from

$$U'(C^*) = e^{(\rho-\gamma)t_2}\,\hat{\lambda}/p(0) .$$

This proves the lemma. □

A consequence of this lemma is that, for $\rho > \gamma$ and $K(0) < K_{\gamma+\mu}$, along an optimal program $\hat{K}(t) \leqq K_{\gamma+\mu}$. For if the economy would arrive at $\hat{K} = K_{\gamma+\mu}$, then it cannot continue with maximal exploitation (lemma 3). And if, at that moment, it starts with interior exploitation, $\hat{K}$ will never exceed $K_{\gamma+\mu}$ (lemma 4). We have then proved:

Theorem 3

Suppose $\rho > \gamma$ and $K(0) < K_{\gamma+\mu}$. The optimal program can be characterized as follows. There exists $\hat{T}_1 > 0$ such that for $0 \leqq t \leqq \hat{T}_1$, $\hat{E}(t) = \bar{E}$ and $\hat{K}(t) \leqq K_{\gamma+\mu}$.

For $t > \hat{T}_1$ either one of the following two propositions holds:

a) $\hat{E}(t) = 0$, $(\hat{K}(t), \hat{C}(t)) \rightarrow (K_{\rho+\mu}, C_{\rho+\mu})$,

b) there exists some $\hat{T}_2 > \hat{T}_1$ such that, for $\hat{T}_2 \geqq t > \hat{T}_1$, $0 < \hat{E}(t) < \bar{E}$, $\hat{K}(t) = K_{\gamma+\mu}$ and, for $t > \hat{T}_2$, $\hat{E}(t) = 0$, $(\hat{K}(t), \hat{C}(t)) \rightarrow (K_{\rho+\mu}, C_{\rho+\mu})$.

The rate of consumption is decreasing for $\hat{T}_2 \geqq t > \hat{T}_1$.

In case a) as well as in case b) the modified golden rule is approached monotonically. □

Whether or not in the case at hand an interior solution for the rate of exploitation will occur obviously depends on the specification of the functions used and the value of the parameters of the model. Nevertheless some more or less intuitive reasoning may help to obtain useful results. Suppose there exists an interval with an interior solution and that the switch to this solution occurs at $T_1 > 0$. $F(\hat{K}) - \mu\hat{K} \leqq F(K_{\gamma+\mu}) - \mu K_{\gamma+\mu}$. Then for $0 \leqq t \leqq T_1$

$$\dot{\hat{K}} \leqq C_{\gamma+\mu} + p(t)\,\bar{E},$$

yielding

$$K_{\gamma+\mu} - K(0) < T_1 C_{\gamma+\mu} + \frac{1}{\gamma}\, p(0)\, \bar{E}\, e^{\gamma T_1}.$$

Obviously, one must have $T_1 < S_o/\bar{E}$ and hence

$$K_{\gamma+\mu} - K(0) < C_{\gamma+\mu}\, S_o/\bar{E} + \frac{1}{\gamma}\, p(0)\, \bar{E}\, e^{\gamma S_o/\bar{E}}.$$

Therefore, a necessary condition for having an interior solution is that S_o or $S_o/\bar{E}$ is sufficiently large or that $K_{\gamma+\mu}$ is sufficiently close to $K(0)$. The role of $\bar{E}$ is ambiguous. The right hand side of the above inequality is decreasing for small $\bar{E}$ and increasing for large $\bar{E}$. Therefore a necessary condition is that $\bar{E}$ is sufficiently small or large. It should be understood that all these statements hold ceteris paribus.

We now proceed to the case $K(0) > K_{\gamma+\mu}$. One would expect the following program to be optimal: initially the rate of exploitation is zero and the stock of capital is reduced up to the level $K_{\gamma+\mu}$. Then there follows an interval with interior exploitation. Finally the economy stops exploitation and approaches the modified golden rule program. It will be shown that in its generality this conjecture is not correct. However it holds for $\bar{E}$ large enough. The excercise will be carried out for a utility function with constant elasticity of marginal utility (η). This is not a serious simplification. Intuitively it is easily seen that the results will hold for more general utility functions, provided that the elasticity of marginal utility is bounded. However, a rigorous proof would require tedious calculations and is therefore omitted here.

Suppose there exists an optimal program $\hat{z} = \{\hat{K}, \hat{S}, \hat{C}, \hat{E}\}$, such that, for $t \leqq \hat{T}_1$, $\hat{E} = 0$, for $\hat{T}_1 < t \leqq \hat{T}_2$, $0 < \hat{E} < \bar{E}$ and, for $t > \hat{T}_2$, $\hat{E} = 0$. See figure 3.4.

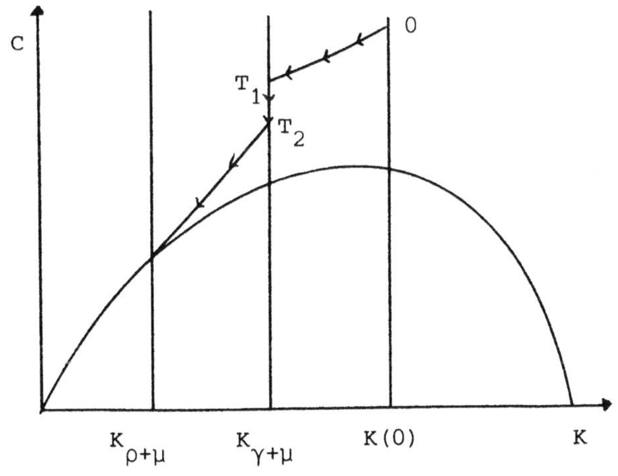

figure 3.4.

Figure 3.4. gives the phase diagram for the neoclassical one-sector optimal growth model. $\hat{T}_2$ is the date of exhaustion. From $\hat{T}_2$ on the economy faces the problem of the neoclassical one-sector growth economy. Hence at $\hat{T}_2$ it will find itself at $K_{\gamma+\mu}$ and $C(\hat{T}_2)=C^*$. From $\hat{T}_1$ on exploitation is interior. Hence $\hat{\alpha} = \hat{\beta} = 0$, $\dot{\hat{\phi}}/\hat{\phi} = -\gamma$ (from 3.11) and $\dot{\hat{C}}/\hat{C} = (\rho-\gamma)/\eta$ (from 3.7), for $\hat{T}_1 \leqq t \leqq \hat{T}_2$. It follows that

$$\hat{C}(t) = C^* e^{(\frac{\rho-\gamma}{\eta})(t-\hat{T}_2)}, \quad \hat{T}_1 \leqq t \leqq \hat{T}_2. \tag{3.17}$$

Using

$$\hat{C}(t) = C_{\gamma+\mu} + p(t)\hat{E}, \quad \hat{T}_1 \leqq t \leqq \hat{T}_2, \tag{3.18}$$

we find

$$\hat{E}(t) = (C^*/p(0))\, e^{\psi t}\, e^{-(\frac{\rho-\gamma}{\eta})\hat{T}_2} - (C_{\gamma+\mu}/p(0))e^{-\gamma t}, \quad \hat{T}_1 \leqq t \leqq \hat{T}_2, \tag{3.19}$$

where $\psi = (\rho-\gamma(1+\eta))/\eta$. Remark that $\psi < 0$ since $\rho > \gamma$ and $\eta < 0$. Between $\hat{T}_1$ and $\hat{T}_2$ the resource is exhausted. Substitution of (3.19) into

$$\int_{\hat{T}_1}^{\hat{T}_2} \hat{E}(t)dt = S_o,$$

yields after straightforward calculations

$$p(0)S_o = e^{-\gamma\hat{T}_2} \{\frac{C^*}{\psi}(1 - e^{-\psi(\hat{T}_2-\hat{T}_1)}) + \frac{C_{\gamma+\mu}}{\gamma}(1 - e^{\gamma(\hat{T}_2-\hat{T}_1)})\}$$

$$= F(\hat{T}_1,\hat{T}_2). \tag{3.20}$$

We are interested in the behaviour of $F(\hat{T}_1, \hat{T}_2)$ for $\hat{T}_2 > \hat{T}_1$. Since $C^* > C_{\gamma+\mu}$ we find

$$\partial F/\partial\hat{T}_1 < 0,\ \partial F/\partial\hat{T}_2 > 0 \text{ and } \partial F/\partial\hat{T}_1 + \partial F/\partial\hat{T}_2 \leqq 0.$$

Furthermore for each $p(0)S_o$ there exist $\hat{T}_1$ and $\hat{T}_2$ such that (3.20) holds for $\hat{T}_2 > \hat{T}_1 > 0$. This is so since $\partial F/\partial\hat{T}_2$, evaluated at $\hat{T}_2 = \hat{T}_1 = 0$, equals $-C_{\gamma+\mu} + C^*$, and it is bounded away from zero for all $T_2 > 0$. For any given $p(0)S_o$ our information about (3.20) is summarized in curve I in figure 3.5.

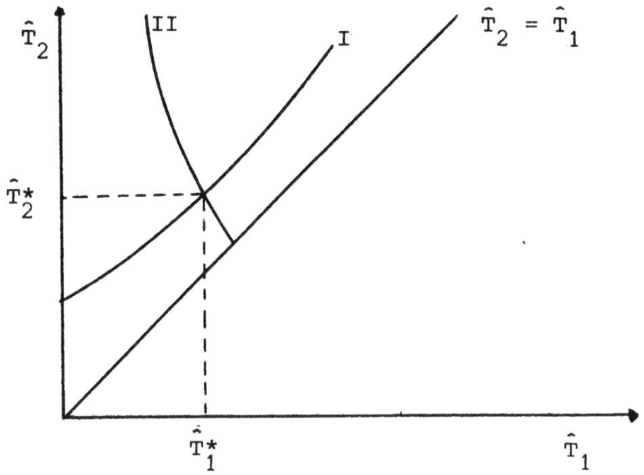

figure 3.5.

Now consider (3.17). Suppose $\hat{T}_1$ is set equal to zero. This means that the economy should "infinitely" fast go from K(0) to $K_{\gamma+\mu}$. This can only be carried out by choosing an infinite initial rate of consumption. Therefore $\hat{T}_2 = \infty$ when $\hat{T}_1 = 0$. Clearly $\hat{T}_2$ decreases as $\hat{T}_1$ increases for if the economy is left more time to arrive at $K_{\gamma+\mu}$, the initial rate of consumption will be smaller, implying that $\hat{C}(\hat{T}_1)$ is smaller. (See appendix A). For $\hat{T}_1 = \hat{T}_2$, $\hat{C}(\hat{T}_1) = C^*$ and $\hat{T}_1$ takes a finite value. In figure 3.5. curve II represents this relation between $\hat{T}_1$ and $\hat{T}_2$. From the previous argument it will be clear that curves I and II have a point of intersection $(\hat{T}_1^*, \hat{T}_2^*)$, such that $\hat{T}_2^* >$ $\hat{T}_1^*$. Hence if the program $\hat{z}$ is optimal $\hat{T}_1 = \hat{T}_1^*$ and $\hat{T}_2 = \hat{T}_2^*$. It is now straightforward to show that $\hat{z}$ is indeed the optimal program, provided that $\bar{E}$ is large enough. This restriction has to be made since there is no guarantee that the solution $\hat{E}(\hat{T}_1^*)$ is smaller than $\bar{E}$ for an arbitrary $\bar{E}$. Presently we can state the following theorem.

Theorem 4

Suppose $\rho > \gamma$ and $K(0) > K_{\gamma+\mu}$. Suppose furthermore that $\bar{E}$ is sufficiently large. The optimal program can be characterized as follows. There exist $0 < \hat{T}_1 < \hat{T}_2$ such that

a) for $0 \leq t \leq \hat{T}_1$, $\hat{E}(t) = 0$, $\dot{\hat{K}}(t) < 0$, $\dot{\hat{C}}(t) < 0$,

b) for $\hat{T}_1 < t \leq \hat{T}_2$, $0 < \hat{E}(t) < \bar{E}$, $\dot{\hat{E}}(t) < 0$, $\hat{K}(t) = K_{\gamma+\mu}$, $\dot{\hat{C}}(t) < 0$,
c) for $t > \hat{T}_2$, $\hat{E}(t) = 0$, $(\hat{K}(t), \hat{C}(t)) \to (K_{\rho+\mu}, C_{\rho+\mu})$. □

Figure 3.6 depicts the time path of $\hat{E}$.

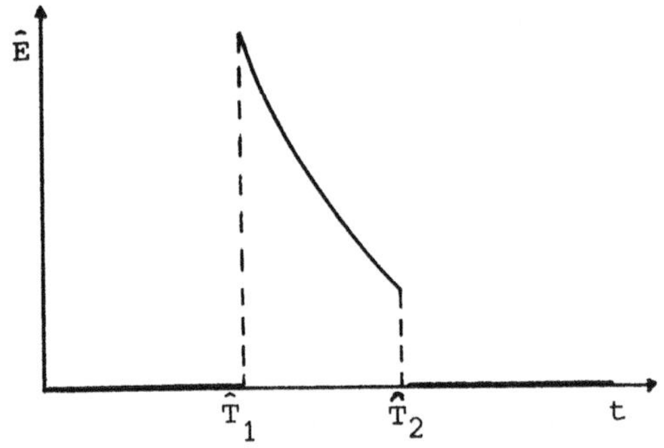

figure 3.6.

A few comments are in order. A feature of the optimal program is that when the resource is discovered, the economy is not starting to increase instantaneous welfare by exploiting the resource. Instead, exploitation is postponed and instantaneous utility is raised by means of a large rate of desinvestment. Secondly one could argue that the case at hand is not very realistic in the sense that relative capital abundance ($K(0) > K_{\rho+\mu}$) is not likely to occur. One should however bear in mind that the discovery of a natural resource could influence the economy's rate of time preference to the extent that this rate is substantially increased. Nonetheless this type of argument is of course rather intuitive and should be tested for its empirical relevance.

3.2.3. The case $\rho < \gamma$

Here we consider the situation where the rate of time preference is smaller than the growth rate of the price of the resource. It turns out to be useful to make a distinction between $K(0) > K_{\gamma+\mu}$ and $K(0) < K_{\gamma+\mu}$. For the ease of exposition we shall continue to work with the constant elasticity of marginal utility type of utility function. It should be recalled that $C_{\gamma+\mu}$ denotes $F(K_{\gamma+\mu}) - \mu K_{\gamma+\mu}$. We shall proceed as follows. First it will be shown that the resource will never be exhausted and that eventually (which means for all instants of time after some given point of time) exploitation will be interior. From this a necessary condition for the existence of an optimal program can be derived. Secondly, optimal programs are characterized for sufficiently large upper bounds on the rate of exploitation. Small upper bounds will be dealt with in subsection 3.2.5.

Theorem 5

Suppose $\gamma > \rho$. Then along an optimal program $\hat{S}(t) > 0$ for all t.

Proof

If the theorem were not correct, then $\hat{E}(t) = 0$ eventually and the economy would face the neoclassical one sector growth problem. Hence the rate of consumption approaches $C_{\rho+\mu}$, a constant. Then, from (3.7), the growth rate of $\hat{\phi}$ approaches ρ. Since eventually $\hat{\beta}(t) = 0$ (in view of $\hat{E}(t) = 0$) $\hat{\alpha}(t)$ must become negative (see (3.9)). This contradicts $\hat{\alpha}(t) \geqq 0$ (3.10). □

Lemma 5

Suppose $\gamma > \rho$. If there exists an optimal program, then $\exists T > 0$ $\forall t > T \quad 0 < \hat{E}(t) < \bar{E}$.

Proof

Suppose that the lemma does not hold. In view of theorem 5 it is not optimal to have $\hat{E} = 0$ eventually. Hence there is an infinite series of intervals of time with $\hat{E} = \bar{E}$. In view, again, of theorem 5 there is also an infinite series of intervals with $0 \leqq \hat{E} < \bar{E}$. We now show that for some point of time, say T, $\hat{C}(T) > C_{\gamma+\mu}$, $\hat{K}(T) = K_{\gamma+\mu}$. Suppose, for some t_1, $\hat{E}(t_1) = 0$. If $\hat{K}(t_1) < K_{\gamma+\mu}$, then $\hat{E}$ will remain zero, at least as long as $\hat{K} \leqq K_{\gamma+\mu}$. Hence there exists $t_2 > t_1$ such that $\hat{E}(t_2) = 0$, $\hat{K}(t_2) > K_{\gamma+\mu}$ (see lemma 2). But it cannot be optimal to have $\hat{K} > K_{\gamma+\mu}$ and $\hat{E} = 0$ eventually, in view of theorem 5. Therefore, either there is some t_3 such that $\hat{K}(t_3) = K_{\gamma+\mu}$ and $\dot{\hat{K}}(t_3) \leqq 0$, implying $\hat{C}(t_3) \geqq C_{\gamma+\mu}$, or for $\hat{K} > K_{\gamma+\mu}$, $\hat{E}$ jumps to $\bar{E}$. But we cannot have $\hat{E} = \bar{E}$ eventually, hence the former statement holds.
Suppose, for some t_1, $\hat{E}(t_1) = \bar{E}$, then this same result is obtained. Denoting t_3 by T, we find $\hat{C}(T) > C_{\gamma+\mu}$, $\hat{K}(T) = K_{\gamma+\mu}$.
At T three possibilities arise. The economy has a choice to make between $\hat{E}(T+) = 0$, $0 < \hat{E}(T+) < \bar{E}$ or $\hat{E}(T+) = \bar{E}$. The first choice is not optimal since then the economy behaves according to the one-

sector optimal growth rule and $\hat{E}(t) = 0$ for all $t \gtrless T$. Remark that here the continuity of $\hat{C}$ is used. In the second option $\hat{K} = K_{\gamma+\mu}$ for an interval of time following T and $\hat{C}$ is increasing during this interval, as can be seen from (3.7) and (3.8). In the final possibility we know that exploitation at the maximal rate must come to an end. This can only happen through a switch to $\hat{E} = 0$, for $\hat{K} < K_{\gamma+\mu}$, or by switching to an interior solution. Let t_2 denote the point of time where the switch takes place. In the former case $\hat{C}(t_2) > C_{\gamma+\mu}$, since $\hat{C}$ is increasing for $\hat{K} < K_{\gamma+\mu}$. (see 3.7 and 3.8) and $\hat{K}(t) \leq K_{\gamma+\mu}$ for $T \leq t \leq t_2$ *or* $\hat{K}(t_1) = K_{\gamma+\mu}$, with $\dot{\hat{K}}(t_1) < 0$ for some t_1, $T < t_1 < t_2$, implying also that $\hat{C}(t_2) > C_{\gamma+\mu}$. We conclude that in the former case the economy behaves according to the one-sector optimal growth rule and $\hat{E}(t) = 0$ eventually. Therefore a switch must occur to an interior solution.

It follows from the previous arguments that $\hat{E}(t) > 0$ eventually. Since it has been assumed that the lemma does not hold true, there exists an infinite series of intervals of time with $\hat{E} = \bar{E}$. Hence a typical $\hat{K}$-trajectory looks as follows.

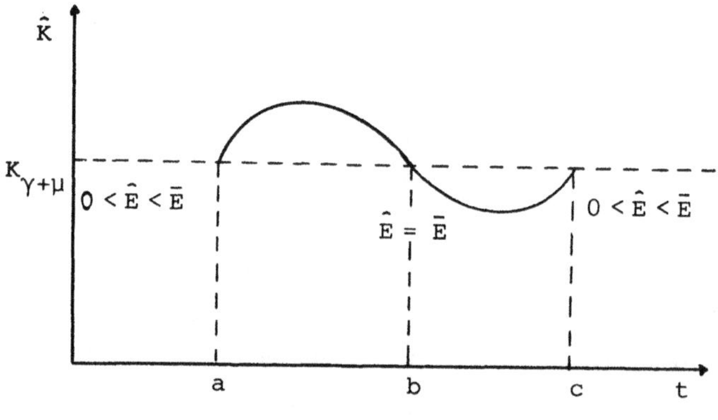

figure 3.7.

Consider a feasible program $\{K^*, C^*, E^*\}$. Suppose that for $t_1 \leq t \leq t_2$, $E^* = \hat{E} = \bar{E}$ and $K^*(t_1) = \hat{K}(t_1) = K^*(t_2) = \hat{K}(t_2) = K_{\gamma+\mu}$.

$$\int_{t_1}^{t_2} e^{-\rho t} \, (U(C^*) - U(\hat{C}))dt \geq$$

$$\int_{t_1}^{t_2} e^{-\rho t} \, U'(C^*)(F'(K^*) - \mu - \rho + \eta \, \dot{C}^*/C^*)(K^*-\hat{K})dt.$$

Now take $K^*(t) = K_{\gamma+\mu}$ for $t_1 \leqq t \leqq t_2$. Then

$$\dot{C}^*/C^* = \gamma/(\frac{C_{\gamma+\mu}}{p(t)\bar{E}} + 1).$$

By choosing $[t_1, t_2]$ far enough in the future, $\dot{C}^*/C^*$ can be made arbitrarily close to γ. Therefore

$$F'(K^*) - \mu - \rho + \eta\dot{C}^*/C^*$$

can be made arbitrarily close to

$$-\rho + \gamma(1+\eta).$$

If this expression is positive, then by taking $t_1 = b$, $t_2 = c$ (see figure 3.7) the optimal path can be improved upon. If the expression is negative, then taking $t_1 = a$ and $t_2 = b$ yields more welfare. Hence, in both cases a contradiction has been obtained. □

Using this lemma it is easy to prove:

Theorem 6

Suppose $\gamma > \rho$. A necessary condition for the existence of an optimal program is that $\rho > \gamma(1+\eta)$.

Proof

Suppose the contrary. It follows from lemma 5 that from, say, T on, there is interior exploitation. Hence from ((3.7)-(3.11)):

$$\hat{C}(t) = \hat{C}(T)\, e^{\frac{\rho-\gamma}{\eta}(t-T)}, \quad t \geqq T, \tag{3.21}$$

and

$$\hat{E}(t) = \hat{C}(T)\, e^{\frac{\rho-\gamma}{\eta}(t-T)}\, e^{-\gamma t}/p(0) - (e^{-\gamma t}/p(0))\, C_{\gamma+\mu}. \tag{3.22}$$

We must have

$$\int_T^\infty \hat{E}(t)\, dt \leqq S_o. \tag{3.23}$$

But the integral diverges, since $\rho \geqq \gamma\ (1+\eta)$. □

The interpretation of the condition given is straightforward. The rate of time preference should not be too small relative to the growth rate of the resource price, otherwise the economy tends to postpone exploitation and consumption until infinity and any program can be overtaken by another program along which consumption takes place further in the future. Henceforth it will be assumed that $\rho > \gamma(1+\eta)$.

In order to characterize optimal programs, it will be supposed, to start with, that along an optimal program there is no exploitation initially and that after finite time exploitation becomes interior. More formally, let $\hat{z} = \{\hat{K}, \hat{S}, \hat{C}, \hat{E}\}$ be the optimal program. Then it is supposed that there exists $\hat{T} > 0$ such that, for $t \leqq \hat{T}$, $\hat{E}(t) = 0$ and, for $t > \hat{T}$, $0 < \hat{E}(t) < \bar{E}$. It follows from the necessary conditions that, for $t > \hat{T}$, (3.22) must hold with T replaced by $\hat{T}$ and that (3.23) must hold with equality, for $T = \hat{T}$. Combination of these two equations yields:

$$\hat{C}(\hat{T}) = -\frac{\rho-\gamma(1+\eta)}{\gamma\eta}\{\gamma p(\hat{T})\ S_o + C_{\gamma+\mu}\}. \tag{3.24}$$

This relation between $\hat{C}(\hat{T})$ and $\hat{T}$ is depicted as curve I in figure 3.8.

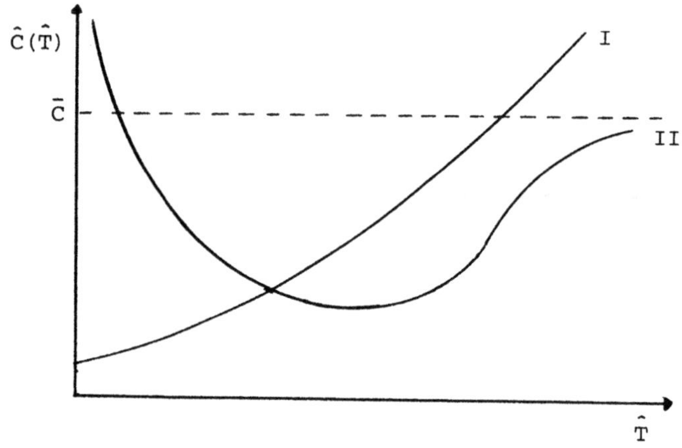

figure 3.8.

It turns out to be convenient to consider first the case $K(0) > K_{\gamma+\mu}$. See figure 3.9.

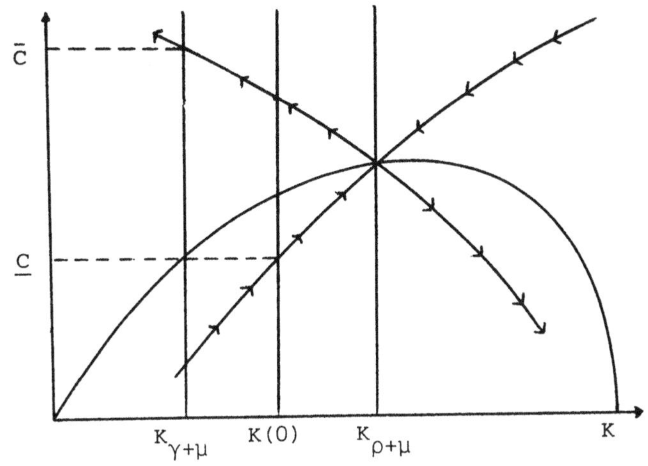

figure 3.9.

From this figure, which is the phase diagram for the neoclassical one-sector optimal growth model, we can derive some information about the way the economy behaves before $K_{\gamma+\mu}$ is reached (see also appendix A). The initial rate of consumption is to be chosen on the line $K = K(0)$. If $\hat{C}(0)$ is very large, it takes little time to reach $K_{\gamma+\mu}$ and the corresponding $\hat{C}(\hat{T})$ is large. The smaller $\hat{C}(0)$ is chosen, the longer it takes to arrive at $K_{\gamma+\mu}$. This does not imply that the corresponding $\hat{C}(\hat{T})$ is getting smaller. On the contrary, it is seen from figure 3.9 that, if the initial rate of consumption is smaller than $F(K(0))-\mu K(0)$, $\hat{C}(\hat{T})$ is larger, the smaller is $\hat{C}(0)$. Clearly, $\hat{C}(0)$ must be above $\underline{C}$, the rate of consumption lying on the unique trajectory, starting from $K(0)$, leading to the modified golden rule. The closer $\hat{C}(0)$ to $\underline{C}$, the closer $\hat{C}(\hat{T})$ to $\bar{C}$. $\hat{C}(\hat{T})$ as function of $\hat{T}$, obtained in this way, is given by curve II in figure 3.8.

Then it is easily seen that curves I and II have a point of intersection. Therefore, we have found the point in time where interior exploitation should start, and the corresponding rate of consumption. By construction, the rate of exploitation is positive since $\hat{C}(\hat{T}) > C_{\gamma+\mu}$. The only thing to worry about is the upper bound on the rate of exploitation.

This problem will be studied in section 3.2.5. For the time being it is assumed that the upper bound is large enough. Now obviously we can find functions $\hat{\alpha}$, $\hat{\beta}$, $\hat{\phi}$ and $\hat{\lambda}$ such that the necessary conditions are satisfied. Furthermore $\hat{S}(t) \to 0$ and $\hat{K}(t)\ e^{-\rho t}\ U'(\hat{C}(t)) \to 0$ as $t \to \infty$. Therefore theorem 1 on sufficiency can be invoked to establish the optimality of the program. It should be remarked that the two curves of figure 3.8 have only one point of intersection since an optimal program is unique.

Theorem 7

Suppose $\gamma > \rho$ and $K(0) > K_{\gamma+\mu}$. Suppose furthermore that $\bar{E}$ is sufficiently large. The optimal program is characterized as follows. There exists $\hat{T} > 0$ such that

a) for $0 \leqq t \leqq \hat{T}$, $\hat{E}(t) = 0$, $\hat{K}(\hat{T}) = K_{\gamma+\mu}$, $\dot{\hat{C}}(t) > 0$,

b) for $t > \hat{T}$, $0 < \hat{E}(t) < \bar{E}$, $\hat{K}(t)=K_{\gamma+\mu}$, $\dot{\hat{C}}(t)/\hat{C}(t) = (\rho-\gamma)/\eta > 0$.

Proof

Existence of an optimal program follows from the arguments given above. That the rate of consumption is increasing during the phase with $\hat{E} = 0$, is clear from figure 3.9. When the rate of exploitation is interior, the growth rate of the rate of consumption is easily derived from the necessary conditions (3.7)-(3.11). □

Next consider the case $K(0) < K_{\gamma+\mu}$. See figure 3.10.

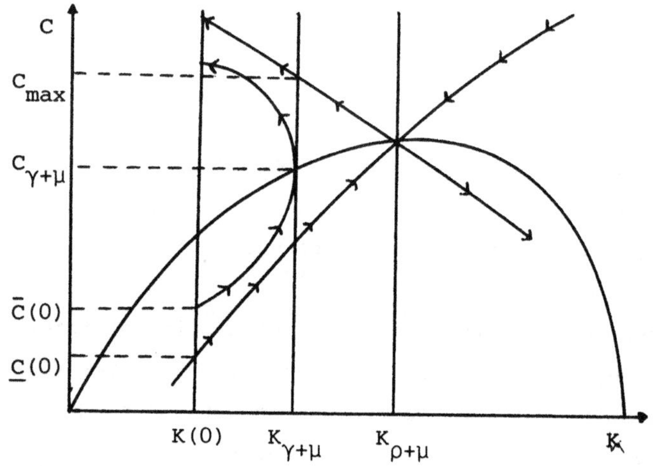

figure 3.10.

We first observe that the initial rate of consumption should lie between $\bar{C}(0)$ and $\underline{C}(0)$, given in figure 3.10. $\underline{C}(0)$ is the rate of consumption lying on the unique trajectory leading from K(0) to the modified golden rule. $\bar{C}(0)$ is such that the trajectory departing from $(\bar{C}(0), K(0))$ passes through the point $(C_{\gamma+\mu}, K_{\gamma+\mu})$. The choice of the initial rate of consumption is restricted to this set for the following reasons. If $\hat{C}(0) > \bar{C}(0)$, then $\hat{E}(t) = 0$ eventually, in view of lemma 2. If $\hat{C}(0) < \underline{C}(0)$, then $K_{\gamma+\mu}$ is approached from the left. At the moment exploitation becomes interior, that is when $K_{\gamma+\mu}$ is reached, $\dot{\hat{K}}$ jumps downwards, implying that the rate of exploitation jumps to a negative value which is clearly ruled out. Consequently, the rates of consumption arrived at, as function of the time necessary to reach them, are given in figure 3.11.

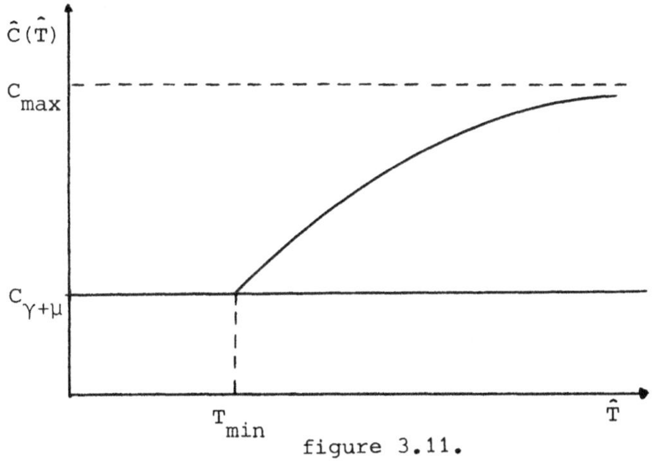

figure 3.11.

In order to see what the optimal $\hat{T}$ (if any) is, the curve in figure 3.11 and curve I in figure 3.8 have to be compared. If the curves displayed have a point of intersection and if the corresponding rate of exploitation is smaller than $\bar{E}$ (which holds true by assumption), the existence of an optimum is established and the characteristics of the optimal program are readily given. If there is no point of intersection, the policy sequence proposed is not optimal. It seems interesting to investigate under which circumstances this would occur. Obviously, the smaller the initial stock of capital relative to $K_{\gamma+\mu}$, the longer is the minimal period of time necessary to reach $K_{\gamma+\mu}$. This implies that the point $(C_{\gamma+\mu}, T_{min})$ in figure 3.11 shifts to the right. Hence the smaller the stock of capital, the more unlikely is a point of intersection to occur. It is easily seen from (3.24) that a relatively large initial value of the resource $(p(0)\ S_o)$ will have the same effect. Figure 3.12 gives in the $p(0)\ S_o$, $K(0)$ plane the region of constellations not allowing for a point of intersection.

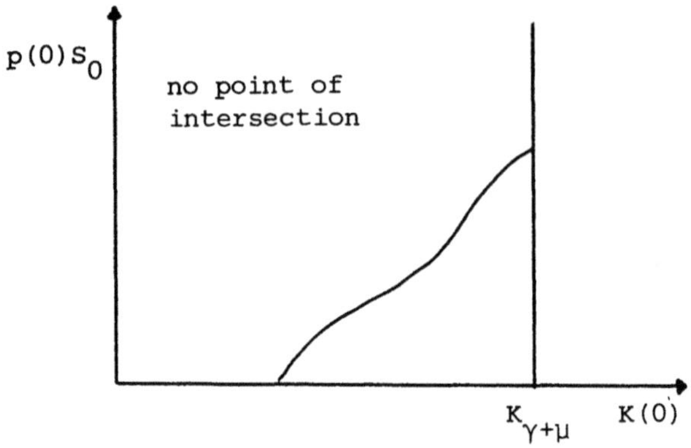

figure 3.12.

What is then the optimal policy sequence when there is no point of intersection? We first remark that the economy should start with exploitation at a maximal rate. For, if it were not, exploitation would be zero for an initial period of time and by virtue of lemma 2 exploitation would still be zero for some t with $\hat{K}(t) > K_{\gamma+\mu}$. But it has been shown that for $\hat{K} > K_{\gamma+\mu}$ there exists an optimal program where initially the rate of exploitation is zero. So if the economy would start with zero exploitation there must be a point of intersection, contradicting our point of departure. Hence there are two possible candidates for an optimal program:

a) maximal exploitation → interior exploitation,

b) maximal exploitation → zero exploitation → interior exploitation.

Both sequences may be optimal as is shown presently. Let $\hat{T}$ denote the point of time where exploitation at the maximal rate comes to an end and suppose sequence a is optimal. At $\hat{T}$ the reserve of the resource equals $S_o - \hat{T}\bar{E}$. Hence we must have

$$\hat{C}(\hat{T}) = \frac{\rho-\gamma(1+\eta)}{\gamma\eta}\{\gamma p(\hat{T})(S_o - \hat{T}\bar{E}) + C_{\gamma+\mu}\}. \tag{3.25}$$

Now suppose

$$-\frac{\rho-\gamma(1+\eta)}{\gamma\eta}(\gamma p(0)\ S_o + C_{\gamma+\mu}) \leq C_{\gamma+\mu}, \tag{3.26}$$

and

$$\bar{E} > \gamma\ S_o\ . \tag{3.27}$$

Then $\hat{C}(\hat{T})$ can be depicted as in figure 3.13.

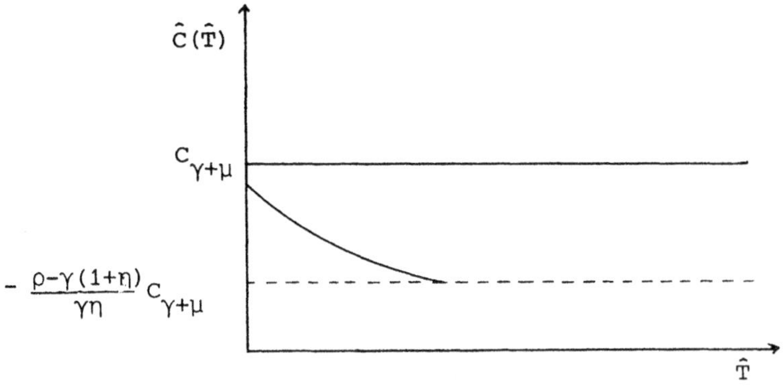

figure 3.13.

At $\hat{T}$ exploitation becomes interior, so it is required that $\hat{C}(\hat{T}) > C_{\gamma+\mu}$. Since $\hat{C}$ is continuous we conclude that policy sequence a is not optimal and that the optimal rate of exploitation should be as in sequence b. If, on the other hand, the initial reserve of the resource is large, then policy sequence a is optimal.
The results are summarized in the following theorem.

Theorem 8

Suppose $\gamma > \rho$ and $K(0) < K_{\gamma+\mu}$. Suppose furthermore that $\bar{E}$ is sufficiently large. The optimal program is characterized as follows.

1) If $p(0)\ S_o$ is small relative to $K(0)$, there exists $\hat{T} > 0$ such that

a) for $0 \leqq t \leqq \hat{T}$, $\hat{E}(t) = 0$, $\hat{K}(\hat{T}) = K_{\gamma+\mu}$, $\dot{\hat{C}}(t) > 0$,

b) for $t > \hat{T}$, $0 < \hat{E}(t) < \bar{E}$, $\hat{K}(t) = K_{\gamma+\mu}$, $\dot{\hat{C}}(t)/\hat{C}(t) = (\rho-\gamma)/\eta$,

c) $\hat{K}(t)$ is increasing initially and decreasing for an interval preceding $\hat{T}$.

2) If $p(0)\ S_o$ is large relative to $K(0)$, there exists $\hat{T}^* > 0$ such that for $0 \leqq t \leqq \hat{T}^*$, $\hat{E}(t) = \bar{E}$. For $t > \hat{T}^*$ the optimal program is of the same type as described under 1a - 1c or as under 1b. □

A final remark concerns the case $K(0) = K_{\gamma+\mu}$. It is not necessarily true that the economy starts with interior exploitation. In fact, it will not do so when the initial reserve of the resource is small in the sense that the solution $\hat{C}(\hat{T})$ of (3.24) is smaller than $C_{\gamma+\mu}$ for $\hat{T} = 0$. It is better for the economy to wait until the resource price is sufficiently large.

3.2.4. The case $\rho = \gamma$

Presently we analyse the case where the rate of time preference coincides with the expected growth rate of the price of the resource commodity. We shall maintain here the assumption that the upper bound on the rate of exploitation is sufficiently large. First the case $K(0) < K_{\gamma+\mu}$ is considered.

It is easily seen that lemma 3 and theorem 2 hold for $\rho = \gamma$. Hence $\hat{K}(t) \leqq K_{\gamma+\mu}$ (lemma 3) and initially $\hat{E}(t) = \bar{E}$. Therefore, if the initial reserve of the resource is "small", the optimal policy is to start with exploitation at a maximal rate. This phase ends within finite time. Afterwards the economy approaches the modified golden rule. When the initial size of the resource is "large", the interval with maximal exploitation is followed by an interval with interior exploitation. This phase will last into infinity. This is seen as follows. It cannot be optimal to jump from an interior solution for the rate of exploitation to exploitation at a zero level, since then exploitation is zero forever and the economy diverges from the modified golden rule. It cannot be optimal either to jump to maximal exploitation, since then lemma 3 would be violated. Hence the resource will last forever. The rate of consumption is constant when exploitation is interior. This constant is larger than the modified golden rule consumption. Along the phase with interior exploitation, exploitation decreases at the rate γ. Hence we have

<u>Theorem 9</u>

Suppose $\gamma = \rho$ and $K(0) < K_{\gamma+\mu}$. The optimal program is characterized as follows.

1) If $p(0)\ S_o$ is small relative to $K(0)$, there exists $\hat{T} > 0$ such that

a) for $0 \leqq t \leqq \hat{T}$, $\hat{E}(t) = \bar{E}$, $\hat{K}(t) < K_{\gamma+\mu}$, $\dot{\hat{C}} > 0$,

b) for $t > \hat{T}$, $\hat{E}(t) = 0$, $\hat{K}(t) \to K_{\rho+\mu}$, $\hat{C}(t) \to C_{\rho+\mu}$.

2) If $p(0)\ S_o$ is large relative to $K(0)$, there exists $\hat{T} > 0$ such that

a) for $0 \leqq t \leqq \hat{T}$, $\hat{E}(t) = \bar{E}$, $\dot{\hat{K}}(t) > 0$, $\dot{\hat{C}}(t) > 0$, $\hat{K}(\hat{T}) = K_{\gamma+\mu}$,

b) for $t > \hat{T}$, $0 < \hat{E}(t) < \bar{E}$, $\dot{\hat{E}}(t)/\hat{E}(t) = -\gamma$, $\hat{K}(t) = K_{\gamma+\mu}$, $\dot{\hat{C}}(t) = 0$. □

Secondly we consider the case $K(0) > K_{\gamma+\mu}$. Then the following holds.

<u>Theorem 10</u>

Suppose $\gamma = \rho$ and $K(0) > K_{\gamma+\mu}$. Suppose furthermore that $\bar{E}$ is sufficiently large. The optimal program can be characterized as follows. There exists $\hat{T} > 0$ such that:

a) for $0 \leqq t \leqq \hat{T}$, $\hat{E}(t) = 0$, $\dot{\hat{K}}(t) < 0$, $\hat{K}(\hat{T}) = K_{\gamma+\mu}$, $\dot{\hat{C}}(t) < 0$,

b) for $t > \hat{T}$, $0 < \hat{E}(t) < \bar{E}$, $\dot{\hat{E}}(t)/\hat{E}(t) = -\gamma$, $\hat{K}(t) = K_{\gamma+\mu}$, $\dot{\hat{C}}(t) = 0$. □

If $K(0) = K_{\gamma+\mu}$, then clearly it is optimal to have interior exploitation forever, provided $\bar{E}$ is large enough.

3.2.5. A small upper bound on the rate of exploitation

In the previous subsections it has been assumed that the upper bound on the rate of exploitation is large enough so as to make interior exploitation optimal, when, at some instant of time, the state of the economy is given by a positive reserve of the resource and a stock of capital equal to $K_{\gamma+\mu}$. Here this assumption will be dropped. Several cases have to be considered.

1) $\rho > \gamma$.

The optimal program for the case $K(0) < K_{\gamma+\mu}$ has been characterized in theorem 3. There it was not necessary to assume that $\bar{E}$ is large enough. Hence this case poses no problems.

We therefore turn to the case $K(0) > K_{\gamma+\mu}$.

In theorem 4 we had to make a proviso with respect to $\bar{E}$. There are only four possible policy sequences with respect to the rate of exploitation when $\bar{E}$ is small. To see this, observe that, if, along an optimal program, exploitation is interior for an interval of time, the resource will be exhausted during that interval. Furthermore, since $K(0) > K_{\gamma+\mu}$ the economy starts with either $\hat{E}(0) = 0$ or $\hat{E}(0) = \bar{E}$. In the former case the interval with $\hat{E} = 0$ must be followed by an interval with $\hat{E} = \bar{E}$ since it is assumed here that $\bar{E}$ will be binding somewhere. In the latter case, the interval with $\hat{E} = \bar{E}$ is followed by an interval with interior exploitation, or by an interval, extending into infinity, with zero exploitation, in view of lemma 2, saying that for $\hat{K} > K_{\gamma+\mu}$ it is impossible to jump from $\hat{E} = \bar{E}$ to $\hat{E} = 0$ and theorem 3, showing that, if $\hat{K} < K_{\gamma+\mu}$ and $\hat{S} > 0$, $\hat{E} = \bar{E}$. Hence the four possible policy sequences are:

a) $\hat{E} = 0 \rightarrow \hat{E} = \bar{E} \rightarrow 0 < \hat{E} < \bar{E} \rightarrow \hat{E} = 0,$

b) $\hat{E} = \bar{E} \rightarrow 0 < \hat{E} < \bar{E} \rightarrow \hat{E} = 0,$

c) $\hat{E} = 0 \rightarrow \hat{E} = \bar{E} \rightarrow \hat{E} = 0,$

d) $\hat{E} = \bar{E} \rightarrow \hat{E} = 0.$

Therefore we can state the following theorem.

Theorem 11

Suppose $\rho > \gamma$. There exist $\hat{T}$ such that $\hat{S}(\hat{T}) = 0$. □

Which one of these policy sequences will be optimal depends obviously on the parameters of the model. It is not the purpose of this subsection to give a full account of the conditions under which each of the sequences is optimal. It seems that this problem is difficult to solve analytically and that a numerical approach is more appropriate. It is however intuitively clear that sequence a is optimal, when the upper bound on the rate of exploitation is not too different from the one the economy would like to prevail. On the other hand, if $\bar{E}$ is very small as well as the initial size of the resource, the optimal policy sequence is d, as the following argument shows.
Suppose, that for some $T_1 > 0$, $\hat{K}(T_1) = K_{\gamma+\mu}$ and $\hat{S}(T_1) > 0$. Define, as before, C^* as the rate of consumption lying on the unique trajectory, starting at $K_{\gamma+\mu}$, leading to the modified golden rule. If $C^* > C_{\gamma+\mu}+p(T_1)\bar{E}$, then the economy will not choose for interior exploitation. This is so since, if the economy did, the rate of consumption after exhaustion of the resource would be smaller than C^* and the modified golden rule cannot be approached, since $\hat{C}$ must be continuous. It is also not optimal to have $\hat{E}(T_1+) = 0$. This contradicts theorem 3 ($\hat{E} = \bar{E}$ for $\hat{K} < K_{\gamma+\mu}$ and $\hat{S} > 0$) or lemma 3 (excluding that $\hat{K}$ is growing for $\hat{K} > K_{\gamma+\mu}$ and $\hat{S} > 0$). Hence if $C^* > C_{\gamma+\mu} + p(T_1)\bar{E}$, then $\hat{E}(T_1+) = \bar{E}$. Suppose then that for some time T_2 ($>T_1$) on the rate of exploitation is interior. The time path of $\hat{K}$ is depicted in figure 3.14.

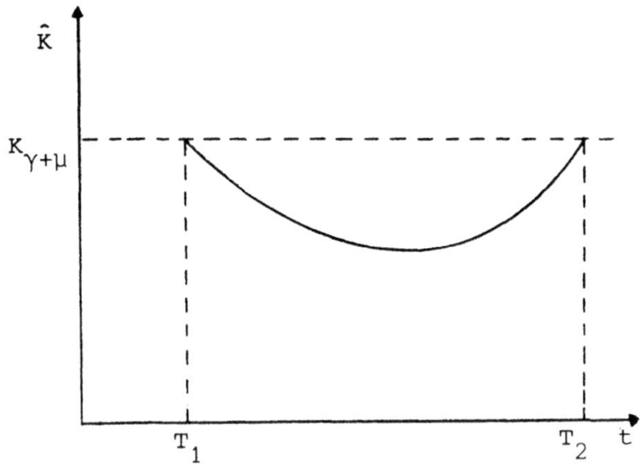

figure 3.14.

$\dot{\hat{K}}(T_2-) > 0$ implying that $\hat{C}(T_2-) < C_{\gamma+\mu} + p(T_2)\bar{E}$. But we must also have $C^* < C_{\gamma+\mu} + p(T_2)\bar{E}$. This implies that $T_2 - T_1 \geqq M$ for some positive M, depending on the difference between C* and $C_{\gamma+\mu} + p(T_1)\bar{E}$. On the other hand $T_2 - T_1 < \hat{S}(T_1)/\bar{E}$ because, at T_2, the resource is not yet exhausted. M can be made arbitrarily close to $C^* - C_{\gamma+\mu}$ by manipulating p(0). Now, if $\hat{S}(T_1)$ is sufficiently small, then we cannot have $C^* < C_{\gamma+\mu} + p(T_2)\bar{E}$. It can therefore be concluded that, if the state of the economy at some instant of time is given by $\hat{K} = K_{\gamma+\mu}$, $\hat{S} > 0$, it is not necessarily optimal to have interior exploitation at some future instant of time.

2) $\rho < \gamma$.

Here we shall not make a distinction according to whether or not $K(0) < K_{\gamma+\mu}$. Let us assume that, along an interval of time, the rate of exploitation is interior. It follows that, along this interval, $\hat{K} = K_{\gamma+\mu}$ and

$$U'(C_{\gamma+\mu} + p\hat{E}) = \hat{\lambda}e^{(\rho-\gamma)t}/p(0). \tag{3.28}$$

Given $\hat{\lambda}$, we can depict the, not necessarily feasible, solution $\hat{E}(t)$ of (3.28) as follows.

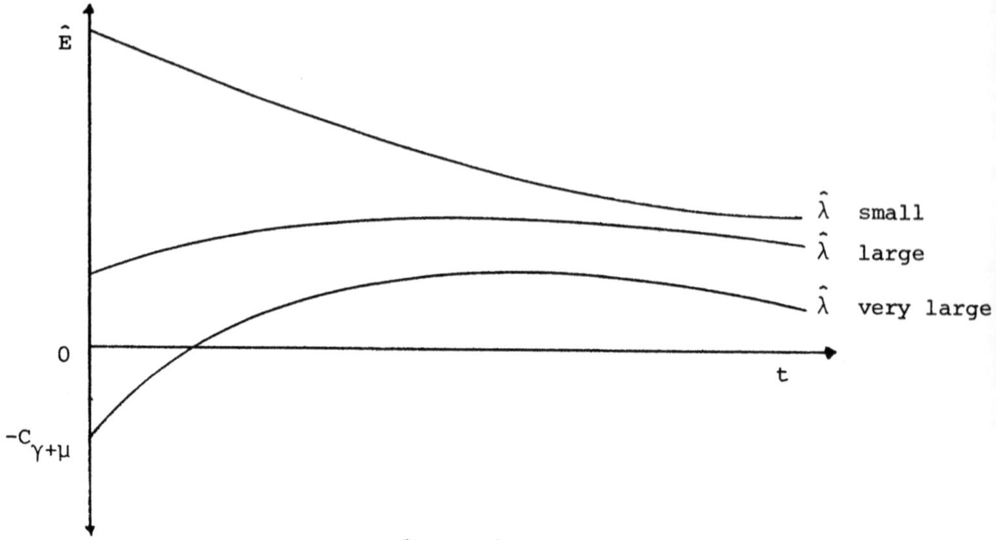

figure 3.15.

Clearly the larger is $\hat{\lambda}$, the smaller is the initial $\hat{E}$. For $\hat{\lambda} \to \infty$, $p(0)\hat{E}(0) \to -C_{\gamma+\mu}$. Differentiation of (3.28) with respect to time yields

$$\eta(\gamma + \dot{\hat{E}}/\hat{E})/(1 + C_{\gamma+\mu}/p\hat{E}) = \rho - \gamma.$$

For $\hat{\lambda}$ very small, $p(0)\hat{E}(0)$ is large. Furthermore, $p\hat{E}$ is increasing in time. Since it has been assumed that $\rho > \gamma\ (1+\eta)$, $\dot{\hat{E}}/\hat{E} < 0$ for small $\hat{\lambda}$. If $\hat{\lambda}$ is large, $p(0)\hat{E}(0)$ is small. Eventually $p\hat{E}$ must become positive in view of (3.28). However $\dot{\hat{E}}/\hat{E} < 0$ eventually. This explains the form of the curves in figure 3.15. We conclude that if, along an optimal program, the rate of exploitation is interior, it is decreasing eventually and that it might increase for an initial interval of time. Next it will be shown that if, along an optimal program, the rate of exploitation is interior and decreasing during some interval of time, then the rate of exploitation will remain interior throughout the program. This is seen as follows. Suppose the statement is not true. Then, at the moment of the transition to maximal exploitation, the rate of investments jumps upwards and there follows an interval with $\hat{K} > K_{\gamma+\mu}$. Along such an interval $\dot{\hat{C}}/\hat{C} < (\rho-\gamma)/\eta$. Therefore, since the rate of consumption is continuous, the "optimal program" can be improved upon by a program, keeping the stock of capital at the $K_{\gamma+\mu}$ level, yielding a growth rate of consumption equal to $(\rho-\gamma)/\eta$. Subsequently, it is shown that if, along an optimal program, the rate of exploitation is interior and increasing for some interval of time, then there follows at most one interval of time with exploitation at a maximal rate. Consider figure 3.16.

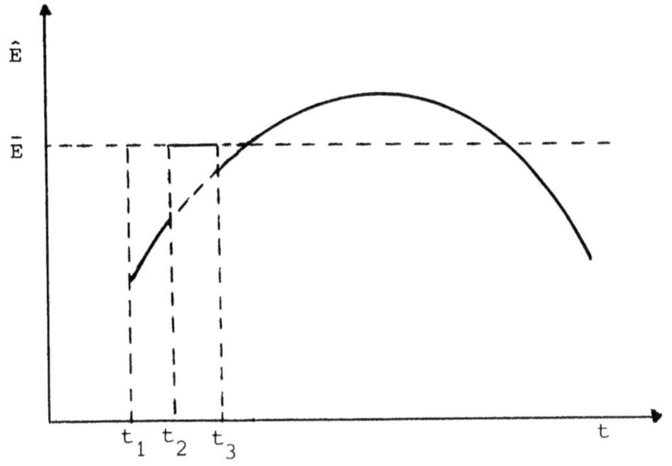

figure 3.16.

Suppose, $0 < \hat{E}(t) < \bar{E}$, for $t_1 < t < t_2$. If $\hat{E}(t_2-) = \bar{E}$, then clearly the statement is proven in view of our previous remarks. So let us suppose that, at t_2, the rate of exploitation jumps upwards to $\bar{E}$ and that, at t_3 ($> t_2$), it becomes interior again. Then the argument used above can be invoked again to show that such a policy is not optimal. These results are summarized in

Theorem 12

Suppose $\rho < \gamma$ and there exists t_1 such that $0 < \hat{E}(t_1) < \bar{E}$. Then $0 < \hat{E}(t) < \bar{E}$ for all $t \geqq t_1$ or $0 < \hat{E}(t) < \bar{E}$ for all $t \geqq t_1$ except for one interval of time where $\hat{E}(t) = \bar{E}$. □

Admittedly, this theorem does not deal with the effects of a small upper bound $\bar{E}$ on the exploitation policy to be pursued initially. We leave this problem to be solved numerically.

3) $\rho = \gamma$.

Since in this case, the rate of exploitation is decreasing whenever it is interior, we have the following theorem.

Theorem 13

Suppose $\rho = \gamma$ and there exists t_1 such that $0 < \hat{E}(t_1) < \bar{E}$. Then $0 < \hat{E}(t) < \bar{E}$ for all $t \geqq t_1$. □

3.3. Markets for stocks

Here we introduce markets for capital stocks and resource reserves, while maintaining the assumption that there is no world market for bonds. Let us first give a motivation for considering this case. In the model of the previous section, the economy will in general wish to adjust its stock of capital to a certain level ($K_{\gamma+\mu}$). The speed of this adjustment is however limited by the continuity requirements on K and S. But it might be interesting to find out what the economy's best policy would be when these constraints were not present. Then it could for example import total industries in exchange for concessions on its resource.

No problem arises when defining markets for capital. A market for capital stocks is a market where property rights on capital stocks are bought and sold. It will be assumed here that capital as a stock is perfectly mobile and can (and will) immediately be used in the buying economy. For this assumption there are some alternatives: one could assume that capital as a stock is immobile and that, therefore, the buyer gets only rights on the flow of revenues derived from it, or that capital is mobile and that the new owner can use it as an input anywhere in the world. We shall not make these assumptions, because we are primarily interested in the optimal size of the domestic stock of capital. It is more difficult to give a definition of a market for property rights onexhaustible resources. If there are no restrictions on the rate of exploitation, no problems occur: buying or selling resources is like trading in pieces of land where the resource finds itself (at least when land does not have any other possible use). But matters become complicated when such restrictions are present. The motivation behind the introduction of $\bar{E}$ in chapter 2 was of a geological nature. Therefore, selling part of the resource cannot be considered irrespective of the exploitation schedule the buyer will follow: the price at which the owner is willing to sell, depends on this schedule, since the geological conditions do not change as a consequence of the sale. (Matters will of course become even more complicated when exploitation requires the input of factors of production). It cannot be hoped to give a full account of all possibilities, so this section will only deal with some special cases.

The analysis will be carried out as follows. We shall compare optimal programs for different initial stocks. From these comparisons conclusions can be drawn with respect to the optimal composition of these initial stocks. Then enter the world markets for stocks and conditions on the relative price of the resource reserves can be derived under which trade will actually occur. The results give sufficient conditions for trade.

A priori it seems worthwile to pay attention to the presence of stock markets not only at the outset of the planning period. There is however a theorem by Arrow and Kurz (1968) saying that, if the Hamiltonian of a control problem is strictly concave, jumps in the state variables will only occur at $t = 0$. Since our U and F are strictly concave, this condition is satisfied here.

We now consider the case $K(0) > K_{\gamma+\mu}$. It follows from theorems 4 and 7, that if $K(0) > K_{\gamma+\mu}$, there is an initial interval with $\hat{E} = 0$. At the end of this interval $\hat{K} = K_{\gamma+\mu}$. Let $\hat{z} = \{\hat{K}, \hat{S}, \hat{C}, \hat{E}\}$ denote the corresponding optimal program and denote by $\hat{T}$ the time where this initial interval ends. Suppose now that, at time zero, there exist stock markets and that the economy were offered an extra reserve of the resource in return for which it has to pay some capital. In particular, the economy is offered $f(t)$ units of the resource to be delivered at time t for $0 \leqq t \leqq \hat{T}$. By $\tilde{K}(0)$ we denote the economy's new stock of capital when the deal is accepted. The economy will accept the offer if, between 0 and $\hat{T}$, it enjoys more welfare and ends up with the same amount of capital. Consider therefore the following problem. Maximize

$$\int_0^{\hat{T}} e^{-\rho t} U(C(t))dt,$$

subject to

$$\dot{K} = F(K) - \mu K - C + pf(t),$$

$$K(0) = \tilde{K}(0),$$

$$K(\hat{T}) = \hat{K}(\hat{T}).$$

Let $\tilde{z} = \{\tilde{K},\tilde{S},\tilde{C},\tilde{E}\}$ be the solution of this problem and let $\tilde{\phi},\tilde{\lambda},\tilde{\alpha}$ and $\tilde{\beta}$ denote the corresponding auxiliary variables. Then

$$J_{\hat{T}} := \int_0^{\hat{T}} e^{-\rho t} (U(\tilde{C})-U(\hat{C}))dt \geq \int_0^{\hat{T}} e^{-\rho t} U'(\tilde{C})(\tilde{C}-\hat{C})dt$$

$$\geq \int_0^{\hat{T}} \tilde{\phi}(F'(\tilde{K})-\mu)(\tilde{K}-\hat{K})dt + \int_0^{\hat{T}} p\tilde{\phi}f(t)dt$$

$$+ \int_0^{\hat{T}} \tilde{\phi}d(\hat{K}-\tilde{K})$$

$$= \int_0^{\hat{T}} p\tilde{\phi}f(t)dt - (\hat{K}(0) - \tilde{K}(0))\tilde{\phi}(0).$$

Since $\tilde{\phi}p$ is non-decreasing for $\tilde{K} \geq K_{\gamma+\mu}$ we have

$$J_{\hat{T}} \geq p(0)\tilde{\phi}(0) \int_0^{\hat{T}} f(t)dt - (\hat{K}(0)-\tilde{K}(0))\tilde{\phi}(0).$$

Therefore the economy will accept the offer if the value of the extra resources, evaluated at p(0), exceeds the stock of capital that has to be sold in return.

We next turn to the case $K(0) < K_{\gamma+\mu}$. The economy is offered a new stock of capital $\tilde{K}(0)$ in return for which it sells an exploitation schedule given by f(t). Suppose that, along the optimal program in the absence of stock markets, $\hat{E}(t) = \bar{E}$ for all t smaller than some $\hat{T}$ and that from $\hat{T}$ on the rate of exploitation is interior, at least for some interval of time. Consider now the following problem. Maximize

$$\int_0^{\hat{T}} e^{-\rho t} U(C(t))dt,$$

subject to

$$\dot{K} = F(K) - \mu K - C + pE,$$

$$0 \leq E \leq \bar{E} - f(t),$$

$$\int_0^{\hat{T}} (E(t) + f(t))dt \leq S_o - \hat{T}\bar{E},$$

$$K(0) = \tilde{K}(0),$$

$$K(\hat{T}) = K_{\gamma+\mu}.$$

Let $\tilde{z} = \{\tilde{K}, \tilde{S}, \tilde{C}, \tilde{E}\}$ be the optimal program and let $\tilde{\phi}$, $\tilde{\lambda}$, $\tilde{\alpha}$ and $\tilde{\beta}$ be the auxiliary variables. Then

$$J_{\hat{T}} := \int_0^{\hat{T}} e^{-\rho t} \, (U(\tilde{C}) - U(\hat{C}))dt$$

$$\geqq \int_0^{\hat{T}} \hat{\phi} \; p(\tilde{E}-\hat{E})dt - (\hat{K}(0) - \tilde{K}(0))\tilde{\phi}(0).$$

Hence the economy will accept the offer if $0 < \tilde{E}(t) < \bar{E} - f(t)$ for $0 \leqq t \leqq \hat{T}$ (and hence $\tilde{K}(0) = K_{\gamma+\mu}$) and

$$K_{\gamma+\mu} - \hat{K}(0) > p(0) \int_0^{\hat{T}} f(t)dt.$$

This is so, since under these conditions $\tilde{\phi}p$ is constant for $0 \leqq t \leqq \hat{T}$. Hence again the economy will engage in trade when the stock of capital newly obtained exceeds the value of the exploitation scheme sold.

3.4. *A perfect world market for bonds*

The model presented here describes a competitive economy that can lend and borrow as much as it wants, provided the present discounted value of total expenditures does not exceed the present discounted value of total income. The world market rate of interest is $r(t)$, which is given to the economy. These assumptions allow for the application of the separation theorem. Hence the economy should aim at the maximization of the present discounted value of the revenues from resource activities. We shall show that such a model leads to rather peculiar outcomes, unless there is some rule relating the interest rate to the growth rate of the price of the resource good. Consider

$$v(t) := - \int_0^t (r(\tau) - \gamma(\tau))d\tau.$$

The economy wishes to maximize

$$\int_0^\infty e^{v(t)} \; p(0)E(t)dt,$$

subject to

$$\int_0^\infty (b\, e^{-bt} \; S_o \; - \; E(t))dt \geqq 0,$$

$$0 \leqq E \leqq \bar{E}.$$

The Lagrangean reads

$$L(E,\lambda,\alpha,\beta) = e^{v(t)} \; p(0)E + \lambda(b\, e^{-bt} \; S_o - E) + \alpha E + \beta(\bar{E}-E).$$

Necessary conditions for an optimum are that there exist a constant $\hat{\lambda}$ and piece-wise continuous $\hat{\alpha}(t)$ and $\hat{\beta}(t)$ (possibly discontinuous at points of discontinuity of $\hat{E}$) such that

$$\partial L/\partial E = 0 : e^{v(t)} \; p(0) - \hat{\lambda} + \hat{\alpha}(t) - \hat{\beta}(t) = 0,$$

$$\hat{\alpha}(t) \; \hat{E}(t) = 0, \; \hat{\alpha}(t) \geqq 0,$$

$$\hat{\beta}(t) \; (\bar{E}-\hat{E}(t)) = 0, \; \hat{\beta}(t) \geqq 0.$$

If $v(t)$ is unbounded, no optimum exists. This is seen as follows. The maximand will attain the value infinity and the original problem of maximizing total welfare will not have a solution. In fact the growth rate of the price of the resource good is too large relative to the rate of interest. Hence we assume that $v(t)$ is bounded from above. The optimal program looks as follows. Take a constant ζ and calculate the total length of time during which $v(t) \geqq \zeta$. If this total length of time equals $T = S_o/\bar{E}$, then put $\hat{E} = \bar{E}$ during these intervals and $\hat{E} = 0$ otherwise. If the total length of time is smaller than T, then take a smaller ζ. Continue this procedure until the total length of intervals equals at least T. If the total length exceeds T, then the optimal policy is to have maximal exploitation during the intervals where v is maximal, taking into account the limitation of the resource. The solution needs obviously not be unique. See figure 3.17.

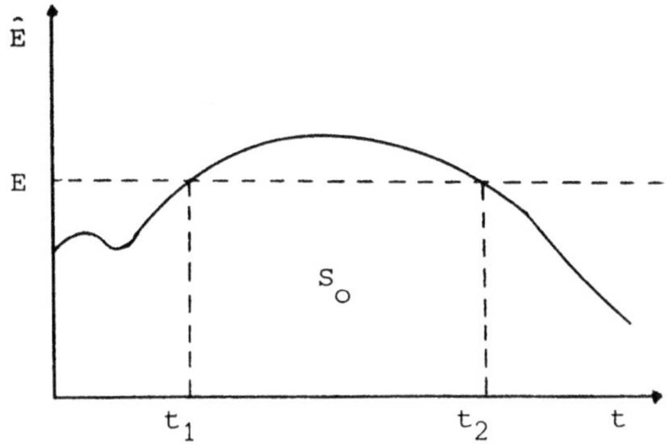

figure 3.17.

Also, when $r(t) = \gamma(t)$ for all t, then an optimal program could be $0 < \hat{E}(t) < \bar{E}$ for all t.

As for the present value of income from non-resource production, the economy will maximize

$$\int_0^\infty q(t)\ (F(K) - (r(t) + \mu)K)dt,$$

where

$$q(t) = e^{-\int_0^t r(\tau)d\tau}.$$

Hence the economy will always employ capital up to the amount equating marginal product and the gross rental rate:

$$F'(\hat{K}(t)) = r(t) + \mu. \tag{3.29}$$

Due to our assumptions on the production function, (3.29) has a solution for any r(t). Denoting the sum of the present discounted values of resource exploitation and non-resource production, carried out in the optimal way, by M, we can formulate the economy's problem with respect to consumption:

$$\text{maximize } J = \int_0^\infty e^{-\rho t}\ U(C(t))dt,$$

subject to

$$\int_0^\infty q(t)\ C(t)dt \leqq M.$$

The Lagrangean reads

$$L(C,\psi) = e^{-\rho t}\, U(C) - \psi(q(t)\, C - b\, e^{-bt}\, M),$$

where b is some positive constant. A necessary condition for an optimal program is that there exists a constant $\hat{\psi}$ such that

$$e^{-\rho t}\, U'(\hat{C}(t)) = \hat{\psi}\, q(t).$$

Hence

$$\dot{\hat{C}}/\hat{C} = (\rho - r(t))/\eta(\hat{C}). \qquad (3.30)$$

Hereby the optimal program has not yet been established. Suppose an optimum exists and denote the initial rate of consumption by $\hat{C}_o$. Then it follows from (3.30) that

$$\int_0^\infty \hat{C}_o\, e^{\int_0^t \frac{\rho - r(\tau)(1+\eta(\hat{C}(\tau)))}{\eta(C(\tau))} d\tau}\, dt \leqq M. \qquad (3.31)$$

If eventually (which means for all $t > T$ for some $T \geqq 0$) $\rho > r(t)$, no problem arises, since the rate of consumption is decreasing eventually and there will exist a $\hat{C}_o$ such that (3.31) is satisfied. If eventually $\rho < r(t)$, then the rate of consumption is increasing. Given that

$$\bar{r} := \lim_{t\to\infty} r(t),$$

$$\bar{\eta} := \lim_{C\to\infty} \eta(C)$$

exist, it is easily seen that a necessary and sufficient condition for the existence of an optimal program for the case at hand, is

$$\rho > \bar{r}(1+\bar{\eta}).$$

It should be remarked that in the analysis no attention has been paid to the amount of bonds the economy starts with. Essentially nothing will change, if we assume the initial bond holdings to differ from zero. Only the value of M, disposable income, will be larger or

smaller depending on whether initially the economy has positive or negative bond holdings.
The results of this section are summarized in

Theorem 14
Suppose there exists a perfect world market for bonds, bearing interest rate $r(t)$. Then necessary conditions for the existence of an optimum are:

i) $-\int_0^t (r(\tau) - \gamma(\tau))d\tau$ is bounded above,

ii) $\rho > \bar{r}(1+\bar{\eta})$.

Condition i) is sufficient for the existence of an optimal exploitation pattern (which needs not be uniquely determined). Condition ii) is (given that condition i) holds) sufficient for the existence of an optimal consumption plan. Along this plan the rate of consumption is increasing (decreasing) if $\rho < r(t)$ $(\rho > r(t))$. □

A final remark is in order with respect to condition i) of this theorem. There are several good reasons to justify the assumption that it holds. It has been postulated that the world market for bonds is competitive as well as the market for the resource good. If condition i) would not hold the market for bonds would not be in equilibrium since the country under consideration would supply an infinite amount of bonds which would not be absorbed in the market. Furthermore, our country would not supply resource goods, but in addition no other owner of the resource would, since each agent is assumed to have perfect knowledge. Hence the resource commodity would not be supplied at all, until infinity. This could never establish world wide general equilibrium since there is always demand for the resource good.

3.5. Conclusions

In this chapter we have analysed the problem of simultaneous optimal exploitation of a natural resource and optimal investments for a small country. It has been shown that the nature of optimal programs heavily depends on which world markets are in existence. We shall here briefly summarize the results and give some conclusions. In the case of no bonds market nor markets for stocks the outcomes drastically differ according to whether or not the growth rate of the world market price of the resource good is larger than the rate of time preference and according to the initial stock of capital relative to $K_{\gamma+\mu}$. Along an optimal program the rate of exploitation is initially either at the maximum level or zero. If $\rho > \gamma$, the resource will be exhausted within finite time, whereas, if $\gamma > \rho$, the resource will last forever. In some cases the upper bound on the rate of exploitation prevents non-existence of optimal programs. When we introduced world markets for stocks, while maintaining the assumption that the world market for bonds is absent, we were able to calculate for some situations the resource-stock price that would provide the economy with an incentive to engage in trade on these markets. Finally, in the presence of a world market for bonds, we characterized the optimal investment/exploitation program. Here the optimal exploitation path typically depends on the course of the real interest rate minus the growth rate of the resource price. In order to have an optimum, the real interest rate should be sufficiently high. What can be learned from the results obtained in this chapter? Before dealing with this question, it should be stressed that here it is necessary to be modest. Although we have been considering several models, it is clear that these models represent extreme cases. In reality the relevant markets are less perfect than we have been postulating here and moreover we have not taken into account any type of uncertainty (see on the problem of uncertainty with respect to e.g. the reserves of the resource, Crabbé (1982)). Nonetheless the very large variety of possible optimal programs, depending on the parameters of the models, will only be increased when more realistic models are studied. Therefore, our general conclusion is that simple rules such as the Hotelling rule can in the case of open economies where physical capital plays a role in non-resource production, not be applied.

4. *RATIONING ON THE BONDS MARKET*

4.1. *Introduction*

In the previous chapter we have been analysing the problem of optimal exploitation and optimal savings of a small, price-taking, economy. With respect to the debt position of the economy two cases have been discussed. Firstly, the case where the economy was a priori held to establish permanent equilibrium on the current account of its balance of payments. Secondly, attention has been paid to a situation where the economy was allowed to lend and borrow at will, provided the sum of discounted exports exceded the sum of discounted imports. Obviously these cases are extremes and not very realistic. It is the objective of the present chapter to give an account of an intermediate possibility.

Such an analysis seems to be important, since in the real world the amount of money a country can borrow or will lend is in some sense limited, in a way different from the cases mentioned above. The explanation of this phenomenon is to be found in the imperfection of the international market for financial capital. This imperfection can on its turn be explained by a large variety of circumstances. One reason could be that transactors on this market do not have uniform expectations with respect to the future prices. One could also think of different attitudes towards risk. Uncertainty with respect to, for example, the size of a natural resource may play a role as well. As a final possibility we mention the phenomenon of dynamic inconsistency, being a result of the non-enforceability of contracts. From this summing-up it follows that the limitation of borrowing facilities can have different grounds. One possible line of research would then be to model each of these reasons of imperfection in order to say something of the type of rationing occurring on the financial market. Such an analysis, however interesting, will not be followed here. The problems mentioned are not specific for natural resources and could be studied in a context not including these resources. We shall, in this chapter, pay attention to the effects credit rationing has on the exploitation scheme of an economy.

Rationing on the world's financial market can be modeled in several ways. One could assume that a country's debt is not allowed to exceed a given proportion of current (per capita) income or that repayments and interest payments should not exceed such a proportion. Another assumption would be that the increase of per capita debt is bounded by some given number (see Aarrestad (1979)). Here we shall simply postulate an upper bound on the indebtedness of the economy. Admittedly this choice is an arbitrary one, but in view of our previous remarks, it is not less plausible than any other, necessarily ad hoc, assumption.

In the sequel we shall adopt a simplified version of the model used in the previous chapter, at least with respect to the features not referring to lending and borrowing. It will be assumed that physical capital does not play a role. This assumption is made in order to facilitate the analysis and to be able to identify in detail the effects of rationing. The objective functional of the economy is simplified in the sense that it is assumed throughout that the elasticity of marginal utility is constant (η). There is no reason why the consumer good, appearing in the utility function, should be the numéraire . We shall assume that the economy takes the price of this good (p_c) given and expects it to grow at a constant rate, denoted by π. As usual, the growth rate of the resource commodity is denoted by γ.

The plan of this chapter is as follows. In sections 4.2. and 4.3. the extreme cases with respect to borrowing facilities, will be analysed. This analysis is concise since the results are contained in the outcomes of the previous chapter. Section 4.4. is devoted to credit rationing. Finally section 4.5. contains the conclusions.

4.2. *Permanent equilibrium on the current account*

The problem of the economy is to maximize

$$J = \int_0^\infty e^{-\rho t}\, U(C(t))dt, \tag{4.1}$$

subject to

$$\int_0^\infty E(t)dt = S_o, \tag{4.2}$$

$$0 \leqq E(t) \leqq \bar{E}, \tag{4.3}$$

$$p_c(t)\; C(t) = p_e(t)\; E(t), \tag{4.4}$$

where $p_e(t)$ stands for the price of the resource commodity the economy expects to prevail at time t. As already mentioned, it is assumed that $\dot{p}_c/p_c = \pi$, $\dot{p}_e/p_e = \gamma$, $U''C/U' = \eta$. This type of utility function guarantees that along an optimal program the rate of consumption and hence the rate of exploitation are positive. Therefore the constraint $E(t) \geqq 0$ will never be active. Then the Lagrangean reads

$$L(C,E,\phi,\lambda,\beta) = e^{-\rho t}\; U(C) + \phi(p_e(t)E - p_c(t)C)$$

$$+ \lambda(be^{-bt}\; S_o - E) + \beta(\bar{E} - E),$$

where b is an arbitrary positive constant. Let $\hat{z}(t) = \{\hat{C}(t), \hat{E}(t)\}$ be an optimal program. Then, according to the maximum principle (see appendix B), there exist a nonnegative constant $\hat{\lambda}$ and piece-wise continuous $\hat{\phi}(t)$ and $\hat{\beta}(t)$, possibly discontinuous at points of discontinuity of $\hat{E}(t)$, such that

$$\partial L/\partial C = 0 \; : \; e^{-\rho t}\; U'(\hat{C}(t)) = \hat{\phi}(t)\; p_c(t), \tag{4.5}$$

$$\partial L/\partial E = 0 \; : \; \hat{\phi}(t)\; p_e(t) - \hat{\beta}(t) = \hat{\lambda}, \tag{4.6}$$

$$\hat{\beta}(t)\; (\bar{E} - \hat{E}(t)) = 0, \qquad \hat{\beta}(t) \geqq 0. \tag{4.7}$$

In the sequel time indices will be omitted when there is no danger of confusion. We first show that an optimal program needs not to exist.

<u>Theorem 1</u>

If $\rho \leqq (\gamma-\pi)(1+\eta)$, then the problem posed has no solution.

<u>Proof</u>

Suppose the contrary. It is convenient to distinguish between the cases $\rho < (\gamma-\pi)(1+\eta)$ and $\rho = (\gamma-\pi)(1+\eta)$. Consider the former case first. Assume that during some interval of time $\hat{E} = \bar{E}$. During such an interval $\hat{\beta}$ and $\hat{\phi}$ are continuous. Differentiation of (4.5) with respect to time and the use of (4.4) gives:

$$\dot{\hat{\phi}}/\hat{\phi}+\gamma = -\rho + (\gamma-\pi)(1+\eta).$$

Since $\hat{\lambda}$ is constant, it then follows from (4.6) that $\hat{\beta}$ is increasing. The phase with $\hat{E} = \bar{E}$ cannot last forever, hence at some point of time a transition to interior exploitation must be made. At that point of time $\hat{\beta}$ jumps downwards and so does $\hat{\phi}$, implying that $\hat{C}$ jumps upwards (see (4.5)). But jumps of $\hat{E}$ and $\hat{C}$ in opposite directions are excluded by (4.4). Therefore, for all instants of time the rate of exploitation is interior. Then it is easily seen that $\hat{\beta} = 0$ (4.7), implying that $\dot{\hat{\phi}}/\hat{\phi} = -\gamma$ (4.6). Upon using this in (4.5) it is found from (4.4) that

$$\dot{\hat{E}}/\hat{E} = \frac{\rho-(\gamma-\pi)(1+\eta)}{\eta} > 0,$$

contradicting (4.2). If $\rho = (\gamma-\pi)(1+\eta)$ and if, during some interval of time, $\hat{E} = \bar{E}$, then, using the same argument as above, we find that $\hat{\phi}p$ is constant along this interval. Suppose $\hat{\beta} > 0$ in this interval. At some instant of time $\hat{E}$ becomes interior. Then $\hat{\beta}$ jumps downwards, $\hat{\phi}$ jumps downwards (4.6) and $\hat{C}$ jumps downwards (4.5), contradicting (4.4). Hence $\hat{\beta} = 0$ along the entire program. Therefore $\hat{\phi}$ is continuous (4.6) and so are $\hat{C}$ (4.5) and $\hat{E}$ (4.4). It then follows from (4.5) and (4.4) that $\hat{E}$ is constant. But there is no positive constant rate of exploitation not violating (4.2). □

Remark that this result is analogous to the outcome of theorem 6 of the previous chapter.

Henceforth it will be assumed that $\omega(:=(\rho-(\gamma-\pi)(1+\eta))/\eta)$ is negative. Then the optimal program is readily established. Consider the equation

$$-\bar{E}/\omega = S_o - \bar{E}T. \tag{4.8}$$

The right hand side of this equation denotes what, at time T, is left of the resource, if, up to T, it is exploited at the maximal rate. The left hand side of (4.8) is the reserve of the resource needed when from T on the rate of exploitation is interior and $\hat{E}(T) = \bar{E}$.

This can be verified as follows

$$E(t) = \bar{E}\, e^{\omega(t-T)} \quad \text{for} \quad t \geqq T\ ,$$

from (4.4)-(4.6). The left hand side of (4.8) then equals:

$$\int_T^\infty \bar{E}\, e^{\omega(t-T)} dt.$$

Now consider figure 4.1.

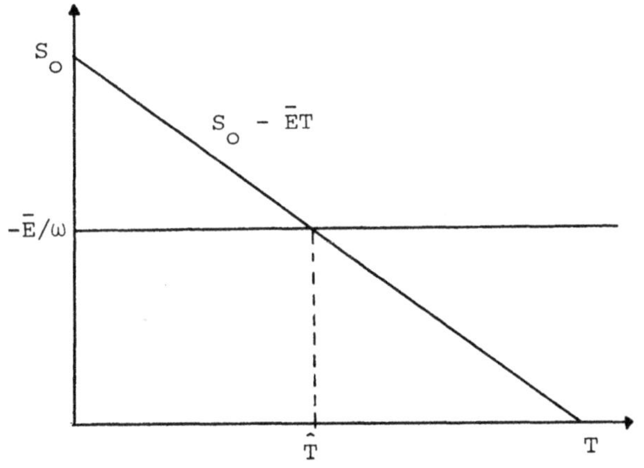

figure 4.1.

If $S_o \geqq -\bar{E}/\omega$, (4.8) has a solution for T, denoted by $\hat{T}$. The optimal exploitation program is to have exploitation at the maximal rate for $0 \leqq t \leqq \hat{T}$ and interior exploitation for $t > \hat{T}$.

If $S_o < -\bar{E}/\omega$ then it is optimal to have interior exploitation for all instants of time. The optimality of these policies is easily seen in view of the concavity of U. Whether or not the rate of consumption is increasing or decreasing depends on the sign of $\pi - \gamma + \rho$. If the rate of time preference is large ($\rho > \gamma - \pi$), consumption decreases, otherwise it increases. The results are summarized in

Theorem 2

Suppose $\rho > (\gamma-\pi)(1+\eta)$. Then the problem posed has a unique solution $\hat{z} = \{\hat{C}, \hat{E}\}$.

If $S_o < -\bar{E}/\omega$, $0 < \hat{E} < \bar{E}$ for all t, $\dot{\hat{C}}/\hat{C} = (\rho-\gamma+\pi)/\eta$, $\hat{E}(0) = -\omega S_o$.

If $S_o \geq -\bar{E}/\omega$, there exists $\hat{T} \geq 0$ such that: $\hat{E} = \bar{E}$ and $\dot{\hat{C}}/\hat{C} = \gamma - \pi$ for $0 \leq t \leq \hat{T}$, and $0 < \hat{E} < \bar{E}$ and $\dot{\hat{C}}/\hat{C} = (\rho-\gamma+\pi)/\eta$ for $t > \hat{T}$. □

4.3. *A perfect world market for bonds*

The problem of the economy is to maximize (4.1) subject to the usual resource constraints (4.2) and (4.3) and subject to

$$\int_0^\infty e^{-rt} p_c(t)\ C(t)dt \leq \int_0^\infty e^{-rt} p_e(t)\ E(t)dt + \int_0^\infty e^{-rt} r\ B_o\ dt, \tag{4.9}$$

where r denotes the interest rate and B_o is the amount of bonds the economy holds at time 0.

The Lagrangean of the problem reads:

$$L(C,E,\mu,\lambda,\alpha,\beta) = e^{-\rho t} U(C) + \mu(e^{-rt} p_e(t)E + e^{-rt} r\ B_o$$

$$-e^{-rt} p_c(t)C) + \lambda(be^{-bt} S_o - E) + \alpha E + \beta(\bar{E} - E),$$

where b is an arbitrary positive constant. Obviously the separation theorem holds in this case. Therefore, we shall mainly deal with optimal exploitation.

Let $\hat{z}(t) = \{\hat{C}(t), \hat{E}(t)\}$ be an optimal program. Then, according to the maximum principle, there exist nonnegative constants $\hat{\mu}$ and $\hat{\lambda}$ and piecewise continuous $\hat{\alpha}(t)$ and $\hat{\beta}(t)$, possibly discontinuous at points of discontinuity of $\hat{E}(t)$, such that

$$\partial L/\partial C = 0 \quad : \quad e^{-\rho t} U'(\hat{C}(t)) = \hat{\mu} e^{-rt} p_c(t), \tag{4.10}$$

$$\partial L/\partial E = 0 \quad : \quad \hat{\mu}\ e^{-rt} p_e(t) + \hat{\alpha}(t) - \hat{\beta}(t) = \hat{\lambda}, \tag{4.11}$$

$$\hat{\alpha}(t)\ \hat{E}(t) = 0,\ \hat{\alpha}(t) \geq 0, \tag{4.12}$$

$$\hat{\beta}(t)\ (\bar{E} - \hat{E}(t)) = 0, \quad \hat{\beta}(t) \geq 0, \tag{4.13}$$

$$\hat{\mu} \int_0^\infty e^{-rt} (p_e(t)\ \hat{E}(t) + rB_o - p_c(t)\ \hat{C}(t))dt = 0. \tag{4.14}$$

Three cases are to be considered now.
If $r > \gamma$, the optimal policy is to extract as fast as possible. Hence $\hat{E} = \bar{E}$ for $0 \leqq t \leqq S_o/\bar{E}$. The optimality of such a program is evident: the economy should invest in bonds, which give a higher rental rate than the resource, kept in the ground. Also the necessary conditions make clear that this should be the optimal exploitation policy. It is seen from (4.11) that it is not optimal to have $0 < \hat{E} < \bar{E}$ for any interval of time. Suppose then, that there is an interval of time, ending at T, with $\hat{E} = 0$, whereas for some interval of time, starting at T, $\hat{E} = \bar{E}$. It follows from (4.11) that up to T $\hat{\alpha}$ is increasing. At T, $\hat{E}$ jumps from 0 to $\bar{E}$. Hence $\hat{\alpha}$ jumps to 0. Then $\hat{\beta}$ must jump downwards, becoming negative and contradicting (4.13).
If $r = \gamma$, the optimal program is indeterminate. Any extraction profile, exhausting the resource, is optimal.
If $r < \gamma$, no optimal extraction policy exists. This is seen as follows. First remark that, for the same reasons as for the case $r > \gamma$, there exists no interval with $0 < \hat{E} < \bar{E}$. Suppose then, that eventually (which means for all $t \geqq T$ for some $T \geqq 0$) $\hat{E} = 0$. Then it follows from (4.11) that eventually $\hat{\alpha}$ becomes negative, contradicting (4.12). Hence for all T there exists an interval of time after T with $\hat{E} = \bar{E}$. But such an interval is finite since the resource is of finite magnitude. At the inevitable jump to $\hat{E} = 0$, $\hat{\alpha}$ becomes negative. Obviously all of this is clear from simple economic reasoning. The economy should exploit as far away in the future as possible, issuing bonds at an infinite rate.
Although $r \geqq \gamma$ is sufficient and necessary for the existence of a profit maximizing extraction policy, an overall optimal program does not necessarily exist, as has been seen in the previous chapter.
We need in addition that the rate of time preference is large enough. To be more specific: if $\rho \leqq (r-\pi)(1+\eta)$, then along an optimal program the total discounted value of consumption would be unbounded, and (4.9) is violated.
The results are summarized in

<u>Theorem 3</u>

a) Suppose $\gamma > r$. Then the problem posed has no solution.

b) Suppose $\gamma \leqq r$ and $\rho > (r-\pi)(1+\eta)$. Then the problem posed has a solution. If $\gamma < r$, $\hat{E} = \bar{E}$ for $0 \leqq t \leqq S_o/\bar{E}$ and $\dot{\hat{C}}/\hat{C} = (\rho - r + \pi)/\eta$. If $\gamma = r$, $\hat{E}$ is indeterminate and $\dot{\hat{C}}/\hat{C} = (\rho - r + \pi)/\eta$.

c) Suppose $\gamma \leqq r$ and $\rho \leqq (r-\pi)(1+\eta)$. Then the problem posed has no solution. □

4.4. *Credit rationing*

4.4.1. Introduction

Here we present the model, give some preliminary results and outline the sequel of this section.

The model resembles the model of the preceding section but with one additional constraint introduced. It requires that at any instant of time the economy's bond holdings exceed some given number $\bar{B}$, where $\bar{B}$ is negative. Defining the bond holdings at time t by B(t) we have:

$$\dot{B}(t) = r\,B(t) + p_e(t)\,E(t) - p_c(t)\,C(t), \tag{4.15}$$

$$B(t) \geqq \bar{B}. \tag{4.16}$$

Hence the problem is to maximize (4.1) subject to the resource constraints, (4.2) and (4.3), (4.9) and the additional constraints (4.15) and (4.16). Condition (4.16) causes some mathematical difficulties. It does not involve any of the instrumental variables and problems may arise at points of time where the constraint becomes effective. If, for some t, $B(t) = \bar{B}$, the right hand side of (4.15) must be nonnegative. We invoke here a theorem on bounded state variables, established by Guinn (1967). First the notion of *junction time* is introduced. Suppose that for $t_o \leqq t < t_1$, $B(t) > \bar{B}$ and that for $t_1 \leqq t \leqq t_2$, $B(t) = \bar{B}$, then t_1 is called a junction time. Next define the Lagrangean:

$$L(B,C,E,\mu,\phi,\lambda,\alpha,\beta,\kappa) = e^{-\rho t}\,U(C)$$

$$+ \mu(e^{-rt}\,p_e(t)E + e^{-rt}\,r\,B_o - e^{-rt}\,p_c(t)C) + \phi(p_e(t)E + rB -$$

$$- p_c(t)C) + \lambda(b\,e^{-bt}\,S_o - E) + \alpha E + \beta(\bar{E} - E) + \kappa(B - \bar{B}),$$

where b is an arbitrary positive constant. Necessary conditions are now readily given. Let $\hat{z}(t) = \{\hat{B}(t), \hat{C}(t), \hat{E}(t)\}$ constitute an optimal program. Then there exist nonnegative constants $\hat{\lambda}$ and $\hat{\mu}$, and functions $\hat{\phi}(t)$, $\hat{\alpha}(t)$, $\hat{\beta}(t)$ and $\hat{\kappa}(t)$ which are continuous, except possibly at junction times or when $\hat{C}(t)$ or $\hat{E}(t)$ are discontinuous, such that:

$$\partial L/\partial C = 0 : e^{-\rho t} U'(\hat{C}(t)) = \hat{\phi}(t)\, p_c(t) + \hat{\mu}\, p_c(t)\, e^{-rt}, \tag{4.17}$$

$$\partial L/\partial E = 0 : \hat{\mu}\, p_e(t)\, e^{-rt} + \hat{\phi}(t)\, p_e(t) + \hat{\alpha}(t) - \hat{\beta}(t) = \hat{\lambda}, \tag{4.18}$$

$$\partial L/\partial B = -\dot{\hat{\phi}}(t) : -\dot{\hat{\phi}}(t) = r\,\hat{\phi}(t) + \hat{\kappa}(t), \tag{4.19}$$

$$\hat{\alpha}(t)\,\hat{E}(t) = 0,\ \hat{\alpha}(t) \geqq 0, \tag{4.20}$$

$$\hat{\beta}(t)\,(\bar{E} - \hat{E}(t)) = 0,\ \hat{\beta}(t) \geqq 0, \tag{4.21}$$

$$\hat{\kappa}(t)\,(\hat{B}(t) - \bar{B}) = 0,\quad \hat{\kappa}(t) \geqq 0, \tag{4.22}$$

$$\hat{\mu}\Big[\int_0^\infty e^{-rt}\,(p_e(t)\,\hat{E}(t) + r\,B_o - p_c(t)\,\hat{C}(t))\,dt\Big] = 0. \tag{4.23}$$

For details on these necessary conditions we refer to appendix C. From here on time indices will be omitted when there is no danger of confusion.

We first prove a sufficiency theorem.

<u>Theorem 4</u>

Let $\hat{z}(t) = \{\hat{B}(t), \hat{C}(t), \hat{E}(t)\}$ be a feasible program. Let along this program $\hat{C}(t)$ be continuous, $\hat{B}(t)$ tend to $\bar{B}$ and the resource be exhausted. If there exist $\hat{\mu}$, $\hat{\phi}(t)$, $\hat{\lambda}$, $\hat{\alpha}(t)$, $\hat{\beta}(t)$, $\hat{\kappa}(t)$, which together with $\hat{z}(t)$ fulfil the necessary conditions given above, then $\hat{z}(t)$ is the unique optimal program.

<u>Proof</u>

Let $\{B(t), C(t), E(t)\}$ constitute an alternative feasible program with $C(t) \neq \hat{C}(t)$ for some interval of time. Then

$$
\begin{aligned}
J_T := &\int_0^T e^{-\rho t}(U(\hat{C})-U(C))\,dt \geq \int_0^T e^{-\rho t}U'(\hat{C})(\hat{C}-C)\,dt \\
= &\int_0^T (\hat{\phi}+\hat{\mu}e^{-rt})(-\dot{\hat{B}}+r\hat{B}+p_e\hat{E}+\dot{B}-rB-p_eE)\,dt \\
= &\int_0^T (\hat{\lambda}-\hat{\alpha}-\hat{\beta})(\hat{E}-E)\,dt + \int_0^T (\hat{\phi}+\hat{\mu}e^{-rt})(r(\hat{B}-B))\,dt \\
&+ (B-\hat{B})(\hat{\mu}e^{-rt}+\hat{\phi})\Big|_0^T - \int_0^T (B-\hat{B})(-\hat{\mu}r\, e^{-rt}-r\hat{\phi}-\hat{\kappa})\,dt \\
= &\int_0^T \hat{\lambda}(\hat{E}-E)\,dt + \int_0^T (\hat{\beta}-\hat{\alpha})(\hat{E}-E)\,dt + \int_0^T (\hat{B}-B)(-\hat{\kappa})\,dt \\
&+ (B(T)-\hat{B}(T))(\hat{\mu}e^{-rT}+\hat{\phi}(T)).
\end{aligned}
$$

The inequality follows from the concavity of U. The equalities are obtained from the feasibility and necessary conditions.
Consider the first term of the right hand side. The resource is completely exhausted, so

$$\lim_{T\to\infty} \int_0^T \hat{E}\,dt = S_o,$$

hence in the limit the first term is nonnegative.
The second term is nonnegative in view of (4.21) and (4.22).
The third term is nonnegative for the following reason. If $\hat{B} > \bar{B}$, then $\hat{\kappa} = 0$ (4.23). If $\hat{B} = \bar{B}$ then $\hat{\kappa}(B-\bar{B}) = 0$.
Finally consider the fourth term. The second factor is positive for all T since the rate of consumption is positive. The first factor tends to a nonnegative number.
As a conclusion we have

$$\lim_{T\to\infty} J_T \geq 0.$$

Furthermore, $\hat{z}$ is the unique optimal program since the utility function is strictly concave. □

In principle six policy regimes are to be considered, according to whether the amount of bonds held is larger than or equal to the minimal amount that is required and according to the rate of exploitation taking one of its extremal values or not. Obviously the case $\hat{B} = \bar{B}$ and $\hat{E} = 0$ cannot occur. Furthermore, for $r \neq \gamma$ we cannot have $\hat{B} > \bar{B}$ and $0 < \hat{E} < E$. In that case $\hat{\alpha} = \hat{\beta} = \hat{\kappa} = 0$, from (4.20)-(4.22) and $\dot{\hat{\phi}}/\hat{\phi} = -r$ from (4.19). But if $r \neq \gamma$, (4.18) cannot hold for any interval of time. The possible regimes are listed below.

table 4.1

$\hat{B}$ \ $\hat{E}$	$\hat{E} = 0$	$0 < \hat{E} < \bar{E}$	$\hat{E} = \bar{E}$
$\hat{B} > \bar{B}$	I	ruled out for $r \neq \gamma$	II
$\hat{B} = \bar{B}$	not pos-sible	III	IV

In the sequel of this section firstly the case $r > \gamma$ is treated (4.4.2). Next attention is paid to the case $r = \gamma$ (4.4.3). Finally we consider the case $r < \gamma$ (4.4.4).

It should be recalled that ω has been defined as $(\rho-(\gamma-\pi)(1+\eta))/\eta$.

ψ is defined as follows:

$$\psi = (\rho-(r-\pi)(1+\eta))/\eta. \tag{4.24}$$

4.4.2. Credit rationing. The case $r > \gamma$

When the rate of interest is large compared with the growth rate of the resource price, it is to be expected that the optimal policy is to exploit as fast as possible. After exhaustion the economy lives out of its bonds holdings. This conjecture is correct as will be shown below.

Theorem 5

Let $\hat{z}(t) = \{\hat{B}(t), \hat{C}(t), \hat{E}(t)\}$ be the solution of the problem posed here. Then $\hat{E}(t) = \bar{E}$ for $0 \leq t \leq S_o/\bar{E}$.

Proof

$$\int_0^\infty e^{-rt} p_e(t) E(t)dt$$

reaches a maximum for $E(t) = \bar{E}$, $0 \leq t \leq S_o/\bar{E}$, since $\gamma < r$. Hence any feasible exploitation policy, different from $\hat{E}(t) = \bar{E}$ for $0 \leq t \leq S_o/\bar{E}$, gives less consumption possibilities (see 4.10) and can therefore not be optimal.

□

Since total discounted profits from exploitation are bounded, it is clear that, as in the previous section, a necessary condition for the existence of an optimum is that the rate of time preference is large enough.

Theorem 6

If $\rho \leq (r-\pi)(1+\eta)$, then the problem posed has no solution.

Proof

Suppose the contrary. Then, from $\hat{T} = S_o/\bar{E}$ on, $\hat{B}(t) > \bar{B}$, otherwise the economy's debt would go to infinity. Hence, for $t > \hat{T}$, $\hat{\kappa}(t) = 0$ (4.22). It then follows from (4.19) that $\dot{\hat{\phi}}/\hat{\phi} = -r$. Using definition (4.24) and differentiation of (4.17) with respect to time yield

$$e^{-rt}\, p_c(t)\, \hat{C}(t) = \hat{C}(\hat{T}+)\, p_c(\hat{T})\, e^{\psi(t-\hat{T})}, \quad \text{for} \quad t \geq \hat{T}.$$

But then condition (4.9) is violated.

□

The final question to be answered is how the optimal trajectories for B and C look like. Define

$$V:= \int_0^{S_o/\bar{E}} e^{-rt}\, p_e(t)\, \bar{E}dt = p_e(0)\, \frac{1}{r-\gamma}\, \{1 - e^{-(r-\gamma)S_o/\bar{E}}\}.$$

Hence the present value of the total income equals: $V + B_o$. Notice that in order to have an optimum we must require $V + B_o > 0$, otherwise consumption is negative in view of (4.9), which is not allowed.

Now suppose that along the optimal program $\hat{B}(t) > \bar{B}$. Then straightforward, but tedious, calculations (using $\hat{\kappa} = 0$ and (4.10) holding with equality) give:

$$B(t) = e^{rt}\, V \left\{ \frac{e^{(\gamma-r)(S_o/\bar{E})} - e^{(\gamma-r)t}}{1 - e^{(\gamma-r)(S_o/\bar{E})}} \right\} + (V+B_o)\, e^{(\psi+r)t},$$

for $\quad 0 \leqq t \leqq S_o/\bar{E},$

$$B(t) = (V+B_o)\, e^{(\psi+r)t} \qquad \text{for } t \geqq S_o/\bar{E}.$$

It follows that

$$\dot{B}(0) = V \frac{r-\gamma}{1 - e^{(\gamma-r)S_o/\bar{E}}} + (\psi+r)B_o + \psi V.$$

Then it is easily seen that, for certain sets of parameters, $\dot{B}(0)$ is negative. And if $\bar{B}$ is sufficiently large, then the assumption $\hat{B}(t) > \bar{B}$ is violated. $\dot{B}(0)$ is negative for example when the rate of time preference is large, or when $S_o/\bar{E}$ is large and $\psi + r < 0$. We therefore conclude that in certain circumstances the borrowing constraint will be binding.

4.4.3. Credit rationing. The case $r = \gamma$

When the rate of interest equals the growth rate of the price of the resource good, the economy would, in the absence of a borrowing constraint, be indifferent with respect to the profile of exploitation. That needs not to be true for the case at hand. Suppose that there exists an optimal program. Then, clearly we must have $\psi \leqq 0$. If, for some t, $\hat{B}(t) = \bar{B}$, whereas, through a reallocation of sales of the resource good, it could be avoided that the borrowing constraint becomes binding, then the proposed program is not optimal. Therefore, in the case at hand, credit rationing could be an incentive to the economy to exploit earlier and faster. If the analysis would be extended to a world-wide scale, then problems might arise when one is interested in general equilibrium. If demand for the resource commodity is smooth, then credit rationing could prevent the establishment of such an equilibruim, even in this case, which is sometimes considered as ideal.

4.4.4. Credit rationing. The case $\gamma > r$

It has been shown in section 4.3, that, when there is no credit rationing and the growth rate of the price of the resource good is larger than the interest rate, the problem of optimal exploitation has no solution. When borrowing is bounded however, a solution could exist, as will be demonstrated in the present subsection. We shall proceeed as follows. The possible policy regimes have been listed in table 4.1. It has already been shown that policies ($\hat{B} = \bar{B}$, $\hat{E} = 0$) and ($\hat{B} > \bar{B}$, $0 < \hat{E} < \bar{E}$) cannot be followed along an optimal program. It will be shown next that transitions from some policies to some other policies are ruled out. This will provide us with a necessary condition (such as $\psi < 0$) for the existence of an optimal program. It then follows that some additional transitions can be ruled out. We then find the policy sequence that is the unique candidate for an optimal program and establish that it is optimal indeed to follow it.

First, consider regime II ($\hat{B} > B$, $\hat{E} = \bar{E}$).
It is not possible to have a transition from this regime to regime I ($\hat{B} > \bar{B}$, $\hat{E} = 0$). The proof of this statement is rather lengthy and therefore given in appendix C. The intuition behind the proof is simple, however. Since $\gamma > r$ it is better to postpone exploitation. It is furthermore not possible to jump to regime III. To show this, let us assume that the statement is incorrect. Let t_1 be the junction time. Then

$$\hat{E}(t_1-) = \bar{E},\ \hat{E}(t_1+) \leq \bar{E},\ \dot{\hat{B}}(t_1-) \leq 0,\ \hat{B}(t_1) = \bar{B}.$$

Since $\gamma > r$, $\hat{\beta}$ increases along regime II (see 4.18 and remark that $\dot{\hat{\phi}}/\hat{\phi} = -r$, because $\hat{B} > \bar{B}$). Hence, $\hat{\beta}(t_1-) \geq \varepsilon$ for some positive ε. $\hat{\beta}(t_1+) = 0$. Hence $\hat{\beta}$ jumps downwards at t_1. In view of the continuity of $\hat{\lambda}$ and μ, $\hat{\phi}$ jumps in the same direction (4.18). Hence, from (4.17), $\hat{C}$ jumps upwards. Now consider (4.15). $\hat{C}(t_1+) > \hat{C}(t_1-)$. Then it follows that $\dot{\hat{B}}(t_1+) < 0$ and $\hat{B}(t_1+) < \bar{B}$, contradicting (4.16).

Second, consider regime III ($\hat{B} = \bar{B}$, $0 < \hat{E} < \bar{E}$).
We show that a transition to regime I ($\hat{B} > \bar{B}$, $\hat{E} = 0$) is not allowed. Suppose the contrary and let t_1 be the junction time,

$$\hat{E}(t_1+) = 0,\ \dot{\hat{B}}(t_1+) \geqq 0,\ \hat{B}(t_1) < 0.$$

It follows from

$$\dot{\hat{B}} = r\hat{B} + p_e\hat{E} - p_c\hat{C}, \tag{4.15}$$

that $\hat{C}(t_1+) < 0$, a contradiction.

Third, consider regime IV ($\hat{B} = \bar{B}$, $\hat{E} = \bar{E}$).
A transition to regime I ($\hat{B} > \bar{B}$, $\hat{E} = 0$) is excluded. Suppose the contrary and let t_1 be the junction time.

$$\dot{\hat{B}}(t_1-) = 0,\ \dot{\hat{B}}(t_1+) > 0,\ \hat{E}(t_1-) = \bar{E},\ \hat{E}(t_1+) = 0,\ \hat{B}(t_1) = \bar{B}.$$

It follows again from (4.15) that $\hat{C}(t_1+) < 0$, a contradiction.

These preliminary results are summarized in table 4.2 below.

Table 4.2. Possible policy switches

From \ to	I $\hat{B}>\bar{B}$, $\hat{E}=0$	II $\hat{B}>B$, $\hat{E}=\bar{E}$	III $\hat{B}=\bar{B}$, $0<\hat{E}<\bar{E}$	IV $\hat{B}=\bar{B}$, $\hat{E}=\bar{E}$
I $\hat{B}>\bar{B}$, $\hat{E}=0$	x			
II $\hat{B}>\bar{B}$, $\hat{E}=\bar{E}$	no	x	no	
III $\hat{B}=\bar{B}$, $0<\hat{E}<\bar{E}$	no		x	
IV $\hat{B}=\bar{B}$, $\hat{E}=\bar{E}$	no			x

It will turn out that regime III is of special interest. Therefore it will be given a close look. Along this regime $\hat{\alpha} = \hat{\beta} = 0$ (from (4.20) and (4.21)). It then follows from (4.18) that

$$\dot{\hat{\phi}} = -\gamma\hat{\phi} - \hat{\mu}(\gamma-r)\ e^{-rt}.$$

The solution of this differential equation is of the type

$$\hat{\phi} = we^{-rt} + ve^{-\gamma t}, \tag{4.25}$$

where w and v are constants. Substitution of (4.25) into (4.17) and differentiation with respect to t yields

$$\dot{\hat{C}}/\hat{C} = (\pi - \gamma + \rho)/\eta. \tag{4.26}$$

It then follows that

$$\dot{p}_c/p_c + \dot{\hat{C}}/\hat{C} = \omega + \gamma. \tag{4.27}$$

Furthermore, $\dot{\hat{B}} = 0$ and $\hat{B} = \bar{B}$. Hence

$$p_e(t)\ \hat{E}(t) = -r\bar{B} + p_c(T)\ \hat{C}(T)\ e^{(\omega+\gamma)(t-T)}, \tag{4.28}$$

where T is the point of time where regime III starts.

Next we pass on to the derivation of a necessary condition for the existence of an optimum.

<u>Theorem 7</u>

If $\rho \leqq (\gamma-\pi)(1+\eta)$, then the problem posed has no solution.

<u>Proof</u>

First, remark that, in view of definition (4.24), $\rho \leqq (\gamma-\pi)(1+\eta)$ is equivalent to $\omega \geqq 0$.

Suppose that the theorem does not hold. Since it has been assumed that $B_o > \bar{B}$, the economy must, at the outset of the planning period, make a choice between regimes I and II.

Suppose first that regime II is chosen. In view of the limited availability of the resource, the regime cannot last forever. Hence a transition will be made to regime IV, since, according to table 4.2, this is the only policy switch allowed. But regime IV cannot last forever either. We infer from this that at some point of time the economy enters into regime III. Just before doing so, the economy is pursuing regime IV (see table 4.2). If, at the switch time, $\hat{E}$ jumps downwards, then $\hat{C}$ jumps downwards (in view of (4.15)), implying that $\hat{\phi}$ jumps upwards (in view of (4.17)). Hence $\hat{\beta}$ would jump upwards (see (4.18)). But, along regime III, $\hat{\beta} = 0$. We have therefore obtained a contradiction. It can be concluded that, at the switch time, $\hat{E}$ is continuous. The economy cannot stay in regime III indefinitely since it follows from (4.28) that then $\hat{E}(t)$ would become arbitrarily large ($\omega > 0$) or $\hat{E}(t)$ would be bounded from below by a positive constant ($\omega = 0$). In both cases a contradiction is obtained. Therefore a transition must be made to regime II or IV and the argument can be repeated. Hence for all $T > 0$ there exists $\tau > T$ such that at τ a switch takes place from regime IV to regime III. At such τ's

$$p_c(\tau)\ \hat{C}(\tau) = r\bar{B} + p_e(\tau)\bar{E}. \tag{4.29}$$

Substitute (4.29) into (4.28) and differentiate with respect to t. Then

$$\dot{E}(t) > 0 \Longleftrightarrow \omega(r\bar{B} + p_e(\tau)\bar{E})\ e^{(\omega+\gamma)(t-\tau)} + \gamma r\bar{B} > 0.$$

Hence, for τ large enough, $\dot{E}(t) > 0$ along regime III. But then for τ large enough $\hat{E}(\tau+) > \bar{E}$, a contradiction.
Suppose then that the economy chooses regime I at the outset of the planning period. One will get into the same difficulties, since it is necessary to enter into one of the regimes II, III or IV. Otherwise bond holdings would become smaller than $\bar{B}$, which is not allowed, or they would go to infinity, which cannot be optimal, since the resource can costlessly be exploited, thereby increasing the rate of consumption and the target function. □

We now turn to the case $\omega < 0$. An additional number of switches from one regime to another can be excluded.

First, a transition from regime III to regime IV is impossible.
This is seen as follows. Along regime III the rate of exploitation is decreasing (see (4.28)). Hence at the point of time where the transition is made, the rate of exploitation jumps upwards and the rate of consumption jumps upwards. Hence, in view of (4.17), $\hat{\phi}$ jumps downwards. Consequently, $\hat{\beta}$ jumps downwards to a negative value. But $\hat{\beta} \geqq 0$.

Second, a transition from regime III to regime II is ruled out.

Suppose that the proposition is not correct and that the transition is made at t_1. Regime II cannot last forever and, according to table 4.2., a transition must be made to regime IV, say at t_2.
Then it follows that

$$\dot{\hat{B}}(t_1+) = r\bar{B} + p_e(t_1)\bar{E} - p_c(t_1)\ \hat{C}(t_1+) \geqq 0,$$

$$\dot{\hat{B}}(t_2-) = r\bar{B} + p_e(t_2)\bar{E} - p_c(t_2)\ \hat{C}(t_2-) \leqq 0.$$

Now consider figure 4.2.

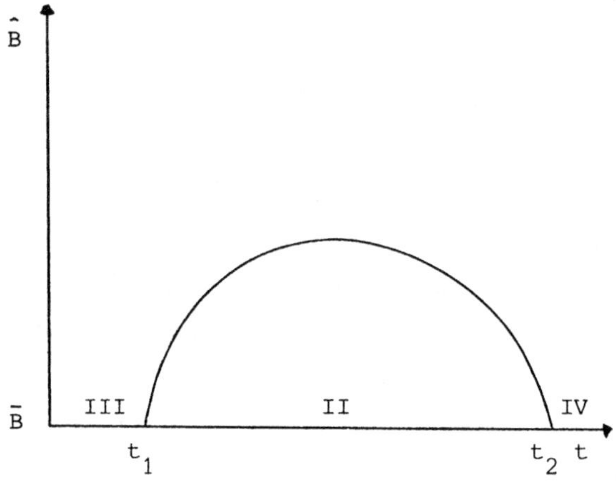

figure 4.2.

Since, along regime II, $\hat{B} > \bar{B}$, we have $\hat{\kappa} = 0$ (4.22). Hence $\dot{\hat{\phi}}/\hat{\phi} = -r$ from (4.19). Substitution into (4.17) yields

$$p_c(t)\ \hat{C}(t) = p_c(t_1)\ \hat{C}(t_1+)\ e^{(\psi+r)(t-t_1)},\quad t_1 < t < t_2\ .$$

We must therefore have

$$\begin{aligned} p_e(t_1)\bar{E} - p_c(t_1)\ \hat{C}(t_1+) &\geqq p_e(t_2)\bar{E} - p_c(t_2)\hat{C}(t_2-) \\ &= p_e(t_1)\bar{E}\ e^{\gamma(t_2-t_1)} - p_c(t_1)\ \hat{C}(t_1+)\ e^{(\psi+r)(t_2-t_1)} \\ &\geqq e^{\gamma(t_2-t_1)}\ \{p_e(t_1)\bar{E} - p_c(t_1)\hat{C}(t_1+)\ e^{(\psi+r-\gamma)(t_2-t_1)}\}. \end{aligned}$$

But

$$\psi + r - \gamma = \omega + (\gamma - r)/\eta < 0,$$

and a contradiction has been obtained.

Third, for the same reasons it is impossible to get into regime II from regime IV.

Fourth, one cannot go from regime IV to regime III. Suppose this statement is incorrect. Let t_1 denote the switch point. Remark first that, at t_1, $\hat{E}$ is continuous. For if $\hat{E}$ would jump downwards, $\hat{C}$ would jump downwards, $\hat{\phi}$ upwards and $\hat{\beta}$ upwards. But $\hat{\beta} = 0$ along regime III. Hence $\hat{E}$, $\hat{C}$, $\hat{\phi}$ and $\hat{\kappa}$ are continuous at t_1. Therefore $\dot{\hat{\phi}}$ and $\dot{\hat{C}}$ are continuous at t_1.

$$(p_c\dot{\hat{C}})/(p_c\hat{C}) = \gamma/((r\bar{B}/p_e\bar{E})+1), \text{ for } t < t_1,$$

$$(p_c\dot{\hat{C}})/(p_c\hat{C}) = \omega + \gamma, \text{ for } t > t_1. \tag{4.27}$$

Hence we must have

$$\omega + \gamma = \gamma/((r\bar{B}/p_e\bar{E}) + 1) \text{ for } t = t_1.$$

Since $\omega < 0$, the left hand side of this expression is smaller than γ, whereas, since $\bar{B} < 0$ and $r\bar{B} + p_e\bar{E} > 0$, the right hand side is larger than γ, a contradiction.

We can now complete table 4.2.

Table 4.3. Possible policy switches for $\omega < 0$.

From \ To	I $\hat{B}>\bar{B}$, $\hat{E}=0$	II $\hat{B}>\bar{B}$, $\hat{E}=\bar{E}$	III $\hat{B}=\bar{B}$, $0<\hat{E}<\bar{E}$	IV $\hat{B}=\bar{B}$, $\hat{E}=\bar{E}$
I $\hat{B}>\bar{B}$, $\hat{E}=0$	x			
II $\hat{B}>\bar{B}$, $\hat{E}=\bar{E}$	no	x	no	
III $\hat{B}=\bar{B}$, $0<\hat{E}<\bar{E}$	no	no	x	no
IV $\hat{B}=\bar{B}$, $\hat{E}=\bar{E}$	no	no	no	x

With the aid of this table the unique candidate for an optimal program is readily found. The economy has to start with either regime I or regime II. From regime II, one can only get into IV, from which no escape is possible. In view of the limited reserve of the resource, this program is not feasible and thus obviously not optimal. Hence the economy should start with regime I. Since the resource can costlessly be exploited, at some point of time a transition must be made to a regime with positive exploitation. A transition to II or IV cannot be optimal since then exploitation would be at its maximal rate forever, thereby violating the feasibility conditions. Hence the economy should switch to regime III.

We can therefore state the following theorem.

Theorem 8

Suppose $\rho > (\gamma-\pi)(1+\eta)$. Then the optimal program can be characterized as follows.

For an initial finite interval of time $\hat{B} > \bar{B}$, $\hat{E} = 0$. Afterwards, $\hat{B} = \bar{B}$, $0 < \hat{E} \leqq \bar{E}$ and $\hat{E}$ is strictly decreasing. □

We next proceed to a more precise description of the program sketched in theorem 8, thereby establishing the existence of an optimal program.

Let regime III ($\hat{B} = \bar{B}$, $0 < \hat{E} < \bar{E}$) start at $\hat{T}$ and suppose that $\hat{C}$ is continuous throughout the program. Then it follows from (4.2) and (4.28) that

$$p_c(\hat{T})\ \hat{C}(\hat{T}) = (-r\bar{B}\omega/\gamma) - \omega S_o p_e(\hat{T}), \tag{4.30}$$

$$\hat{E}(\hat{T}) = -\ \omega S_o - r\bar{B}(\omega+\gamma)/\gamma p_e(\hat{T}). \tag{4.31}$$

So, (4.31) gives the initial rate of exploitation when exploitation starts at $\hat{T}$. This $\hat{E}(\hat{T})$ might not be feasible. It could be that $\bar{E} < \hat{E}(\hat{T})$. We return to this problem below.

For $t < \hat{T}$ regime I rules. Hence

$$\dot{\hat{B}} = r\hat{B} - p_c\ \hat{C},\ \text{for } 0 \leqq t < \hat{T}.$$

It follows from (4.17)-(4.22) that

$$\dot{\hat{C}}/\hat{C} = (\pi - r + \rho)/\eta, \text{ for } 0 \leq t < \hat{T}. \tag{4.32}$$

Hence

$$\hat{B}(t) = e^{rt}\{B_o + (1-e^{\psi t})p_c(0)\ \hat{C}(0)/\psi\},\ 0 \leq t \leq \hat{T}.$$

Using (4.32) again and realizing that $B(\hat{T}) = \bar{B}$ we find

$$p_c(\hat{T})\ \hat{C}(\hat{T}) = \psi(-\bar{B} + e^{r\hat{T}}\ B_o)/(1 - e^{-\psi\hat{T}}). \tag{4.33}$$

Theorem 4 on sufficiency guarantees that we have found the optimum if there exists $\hat{T}$ such that the right hand side of (4.30) equals the right hand side of (4.33) and if, moreover, the corresponding rate of extraction is feasible. The former condition implies the overall continuity of the rate of consumption and the latter is obvious.

Now several problems arise.

First of all it might be that the right hand side of (4.31) is larger than $\bar{E}$ for all positive $\hat{T}$. This occurs for example when S_0 is large relative to $\bar{E}$ (recall that $\omega > 0$). In that case no optimum exists: at the start of the period of interior exploitation the rate of consumption might assume a large value which cannot be matched by $\bar{E}$.

Second, the right hand side of (4.30) is increasing without bound, but it might be negative for small $\hat{T}$. The right hand side of (4.33) can have several forms: it is large for small T but (when B_0 is not equal to 0) it either goes to $-\infty$ or $+\infty$. In general however there does not need to exist a point of intersection of the two curves with positive corresponding rates of consumption. It is easily seen that such a point does exist when $B_0 < 0$. If $B_0 > 0$ the economy will quickly reach its maximal debt and at that point in time the resource price may not be high enough to pay the interest from the revenues of selling the exploited commodity. Also in this case no optimum exists.

Finally, when at the intersection point $\hat{T}$ the rate of consumption is positive but $E(\hat{T}) > \bar{E}$ then there is no optimum either. The transition time should be larger or smaller than $\hat{T}$ and thereby a discontinuity in the rate of consumption is induced. This is not allowed. An upward jump gives a downward discontinuity in $\hat{\phi}$ (4.17), but then $\hat{\alpha}$ jumps upwards, which contradicts that $\hat{E}$ becomes interior. A downward discontinuity is excluded as well. Since U is strictly concave a small reduction of $\hat{C}(\hat{T}-)$ is more than compensated in terms of discounted utility by an equal increase in $\hat{C}(\hat{T}+)$. Moreover, such a reallocation is feasible because it will then take the economy longer to reach the maximal debt, on which the interest can be paid from larger revenues of the exploited commodity.

From the above analysis we infer that an optimum may exist in the case of credit rationing with $\gamma>r$. This is the more likely to occur the larger is the upper bound $\bar{E}$ relative to S_0 and the larger is the initial wealth of the economy.

4.5. Summary and conclusions

In the present chapter three possible kinds of borrowing facilities for a country in the possession of an exhaustible resource have been examined. Before giving the conclusions of this study, we summarize the results.

A. No borrowing facilities.

A necessary and sufficient condition for the existence of an optimal program is $\rho > (\gamma-\pi)(1+\eta)$. The optimal policy with respect to exploitation is:

for $\bar{E}$ "large": $\hat{E}$ is interior for all $t \geq 0$, and decreasing at a constant rate,

for $\bar{E}$ "small": $\hat{E}$ is maximal for an initial period of time, and decreases eventually at a constant rate.

Exhaustion does not take place.

B. Perfect world market for financial capital.

For $\gamma > r$ and for $\gamma \leq r$ and $\rho \leq (r-\pi)(1+\eta)$ there exists no optimal program.

If $\gamma < r$ and $\rho > (r-\pi)(1+\eta)$, $\hat{E} = \bar{E}$ until the resource is exhausted.

If $\gamma = r$ and $\rho > (r-\pi)(1+\eta)$, $\hat{E}$ is indeterminate.

C. Credit rationing.

For $\gamma \leqq r$ and $\rho \leqq (r-\pi)(1+\eta)$, there exists no optimal program.

If $\gamma < r$ and $\rho > (r-\pi)(1+\eta)$, $\hat{E} = \bar{E}$ until the resource is exhausted.

If $\gamma = r$ and $\rho > (r-\pi)(1+\eta)$, $\hat{E}$ is possibly not indeterminate.

If $\gamma > r$ then a necessary condition for the existence of an optimal program is that $\rho > (\gamma-\pi)(1+\eta)$. The optimal exploitation policy is: $\hat{E} = 0$ for an initial period of time. After this period the rate of exploitation becomes interior and the economy's debt is maximal. This exploitation profile will last ad infinitum.

What conclusion can be drawn? It does not seem very interesting to comment on conditions such as $\rho > (r-\pi)(1+\eta)$, since these are familiar from traditional growth theory and not especially related to the problem at hand. Moreover, an intuitive guess says that they are satisfied in the real world (take $\pi = 0{,}02$, $r = 0{,}04$, $\gamma = 0{,}06$, $\rho = 0{,}03$, $\eta < -0{,}25$).

If the two extreme cases studied are compared, the differences in extraction policies are striking, as one would expect from the analysis in the preceding chapter. When world supply of the resource commodity is taken into consideration, then the first case guarantees a steady stream of the good to the world market. In the second case this is not so: equilibrium on the world market can only occur when the expected growth rate of the price coincides with the interest rate. When there is credit rationing, then equilibrium on the world market might be established, also when $\gamma > r$. But then it has to be accepted that the resource exporting economy has a debt until infinity.

We conclude that exploitation policies of resource exporting countries heavily depend on the way these countries can invest there earnings and that it is recommendable to investigate further the conditions that would allow for world-wide equilibrium.

5. A GENERAL EQUILIBRIUM MODEL OF INTERNATIONAL TRADE IN EXHAUSTIBLE RESOURCES

5.1. *Introduction*

In the preceding two chapters of the present monograph we have been studying international trade in exhaustible resources from a partial equilibrium point of view. It has been remarked in several places that a general equilibrium type analysis would be more appropriate. This has also been stressed in the survey of the existing literature in chapter 2. Here we shall adopt the approach proposed: the aim of the present chapter is to study general equilibrium in a world with two open economies, both in the possession of a natural resource. The plan of the chapter is as follows. In section 5.2 the model is described. In 5.3 we derive the necessary conditions for equilibrium and give some preliminary results. Section 5.4 is devoted to the characterization of general equilibrium. In 5.5 the outcomes will be compared with those obtained in earlier studies and the conclusions and some recommendations for further research are given.

5.2. *The model*

We consider two economies, which can be described as follows. Economy i (i = 1,2) maximizes its social welfare function:

$$J^i(C_i) := \int_0^\infty e^{-\rho_i t} U_i(C_i(t))dt, \tag{5.1}$$

where, as usual, t denotes time, ρ_i is the rate of time preference ($\rho_i \geqq 0$), C_i is the rate of consumption and U_i is the instantaneous utility function. It is assumed that

$$U_i'(C_i) > 0 \quad \text{and} \quad U_i''(C_i) < 0 \quad \text{for all} \quad C_i \geqq 0 \quad \text{and} \quad U_i'(0) = \infty.$$

Maximization of (5.1) takes place subject to a number of constraints, referring to the resource technology, the non-resource technology and the world markets.

The initial (i.e. at $t = 0$) reserve of the *resource* of economy i is denoted by S_{oi}. The resource is not replenishable. Denoting the rate of exploitation by E_i, we have

$$\int_0^\infty E_i(t)dt \leqq S_{oi}, \qquad (5.2)$$

$$E_i(t) \geqq 0. \qquad (5.3)$$

Exploitation is not costless. It is assumed that, in order to exploit, one has to use capital (which is perfectly malleable with the consumer good) as an input. In particular, we postulate an extraction technology of the fixed proportions type:

$$E_i(t) = K_i^e(t)/a_i, \qquad (5.4)$$

where a_i is a positive constant and K_i^e is the amount of capital. This specification is widely used in exhaustible resource models (see for example Heal (1976), Kay and Mirrlees (1975) and Kemp and Long (1980b)).

Capital can also, together with the resource commodity, be allocated to *non-resource production*. Let R_i denote the rate of use of the resource good, K_i^Y the use of capital, Y_i the rate of non-resource production and F_i the technology. Then

$$Y_i(t) = F_i(K_i^Y(t), R_i(t)). \qquad (5.5)$$

About F_i the following assumptions, customary in models of international trade, are made:

A1) both inputs are necessary for production:

$$\forall_{R_i>0} \lim_{K_i^Y \to 0} F_i(K_i^Y, R_i) = 0; \quad \forall_{K_i^Y>0} \lim_{R_i \to 0} F_i(K_i^Y, R_i) = 0,$$

A2) F_i exhibits constant returns to scale,

A3) positive marginal products:

$$\forall_{K_i^y>0}\ \forall_{R_i>0}\ F_{iK}(K_i^y,R_i) > 0,\ F_{iR}(K_i^y,R_i) > 0,$$

A4) F_i is concave.

In A3), F_{iK} and F_{iR} denote the partial derivative of F_i with respect to K_i^y and R_i respectively.

The open character of the economy finds its expression in the *balance of payments*. There is trade in the resource good as well as in the non-resource good. Since we wish to describe general competitive equilibrium, the economy is assumed to take the prices at which trade takes place, as given. Furthermore, it has fixed and firm expectations of the time-path of these prices. The non-resource commodity is taken as the numéraire. $p_i(t)$ denotes the price of the resource good the economy expects to prevail at time t, where the expectation is formed at time 0. In addition to the existence of the markets for the extracted commodity and the non-resource commodity, we assume that there is a perfect world market for lending and borrowing. The interest rate economy i expects to rule at time t is given by $r_i(t)$. Then the time-path of the total stock of capital is

$$\dot{K}_i(t) = r_i(t)(K_i(t) - K_i^e(t) - K_i^y(t)) +$$

$$+ p_i(t)(E_i(t) - R_i(t)) + Y_i(t) - C_i(t), \tag{5.6}$$

$$K_i(0) = K_{io}, \text{ given.} \tag{5.7}$$

The interpretation of these equations is straightforward. The economy rents all its capital (K_i), sells all that is extracted and total non-resource production: this generates expected earnings at time t amounting to $r_i(t)K_i(t) + p_i(t)E_i(t) + Y_i(t)$. Subsequently, it hires capital, buys resource goods for production purposes and consumer goods: total expected expenditures at time t are then $r_i(t)(K_i^e(t) + K_i^y(t)) + p_i(t)R_i(t) + C_i(t)$. If the difference is positive, the economy's wealth ($K_i(t)$) is increased, otherwise it is decreased. Remark that $K_i(t)$ might be negative for some instant of time. Given its price expectations, the economy makes a consumption-production plan. This may and, in the model presented sofar, will exhibit borrowing at an unbounded amount. In order to prevent this, we force the economy to perceive the following constraint:

$$\lim_{t \to \infty} K_i(t) \geqq 0 \tag{5.8}$$

Finally, there are the obvious nonnegativity conditions

$$(C_i(t), Y_i(t), K_i^y(t), R_i(t), K_i^e(t)) \geqq 0. \tag{5.9}$$

Given $p_i(t)$ and $r_i(t)$, $\{K_i(t), z_i(t)\} := \{K_i(t), C_i(t), Y_i(t), K_i^y(t), R_i(t), K_i^e(t), E_i(t)\}$, defined for all $t \geqq 0$, is called a *feasible program* if it satisfies (5.2)-(5.9). A feasible program is called *optimal* if it maximizes (5.1).

Next we define *general competitive equilibrium*.

$\{\hat{K}_1(t), \hat{K}_2(t), \hat{z}_1(t), \hat{z}_2(t), \hat{p}(t), \hat{r}(t)\}$, with $\hat{p}(t) \geqq 0$ and $\hat{r}(t) \geqq 0$, constitutes a general equilibrium if

i) $\{\hat{K}_i(t), \hat{z}_i(t)\}$ is optimal for economy i (i = 1,2), when it expects $\hat{p}(t)$ and $\hat{r}(t)$ to prevail,

ii) no excess demand on the resource market, capital market and non-resource (flow) market:

$$\hat{R}_1(t) + \hat{R}_2(t) \leqq \hat{E}_1(t) + \hat{E}_2(t), \tag{5.10}$$

$$\hat{K}_1^e(t) + \hat{K}_2^e(t) + \hat{K}_1^y(t) + \hat{K}_2^y(t) \leqq \hat{K}_1(t) + \hat{K}_2(t), \tag{5.11}$$

$$\hat{C}_1(t) + \hat{C}_2(t) + \dot{\hat{K}}_1(t) + \dot{\hat{K}}_2(t) \leqq \hat{Y}_1(t) + \hat{Y}_2(t) \quad \text{(Walras' law)},$$

iii) $\hat{p}(t) = 0$ when (5.10) holds with strict inequality, $\hat{r}(t) = 0$ when (5.11) holds with strict inequality.

Before we proceed a few remarks are in order. Imagine a single closed economy with many resource owners, whose deposits can be exploited according to extraction technology (5.4). Hence some of them need a_1 units of capital to extract one unit of the resource and others need a_2 units of capital for the same purpose. Furthermore, in this economy

there are many non-resource producers which can employ the F_1 technology and others that use the F_2 production possibilities. Consumers earn all the profits from resource exploitation and non-resource production, in some way. They dispose of the initial capital endowments and are characterized by preference relations, given by (5.1). Then the definition of general equilibrium given above applies to this economy provided that resource and non-resource producers aim at the maximization of the present discounted value of their profits. This observation is of course not very striking but it might help understanding the sequel of this chapter.
Second, the model of each economy i can be looked upon as the aggregate of models describing individual agents in this economy. Then an optimal program of such an economy constitutes a general equilibrium in the sense described above.

5.3. *Necessary conditions for an equilibrium and some preliminary results*

In this section we start by deriving necessary conditions for an optimal program for an individual economy. Subsequently we prove a sufficiency theorem and show that a general equilibrium is Pareto-efficient.
In the sequel we shall often omit the index i and the time variable t will be suppressed when there is no danger of confusion. It will be assumed that the economy expects the prices to be piece-wise continuous and, on a priori grounds, desires an optimal program to exhibit continuous K and piece-wise continuous z.
Remark that resource constraint (5.2) can be written as

$$\int_0^\infty (be^{-bt} S_o - E(t))dt \geqq 0, \tag{5.12}$$

where b is an arbitrary positive constant. (5.6)-(5.8) imply

$$\int_0^\infty e^{-\int_0^t r(\tau)d\tau} \{Y + p(E - R) - C - r(K^e + K^y) + me^{-mt} K_o\}dt \geqq 0, \tag{5.13}$$

where m is an arbitrary positive constant.

The Lagrangean of the (modified) problem is:

$$L(C,Y,K^Y,R,K^e,E,\lambda,\mu,\phi,\omega,\alpha_1,\alpha_2,\alpha_3,\alpha_4,\alpha_5,\alpha_6) =$$

$$= e^{-\rho t} U(C) + \lambda(be^{-bt} S_o - E) + \mu e^{-\int_0^t r(\tau)d\tau} \{Y + p(E-R) - C$$

$$- r(K^e + K^Y) + me^{-mt} K_o\} + \phi(F(K^Y,R) - Y) + \omega(-E + K^e/a)$$

$$+ \alpha_1 C_1 + \alpha_2 Y + \alpha_3 K^Y + \alpha_4 R + \alpha_5 K^e + \alpha_6 E.$$

Let $\{\hat{K},\hat{z}\} = \{\hat{K},\hat{C},\hat{Y},\hat{K}^Y,\hat{R},\hat{K}^e,\hat{E}\}$ constitute an optimal program. Then, according to Pontryagin's maximum principle, there exist multipliers

$$\hat{\lambda},\ \hat{\mu},\ \hat{\phi},\ \hat{\omega},\ \hat{\alpha}_i \quad (i = 1,2,\ldots,6),$$

such that

i) $\hat{\lambda}$ and $\hat{\mu}$ are nonnegative constants and

$$\hat{\lambda}\left[S_o - \int_0^\infty \hat{E}(t)dt\right] = 0,$$

$$\hat{\mu}\left[\int_0^\infty e^{-\int_0^t r(\tau)d\tau} \{\hat{Y} + p(\hat{E} - \hat{R}) - \hat{C} - r(\hat{K}^e + \hat{K}^Y)\}dt + K_o\right] = 0.$$

ii) $\hat{\phi}$, $\hat{\omega}$ and $\hat{\alpha}_i$ $(i = 1,2,\ldots,6)$ are continuous functions of time, except possibly at points of discontinuity of $\hat{z}$.

$$\partial\hat{L}/\partial C = 0 \ :\ e^{-\rho t} U'(\hat{C}) + \hat{\alpha}_1 = \hat{\pi}, \tag{5.14}$$

$$\partial\hat{L}/\partial Y = 0 \ :\ \hat{\pi} - \hat{\phi} + \hat{\alpha}_2 = 0, \tag{5.15}$$

$$\partial\hat{L}/\partial K^Y = 0 \ :\ -\hat{\pi}r + \hat{\phi}\hat{F}_K + \hat{\alpha}_3 = 0, \tag{5.16}$$

$$\partial\hat{L}/\partial R = 0 \ :\ -\hat{\pi}p + \hat{\phi}\hat{F}_R + \hat{\alpha}_4 = 0, \tag{5.17}$$

$$\partial\hat{L}/\partial K_e = 0 \ :\ -\hat{\pi}r + \hat{\omega}/a + \hat{\alpha}_5 = 0, \tag{5.18}$$

$$\partial\hat{L}/\partial E = 0 \ :\ -\hat{\lambda} + \hat{\pi}p - \hat{\omega} + \hat{\alpha}_6 = 0, \tag{5.19}$$

where $\hat{\pi}(t)$ is defined as $\hat{\mu} e^{-\int_0^t r(\tau)d\tau}$, $\hat{F}_K$ is the derivative of F with respect to K^Y, evaluated at $(\hat{K}^Y, \hat{R})$ and $\hat{F}_R$ is defined in an analogous way.

iii) $\hat{\alpha}_1 \hat{C} = 0 \ , \quad \hat{\alpha}_1 \geqq 0,$ (5.20)

$$\hat{\alpha}_2 \hat{Y} = 0 \ , \quad \hat{\alpha}_2 \geqq 0, \tag{5.21}$$

$$\hat{\alpha}_3 \hat{K}^Y = 0, \quad \hat{\alpha}_3 \geqq 0, \tag{5.22}$$

$$\hat{\alpha}_4 \hat{R} = 0 \ , \quad \hat{\alpha}_4 \geqq 0, \tag{5.23}$$

$$\hat{\alpha}_5 \hat{K}^e = 0, \quad \hat{\alpha}_5 \geqq 0, \tag{5.24}$$

$$\hat{\alpha}_6 \hat{E} = 0 \ , \quad \hat{\alpha}_6 \geqq 0. \tag{5.25}$$

Since all functions involved are concave, we have not explicitly mentioned conditions saying that the Hamiltonean is maximized. The multipliers $\hat{\lambda}$, $\hat{\mu}$ and $\hat{\pi}$ have a nice economic interpretation. $\hat{\lambda}$ is the shadow-price of the resource. It gives the value (in terms of 'utils' discounted at the rate of time preference) that the economy attaches to an increase of the initial stock of the resource with one unit. Similarly, $\hat{\mu}$ is the value of an extra dollar of initial wealth. Since $\hat{\pi}/\hat{\mu}$ is defined as the present market value of the consumer good, (5.14) says that the intertemporal rate of substitution should equal the price ratio (of course as long as the rate of consumption is positive, as will be the case). See also the discussion in chapter 3 after equation (3.11).

We shall now reduce the system (5.14)-(5.25) to a more amenable form. We proceed step by step.

1) Since $U'(0) = \infty$, $\hat{C}(t) > 0$ for all $t \geqq 0$. It follows from (5.20), that $\hat{\alpha}_1 = 0$ and, from (5.14), that $\hat{\mu} > 0$. This implies that, along an optimal program, the budget constraint holds with equality.

2) It follows from the definition of $\hat{\pi}$, that $\dot{\hat{\pi}}/\hat{\pi} = -r$.

3) For $i = 1,2,\dots,6$ define $\hat{\beta}_i = \hat{\alpha}_i/\hat{\pi}$. Then $\hat{\alpha}_i > 0$ if and only if $\hat{\beta}_i > 0$. It follows from (5.15) that $\hat{\phi}/\hat{\pi} = 1 + \hat{\beta}_2$. Substitution into (5.16) and (5.17) yields:

$$\hat{F}_K + \hat{\gamma}_1 = r, \quad \hat{F}_R + \hat{\gamma}_2 = p,$$

where $\hat{\gamma}_1 = \hat{\beta}_2\hat{F}_K + \hat{\beta}_3$ and $\hat{\gamma}_2 = \hat{\beta}_2\hat{F}_R + \hat{\beta}_4$. Obviously, $\hat{\gamma}_1$ and $\hat{\gamma}_2$ are nonnegative. If $\hat{K}^Y > 0$, then $\hat{\beta}_3 = 0$ from (5.22). Then $\hat{Y} > 0$ as well since it cannot be optimal to use capital unproductively. But in order to have $\hat{Y} > 0$, $\hat{R}$ must be positive. Hence: $\hat{\gamma}_1 \geqq 0$, $\hat{\gamma}_1\hat{K}^Y = 0$, $\hat{\gamma}_2 \geqq 0$, $\hat{\gamma}_2\hat{R} = 0$.

4) It follows from (5.19) that $\hat{\omega}/\hat{\pi} = p + \hat{\alpha}_6 - \hat{\lambda}/\hat{\pi}$. Substitution into (5.18) yields $\hat{\lambda} = \hat{\pi}(p - ar) + \hat{\gamma}_3$, where $\hat{\gamma}_3 = \hat{\alpha}_5\hat{\pi} + \hat{\alpha}_6\hat{\pi}/a$.

For convenience the reduced set of necessary conditions is listed below. It should be recalled that $\hat{\lambda}$ is a nonnegative constant, $\hat{\pi}$ is continuous and $\hat{\gamma}_1$, $\hat{\gamma}_2$ and $\hat{\gamma}_3$ are piece-wise continuous.

$$e^{-\rho t}\, U'(\hat{C}) = \hat{\pi}, \tag{5.26}$$

$$\dot{\hat{\pi}}/\hat{\pi} = -r, \tag{5.27}$$

$$\hat{F}_K + \hat{\gamma}_1 = r, \quad \hat{\gamma}_1 \geqq 0, \quad \hat{\gamma}_1\hat{K}^Y = 0, \tag{5.28}$$

$$\hat{F}_R + \hat{\gamma}_2 = p, \quad \hat{\gamma}_2 \geqq 0, \quad \hat{\gamma}_2\hat{R} = 0, \tag{5.29}$$

$$\hat{\lambda} = \hat{\pi}(p - ar) + \hat{\gamma}_3, \quad \hat{\gamma}_3 \geqq 0, \quad \hat{\gamma}_3\hat{E} = \hat{\gamma}_3\hat{K}^e = 0. \tag{5.30}$$

We next prove a sufficiency theorem.

<u>Theorem 1</u>

Let there exist a program $\{\hat{K},\hat{z}\} = \{\hat{K},\hat{C},\hat{Y},\hat{K}^Y,\hat{R},\hat{K}^e,\hat{E}\}$, which together with $\hat{\lambda}$, $\hat{\mu}$, $\hat{\gamma}_1$, $\hat{\gamma}_2$ and $\hat{\gamma}_3$ solves (5.1)-(5.9) and (5.26)-(5.30) for given (p,r). Then $\{\hat{K},\hat{z}\}$ is an optimal program.

<u>Proof</u>

Let $\{K,z\} \neq \{\hat{K},\hat{z}\}$ be an alternative feasible program. It follows from standard arguments (using the concavity of U and F and the equations mentioned) that

$$J_T := \int_0^T e^{-\rho t}(U(\hat{C}) - U(C))dt \geq$$

$$\geq \hat{\lambda}(S(T) - \hat{S}(T)) + \hat{\pi}(T)(K(T) - \hat{K}(T)),$$

where S(T) denotes the reserve of the resource at time T. Along an optimal program $\hat{S}(T) \to 0$ as $T \to \infty$, or $\hat{\lambda} = 0$. Since (5.8) must hold, $\hat{\pi}(T)\hat{K}(T) \to 0$ as $T \to \infty$. Therefore

$$\lim_{T\to\infty} J_T \geq 0. \qquad \square$$

As a final preliminary result we prove that a general equilibrium is Pareto-efficient.

Theorem 2

Let $\{\hat{K}_1, \hat{K}_2, \hat{z}_1, \hat{z}_2, \hat{p}, \hat{r}\}$ constitute a general equilibrium. Then the corresponding allocation is Pareto-efficient.

Proof

Suppose the theorem does not hold true. Then there exist feasible programs $\{K_1, z_1\}$ and $\{K_2, z_2\}$ such that

$$\int_0^\infty e^{-\rho_1 t} U_1(C_1)dt \geq \int_0^\infty e^{-\rho_1 t} U_1(\hat{C}_1)dt,$$

$$\int_0^\infty e^{-\rho_2 t} U_2(C_2)dt \geq \int_0^\infty e^{-\rho_2 t} U_2(\hat{C}_2)dt,$$

with one inequality holding strictly. Take $\alpha = \hat{\pi}_1/\hat{\pi}_2 = \hat{\mu}_1/\hat{\mu}_2$. α is positive and constant.

$$J_T := \int_0^T e^{-\rho_1 t}(U_1(\hat{C}_1) - U_1(C_1))dt + \alpha \int_0^T e^{-\rho_2 t}(U_2(\hat{C}_2) - U(C_2))dt$$

(a) $$\geq \int_0^T \hat{\pi}_1(\hat{C}_1 - C_1 + \hat{C}_2 - C_2)dt$$

(b) $$= \int_0^T \hat{\pi}_1\{\hat{r}(\hat{K}_1 - \hat{K}_1^e - \hat{K}_1^y + \hat{K}_2 - \hat{K}_2^e - \hat{K}_2^y) - \hat{r}(K_1 - K_1^e - K_1^y +$$

$$+ K_2 - K_2^e - K_2^y) + \hat{p}(\hat{E}_1 + \hat{E}_2 - \hat{R}_1 - \hat{R}_2) - \hat{p}(E_1 + E_2 - R_1 - R_2)$$

$$+ (\hat{Y}_1 + \hat{Y}_2 - Y_1 - Y_2) - (\dot{\hat{K}}_1 + \dot{\hat{K}}_2 - \dot{K}_1 - \dot{K}_2)\}dt$$

(c) $$\geq \int_0^T \hat{\pi}_1\{\hat{r}(\hat{K}_1 + \hat{K}_2 - K_1 - K_2) - \hat{r}(\hat{K}_1^y + \hat{K}_2^y - K_1^y - K_2^y)$$

$$- \hat{r}a_1(\hat{E}_1 - E_1) - \hat{r}a_2(\hat{E}_2 - E_2) + \hat{p}(\hat{E}_1 - E_1) + \hat{p}(\hat{E}_2 - E_2)$$

$$- \hat{p}(\hat{R}_1 - R_1) - \hat{p}(\hat{R}_2 - R_2) + \hat{F}_{1K}(\hat{K}_1^y - K_1^y) + \hat{F}_{1R}(\hat{R}_1 - R_1)$$

$$+ \hat{F}_{2K}(\hat{K}_2^y - K_2^y) + \hat{F}_{2R}(\hat{R}_2 - R_2)\}dt$$

$$- \int_0^T \hat{\pi}_1 d(\hat{K}_1 + \hat{K}_2 - K_1 - K_2)$$

(d) $$\geq \int_0^T \hat{\pi}_1\{\hat{r}(\hat{K}_1 + \hat{K}_2 - K_1 - K_2)$$

$$+ \hat{\lambda}_1(\hat{E}_1 - E_1)/\hat{\pi}_1 + \hat{\lambda}_2(\hat{E}_2 - E_2)/\hat{\pi}_2\}dt$$

$$+ \hat{\pi}_1(T)(K_1(T) + K_2(T) - \hat{K}_1(T) - \hat{K}_2(T))$$

$$+ \int_0^T (\hat{K}_1 + \hat{K}_2 - K_1 - K_2)(-\hat{r})\hat{\pi}_1 dt$$

$$= \int_0^T \{\hat{\lambda}_1(\hat{E}_1 - E_1) + \alpha\hat{\lambda}_2(\hat{E}_2 - E_2)\}dt$$

$$+ \hat{\pi}_1(T)(K_1(T) + K_2(T) - \hat{K}_1(T) - \hat{K}_2(T)).$$

The (in)equalities are arrived at as follows:

(a) using concavity of U_i, and (5.26);

(b) from (5.6);

(c) using concavity of F_i, and (5.4);

(d) from (5.28)-(5.30), and (5.27).

Along general equilibrium, $\hat{\pi}_i(T)\hat{K}_i(T)$ tends to zero as T goes to infinity (see (5.8)) and $\hat{\lambda}_i$ equals zero or resource i is completely exhausted in infinity. Hence

$$\lim_{T\to\infty} J_T \geq 0,$$

contradicting our point of departure. □

5.4. *The equilibrium solution*

In this section we shall proceed as follows. First the concept of cost functions is introduced. It will turn out that this concept is very valuable for the subsequent analysis. Second, it will be shown that, along general equilibrium, there is no simultaneous non-resource production, provided the production functions differ. There will, furthermore, not occur simultaneous extraction, if the a_i's differ. Third, the general equilibrium price-paths are sketched. Finally, some remarks are devoted to the existence of a general equilibrium.

Nowadays it is widely recognized that the concept of duality is a useful tool in economic analysis. See Diewert (1982a) for an excellent survey and Ruys (1974) and Weddepohl (1970) for early applications. It is also helpful for the solution of the problem studied here. We start with a brief digression on the *cost function*.

Consider a production function $F(K^Y,R)$. Input prices are denoted by r and p respectively. The cost function, $c(Y,r,p)$, is defined as:

$$c(Y,r,p) = \min_{K^Y,R} \{rK^Y + pR \mid F(K^Y,R) \geq Y\}.$$

It has been proved by a.o. Diewert (1982b) that, if F is increasing, quasi concave and continuous for $(K^Y,R) \geq 0$, then $c(Y,r,p)$ is increasing, linearly homogeneous in (r,p), concave in (r,p) and continuous for positive (r,p). If, moreover, F exhibits constant returns to scale, $c(\lambda Y,r,p) = \lambda c(Y,r,p)$ for all $\lambda > 0$. Our assumptions on the production functions F_i satisfy the conditions given, so the listed properties of the cost function hold. Moreover, in competitive equilibrium with constant returns to scale, we must have $c_i(\hat{Y}_i,\hat{r},\hat{p}) = \hat{Y}_i$ $(i = 1,2)$, since otherwise profits could be made arbitrarily large. Then, from the linear homogeneity: $c_i(1,\hat{r},\hat{p}) = 1$, $i = 1,2$. The graphs of these relations are called the factor-price frontiers (fpf). The fpf's can have several configurations. They may or may not intersect or they may or may not have (one of) the axes as an asymptote. For the ease of exposition (and only for that reason) one additional assumption will be made.

A5) There are at most two positive (r,p) configurations for which the fpf of country 1 intersects the fpf of country 2. Furthermore, at points of intersection $p \neq a_i r$ (i = 1,2).

Some elucidation of A5 is in order. A5 in fact excludes some pathological cases. Consider figure 5.1.

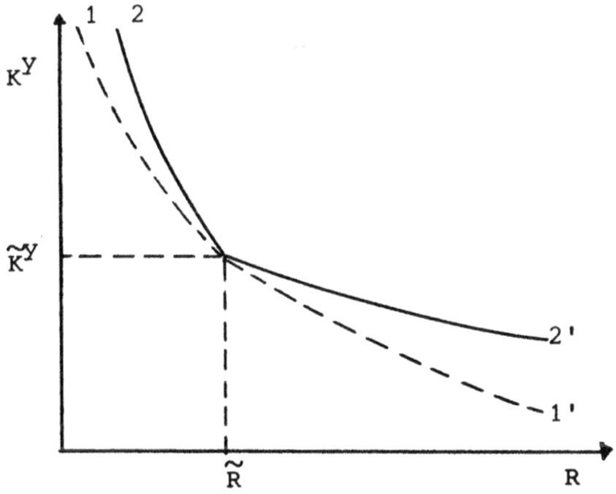

figure 5.1.

The dotted curve represents an isoquant of, say, country 1 and the curve 2-2' is the isoquant for the second country at the same output level. Both curves display a kink at the point $(\tilde{K}^y, \tilde{R})$. This implies that the fpf's coincide for (r,p)'s on a line segment. This is excluded by assumption A5. Obviously, also the case where isoquants coincide cannot occur under assumption A5. Hence, our fpf's will typically look like the ones depicted in figure 5.2.

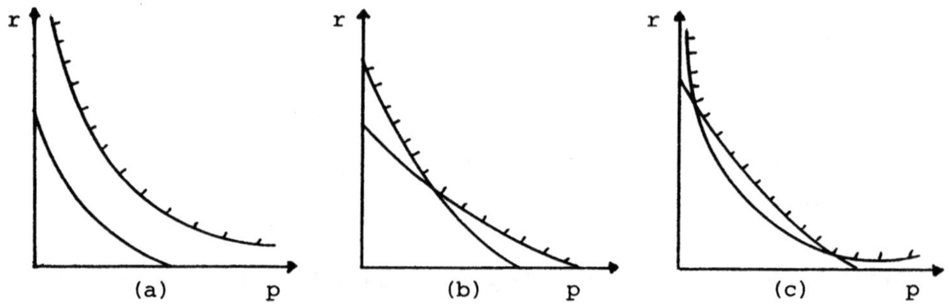

figure 5.2.

So A5 guarantees that the non-resource technologies differ between countries. The second part of A5 rules out that intersections occur at specific points. The meaning of this will be made clear below. Straightforward calculations show that for a Cobb-Douglas technology with parameter α, the fpf is given by

$$(r/\alpha)^{\alpha}(p/(1-\alpha))^{1-\alpha} = 1.$$

For a C.E.S. production function, with elasticity of substitution equal to $1/(1+\alpha)$ and share parameter δ, it is

$$\{\delta(r/\delta)^{\alpha/(1+\alpha)} + (1-\delta)(p/(1-\delta))^{\alpha/(1+\alpha)}\}=1.$$

Remark here that in order to satisfy A1 (necessity of both inputs), we must have $\alpha > 0$.

The following two theorems assert that, along general equilibrium, production of non-resource commodities and exploitation are always specialized.

<u>Theorem 3</u>

For all non-degenerate intervals of time $\hat{Y}_1=0$ or $\hat{Y}_2=0$.

<u>Proof</u>

Suppose the contrary. Let $V := [t_1,t_2]$, with $t_2 > t_1$, be an interval of time such that for all $t \in V$, $\hat{Y}_1(t) > 0$ and $\hat{Y}_2(t) > 0$. Since both inputs are necessary (A1), it follows from (5.28) and (5.29) that

$$\hat{F}_{1K} = \hat{F}_{2K} = \hat{r}, \quad \hat{F}_{1R} = \hat{F}_{2R} = \hat{p}. \tag{5.31}$$

A3 (positive marginal products) implies that $\hat{r} > 0$ and $\hat{p} > 0$. Since F_1 and F_2 exhibit constant returns to scale, marginal products are functions of the input ratio (K_i^Y/R_i) only. In view of A5 the fpf's intersect for positive $\hat{r}$ and $\hat{p}$ in at most two isolated points. Hence along V $\hat{r}$ and $\hat{p}$ are constants. At least one of the economies exploits its resource, because the exploited commodity is a necessary input. Assume, without loss of generality, this is the first economy. Then, along V, $\hat{\lambda}_1 = \hat{\pi}_1(\hat{p} - a_1\hat{r})$. Since, by virtue of A5, $\hat{\lambda}_1$ is a positive constant, we must have that $\hat{\pi}_1$ is constant, implying from (5.27) that $\hat{r} = 0$, a contradiction. □

Theorem 4

Suppose $a_1 \neq a_2$. Then, for all non-degenerate intervals of time, $\hat{E}_1 = 0$ or $\hat{E}_2 = 0$.

Proof

Suppose the contrary. Let $V := [t_1, t_2]$, with $t_2 > t_1$, be an interval of time, such that for all $t \in V$, $\hat{E}_1(t) > 0$ and $\hat{E}_2(t) > 0$. Along V we have from (5.30):

$$\hat{\lambda}_1 = \hat{\pi}_1(\hat{p} - a_1\hat{r}), \quad \hat{\lambda}_2 = \hat{\pi}_2(\hat{p} - a_2\hat{r}).$$

Since $\hat{\lambda}_1$ and $\hat{\lambda}_2$ are constants and $\dot{\hat{\pi}}_1/\hat{\pi}_1 = \dot{\hat{\pi}}_2/\hat{\pi}_2 = -\hat{r}$, it follows that

$$-\hat{r}(\hat{p} - a_1\hat{r}) + \dot{\hat{p}} - a_1\dot{\hat{r}} = 0,$$

$$-\hat{r}(\hat{p} - a_2\hat{r}) + \dot{\hat{p}} - a_2\dot{\hat{r}} = 0.$$

Substraction yields $\dot{\hat{r}}/\hat{r} = \hat{r}$ and substitution gives $\dot{\hat{p}}/\hat{p} = \hat{r}$. Hence both $\hat{r}$ and $\hat{p}$ are increasing. At least one of the economies is engaged in non-resource production, since, in equilibrium, supply of the resource good should equal demand. Assume that the first country is producing. Define $\hat{k}_1 = \hat{K}_1^Y/\hat{R}_1$ and $f_1(\hat{k}_1) = F_1(\hat{k}_1, 1)$. Then

$$\hat{F}_{1K} = f_1', \quad \hat{F}_{1R} = f_1 - f_1' * \hat{k}_1.$$

It follows that

$$\text{SIGN } \dot{\hat{r}} = \text{SIGN } f_1'' * \dot{\hat{k}}_1 = - \text{SIGN } f_1'' * \dot{\hat{k}}_1 * \hat{k}_1 = - \text{SIGN } \dot{\hat{p}},$$

contradicting that both $\hat{r}$ and $\hat{p}$ are increasing along V. □

Theorems 3 and 4 assert that, in equilibrium, production and exploitation are specialized. The next theorem goes into the problem of the order of exploitation. A well-known outcome of partial equilibrium models is that the 'cheap' resource should be exhausted before exploitation of the 'expensive' resource starts. It is shown presently that this statement holds true in general equilibrium.

<u>Theorem 5</u>

Suppose $a_1 < a_2$. Then $\hat{E}_2(t) > 0$ implies $\int_0^t \hat{E}_1(t)dt = S_{1o}$.

<u>Proof</u>

Suppose that the statement is incorrect. In view of the previous theorem this means that there exist t_1 and t_2, with $t_2 > t_1$, such that $\hat{E}_1(t_1) = 0$, $\hat{E}_2(t_1) > 0$, $\hat{E}_1(t_2) > 0$ and $\hat{E}_2(t_2) = 0$. It follows from (5.30) that

i) $\hat{\lambda}_1 \geq \hat{\pi}_1(t_1)(\hat{p}(t_1) - a_1\hat{r}(t_1))$,

ii) $\hat{\lambda}_2 = \hat{\pi}_2(t_1)(\hat{p}(t_1) - a_2\hat{r}(t_1))$,

iii) $\hat{\lambda}_1 = \hat{\pi}_1(t_2)(\hat{p}(t_2) - a_1\hat{r}(t_2))$,

iv) $\hat{\lambda}_2 \geq \hat{\pi}_2(t_2)(\hat{p}(t_2) - a_2\hat{r}(t_2))$.

From i) and ii) and iii) and iv) respectively, it follows that

$$\hat{\lambda}_2/\hat{\pi}_2(t_1) - \hat{\lambda}_1/\hat{\pi}_1(t_1) \leq (a_1 - a_2)\hat{r}(t_1) < 0,$$

$$\hat{\lambda}_2/\hat{\pi}_2(t_2) - \hat{\lambda}_1/\hat{\pi}_1(t_2) \geq (a_1 - a_2)\hat{r}(t_2).$$

Since $\dot{\hat{\pi}}_i = -\hat{r}\hat{\pi}_i$, for i = 1,2: $\hat{r}(t_2) \geq \hat{r}(t_1)$. From i) and iii) we have

$$\hat{p}(t_2) - \frac{\hat{\pi}_1(t_1)}{\hat{\pi}_1(t_2)}\hat{p}(t_1) - a_1\hat{r}(t_2) + a_1\frac{\hat{\pi}_1(t_1)}{\hat{\pi}_1(t_2)}\hat{r}(t_1) \geq 0.$$

Therefore $\hat{p}(t_2) > \hat{p}(t_1)$. But then $\hat{p}$ and $\hat{r}$ have increased simultaneously which is ruled out since the fpf's are negatively sloped. □

We now proceed to a discussion of the equilibrium price paths. It has already been remarked that the fpf's can have several forms. However, in any case, if non-resource production takes place, the cheapest country is producing. This is a consequence of the fact that general equilibrium is Pareto efficient. But it can also be seen as follows. Suppose $\hat{p}$ is an equilibrium price and let r_1 and r_2 be the corresponding rental rates on the fpf of the first and the second country respectively. If $r_1 > r_2$, then $(\hat{p}, r_2)$ cannot constitute an equilibrium price pair. For, if it did, the first economy would make arbitrarily large profits in production, which is ruled out in equilibrium. We conclude that if non-resource production takes place, the equilibrium prices should lie on the outer envelope of the fpf's (seen from the origin). If the frontiers do not have points in common, one of the economies will never be engaged in non-resource production. Consider, by way of example, figure 5.3.

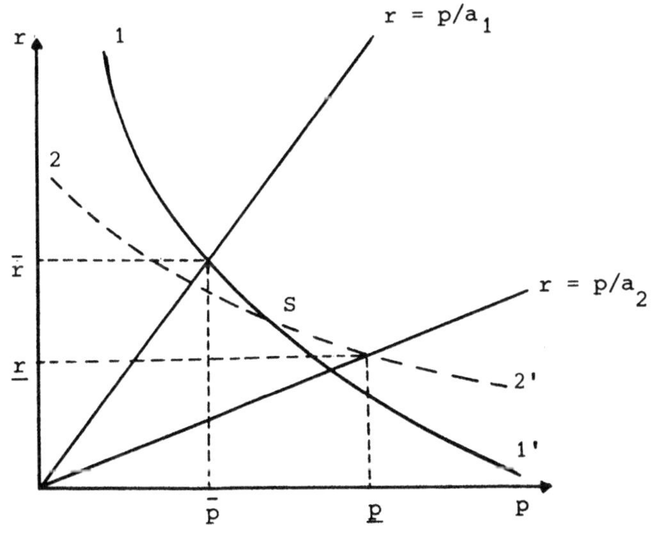

figure 5.3.

In this figure the curves 1-1' and 2-2' represent the fpf's of economy 1 and economy 2 respectively. They intersect at point S. The straight lines represent the prices at which exploitation yields zero profits. In the figure, and also in the sequel, it is assumed that the first economy is relatively cheap in exploitation. We define some notions to be used below.

$(\bar{r},\bar{p})$ is the point where the line $r = p/a_1$ intersects the outer envelope of the fpf's.

$(\underline{r},\underline{p})$ is the point where the line $r = p/a_2$ intersects the outer envelope of the fpf's.

p^* is the point where the outer envelope of the fpf's intersects the p-axis.

By virtue of our assumptions on the non-resource technologies $(\bar{r},\bar{p})$ and $(\underline{r},\underline{p})$ exist. p^* might not exist. This occurs for example when both technologies are Cobb-Douglas.

In order to prove our main theorems 6 and 7, some lemmas are established first.

Lemma 1

Let $\{\hat{r}(t),\hat{p}(t)\}$ be equilibrium prices. Then $\hat{r}(t) \leqq \bar{r}$ for all $t \geqq 0$.

Proof

Suppose the lemma is not correct. If, for some t, $\hat{r}(t) > \bar{r}$, then, at t, exploitation is not profitable and will not be carried out. Hence there is no non-resource production either. Therefore, demand for capital equals zero, which, from the definition of general equilibrium, implies $\hat{r}(t) = 0$, a contradiction. □

Lemma 2

Let $\{\hat{r}(t),\hat{p}(t)\}$ be equilibrium prices. If $\hat{r}(t_1) = 0$ for some $t_1 \geqq 0$, then $\hat{r}(t) = 0$ for all $t \geqq t_1$.

Proof

Suppose that $\hat{r}(t_1)=0$ and that for some $t_2>t_1$ $\hat{r}(t_2)>0$. Since each economy is a profit maximizer in non-resource production, $\hat{p}(t_1)>p^*$. Otherwise profits could be made arbitrarily large by exerting infinite demand for capital. At t_2 $\hat{p}(t_2) > p^*$ for the same reason. Furthermore there is demand for capital at t_2 and hence non-resource production is carried out, implying demand for resource goods. Suppose that the first economy is exploiting at t_2. Then

$$\hat{\pi}_1(t_2)(\hat{p}(t_2)-a_1\hat{r}(t_2)) \geqq \hat{\pi}_1(t_1)\hat{p}(t_1).$$

This follows from (5.30). $\hat{\pi}_1(t_1) \geqq \hat{\pi}_1(t_2)$ since $\hat{\pi}_1$ is continuous and decreasing. Hence

$$-a_1\hat{r}(t_2)\hat{\pi}_1(t_2) \geqq 0,$$

implying that $\hat{r}(t_2) \doteq 0$, a contradiction.

Lemma 3

Let $\{\hat{r}(t),\hat{p}(t)\}$ be equilibrium prices. Then $\hat{r}(0) > 0$.

Proof

If $\hat{r}(0) = 0$, then $\hat{r}(t) = 0$ for all $t \geqq 0$, from the previous lemma. If $\hat{p}(t_1) = 0$ for some t_1, then demand for capital and the resource good would be unbounded, since profits from non-resource production can be made arbitrarily large. This is not feasible. Hence $\hat{p}(t) \geqq p^*$. But since resource suppliers aim at profit maximization, there will, along general equilibrium, resource goods be supplied, which however are not demanded. This contradicts $\hat{p}(t) \geqq p^* > 0$. □

Lemma 4

Let $\{\hat{r}(t),\hat{p}(t)\}$ be equilibrium prices. Suppose $(\hat{r}(0),\hat{p}(0)) = (\bar{r},\bar{p})$. Then $\{\hat{r}(t),\hat{p}(t)\} = (\bar{r},\bar{p})$ for all $t \geqq 0$.

Proof

Exploitation at time zero is not profitable for the second country. Since $\hat{r}(0) > 0$, there is demand for the exploited commodity, which has to be satisfied by the first economy. It follows from (5.30) that $\hat{\lambda}_1 = 0$. In view of lemma 1 this proves the lemma. □

Lemma 5

Let $\{\hat{r}(t),\hat{p}(t)\}$ be equilibrium prices. Suppose $\hat{r}(0) < \hat{p}(0)/a_1$. Then there exists $t_1 \geqq 0$ such that for all $t \geqq t_1$, $\hat{r}(t) \leqq \underline{r}$.

Proof

Two cases are to be considered.

1) Suppose there exists $\varepsilon > 0$ such that, for all t, $\hat{r}(t) \geqq \underline{r}+\varepsilon$. Then $\hat{p}(t) < \underline{p}$ for all t. We are in a region (between $r = p/a_1$ and $r = p/a_2$) where it is not profitable for the second country to extract. Hence the first country will exploit its resource, since there is demand for it. Therefore, by (5.30)

$$(\dot{\hat{p}} - a_1\dot{\hat{r}})/(\hat{p} - a_1\hat{r}) = \hat{r} \geqq \underline{r} + \varepsilon$$

and $\hat{p}$ goes to infinity as t goes to infinity, a contradiction.

2) If, for some t_1, $\hat{r}(t_1) < \underline{r}$, then either the first or the second economy is exploiting (except when $r(t_1) = 0$, which in view of the lemma stated is not interesting). In both cases the resource price is increasing and the rental rate is decreasing, according to (5.30). □

It should be remarked that lemmata 4 and 5 do not exclude the possibility that in equilibrium $\hat{r}(t) = \bar{r}$ and $\hat{p}(t) = \bar{p}$ or $\hat{r}(t) = \underline{r}$ and $\hat{p}(t) = \underline{p}$ for all t. The following lemma provides necessary conditions for the first possibility to occur.

Lemma 6

Let $\{\hat{r}(t),\hat{p}(t)\}$ be equilibrium prices. If for all $t \geqq 0$, $\hat{r}(t) = \bar{r}$ and $\hat{p}(t) = \bar{p}$, then $\rho_1 > \bar{r}$ and $\rho_2 > \bar{r}$.

Proof

For all $t \geqq 0$ the second economy incurs losses if it were to engage in exploitation activities. The first economy will not make profits in exploitation. Whichever economy produces the non-resource commodity, it earns no profits from this activity since F_i is linearly homogeneous. It follows from (5.6) that

$$\dot{\hat{K}}_i(t) = \bar{r}\hat{K}_i(t) - \hat{C}_i(t), \quad i = 1,2, \quad t \geqq 0.$$

The input ratio in non-resource production is constant. Since the reserve of the first economy's resource is limited, the rate of extraction and hence also the amount of capital in use should decrease, towards zero. But then it is necessary that both rates of consumption decrease. It follows from (5.26) and (5.27) that

$$\eta_i(\hat{C}_i)\dot{\hat{C}}_i/\hat{C}_i = \rho_i - \bar{r}, \quad i = 1,2,$$

where $\eta_i(\hat{C}_i)$ denotes the elasticity of marginal utility of economy i. Since U_i is concave, η_i is negative. Therefore we must have $\rho_i > \bar{r}$, $i = 1,2.$ □

Now we proceed to the characterization of the equilibrium prices. It is first shown that they are continuous.

<u>Theorem 6</u>

Let $\{\hat{r}(t),\hat{p}(t)\}$ be equilibrium prices. Then $\hat{r}(t)$ and $\hat{p}(t)$ are continuous.

<u>Proof</u>

Suppose the theorem is false. Let there occur a discontinuity in $\hat{r}$ at, say, t_1. Then several possibilities are to be considered.

1) $\hat{r}(t_1-) > \hat{r}(t_1+)$. Since, in equilibrium, prices must move along smooth factor-price frontiers, the downward jump in $\bar{r}$ must be accompanied by an upward jump in $\hat{p}$. Since, at t_1 -, at least one of the resources is being exploited and since $\hat{\pi}_i$ is continuous, at least one of the $\hat{\gamma}_3$'s jumps to a negative value, which is not allowed.

2) $\hat{r}(t_1-) > 0$, $\hat{r}(t_1+) > \hat{r}(t_1-)$. The upward jump in $\hat{r}$ must be accompanied by a downward jump in $\hat{p}$. Hence both $\hat{\gamma}_3$'s jump upwards, implying that, at t_1 +, no resource is being exploited, contradicting that, for $\hat{r} > 0$, there is demand for the resource good, which must be met in equilibrium.

3) $\hat{r}(t_1-) = 0$, $\hat{r}(t_1+) > 0$. This possibility cannot occur in view of lemma 2.

These observations lead to the conclusion that discontinuities in $\hat{p}$ can occur only for $\hat{r} = 0$. But since $\hat{r}$ is continuous at the point of time where it reaches zero, say at t_2, $\hat{p}$ is continuous at t_2. Therefore $\hat{E}_i(t_2 -) > 0$ for some i and the corresponding γ_3 is continuous at t_2 and equals zero. We conclude that, also for $\hat{r} = 0$, $\hat{p}$ is continuous. □

At first sight it might seem that $\{\hat{r}(t),\hat{p}(t)\} = (\bar{r},\bar{p})$ cannot constitute equilibrium prices. Below we shall provide an example to show that this conjecture is not correct. The idea is basically that there are situations where the cheaper resource is abundant. Then $\hat{\lambda}_1 = 0$ and a fortiori $\hat{\lambda}_2 = 0$.

Suppose that $\eta_i(C_i) := U_i'' * C_i/U_i'$ is constant and denote it by η_i. Assume $\rho_i > \bar{r}$ $(> \bar{r}(1 + \eta_i))$ for i = 1,2. If $(\bar{r},\bar{p})$ are equilibrium prices, the second country would incur a loss when it engages in exploitation activities. Therefore, the first economy is extracting. No economy, however, earns profits, neither from non-resource production nor from exploitation. It follows from (5.6) that for all $t \geqq 0$:

$$\dot{\hat{K}}_i(t) = \bar{r}\hat{K}_i(t) - \hat{C}_i(t), \quad i = 1,2,$$

and from (5.26) and (5.27) that

$$\dot{\hat{C}}_i(t)/\hat{C}_i(t) = (\rho_i - \bar{r})/\eta_i, \quad i = 1,2.$$

Take

$$\hat{C}_i(0) = -\frac{\rho_i - \bar{r}(1 + \eta_i)}{\eta_i} K_{io}, \quad i = 1,2.$$

Then it is found that

$$\hat{K}_i(t) = K_{io}\, e^{\frac{\rho_i - \bar{r}}{\eta_i} t}, \quad i = 1,2.$$

Hence (5.7) is satisfied. Moreover, $\hat{K}_i(t) \to 0$ as $t \to \infty$, i = 1,2.

$$\hat{K}(t) := \hat{K}_1(t) + \hat{K}_2(t).$$

Without loss of generality it is assumed that the second country is producing the non-resource goods. Since F_2 is linearly homogeneous it follows that

$$f_2'(\hat{K}_2^y/\hat{R}_2) := F_{2K}(\hat{K}_2^y, \hat{R}_2) = \bar{r},$$

and

$$\hat{K}_2^y(t) = g(\bar{r})\hat{R}_2(t) = g(\bar{r})\hat{E}_1(t),$$

where g is the inverse of f_2'. Since $\hat{K}(t) = \hat{K}_2^y(t) + \hat{K}_1^e(t)$, it follows that

$$\hat{E}_1(t) = \frac{K_{10}\, e^{\frac{\rho_1 - \bar{r}}{\eta_1} t} + K_{20}\, e^{\frac{\rho_2 - \bar{r}}{\eta_2} t}}{a_1 + g(\bar{r})}.$$

Then

$$\int_0^\infty \hat{E}_1(t)dt$$

is easily calculated. If the outcome is equal to or smaller than S_{1o}, all the conditions for a general competitive equilibrium are satisfied. This will occur for small initial capital stocks and a large initial reserve of the resource of the first economy.

The result is summarized in

Theorem 7

Suppose $\rho_i > \bar{r}$, i = 1,2. Let K_{io} be 'small' and/or S_{1o} be 'large'. Then the equilibrium prices are given by $\hat{p}(t) = \bar{p}$ and $\hat{r}(t) = \bar{r}$ for all t.

Proof

The proof has been given above for constant elasticities of marginal utility. An extension to variable elasticities is straightforward but is omitted here. □

What is, then, the equilibrium price-path when one of the conditions mentioned in the previous theorem does not hold? It is shown below that in that case the prices are not constant and that the interest rate converges towards zero and the resource price converges to p*, if it exists, and goes to infinity otherwise.

Theorem 8

Suppose that one of the conditions given in theorem 7 does not hold. Let $\{\hat{r}(t),\hat{p}(t)\}$ be equilibrium prices. Then

1) $0 < \hat{r}(0) < \bar{r}, \quad \hat{p}(0) > \bar{p}$,

2) $\dot{\hat{r}}(t) < 0, \quad \dot{\hat{p}}(t) > 0$ for all t, as long as $\hat{r}(t) > 0$ and $\hat{p}(t) > 0$,

3) $\hat{r}(t) \to 0$ and $\hat{p}(t) \to p^*$ or $\hat{p}(t) \to \infty$ as $t \to \infty$.

Proof

ad 1. This follows from lemma 3, lemma 4 and theorem 7.

ad 2. Suppose that for an interval of time during which $\hat{r} > 0$ and $\hat{p} > 0$, $\dot{\hat{r}}(t) = 0$. One of the countries is carrying out non-resource production. This implies through (5.28) and (5.29) that $\dot{\hat{p}}(t) = 0$ along that interval. Since non-resource production takes place, there is also exploitation. But in view of (5.30) and because the $\hat{\pi}$ of the exploiting country is decreasing this implies that the corresponding $\hat{\gamma}_3$ is increasing, unless of course $\hat{p} = a\hat{r}$, or, to be more specific, $\hat{p} = a_2\hat{r}$ in the interval. By the same argument it can be seen that a constant $\hat{p}$ along some interval can only occur when $\hat{p} = a_2\hat{r}$. It therefore suffices to show that there cannot be a non-degenerate interval of time, along which $\hat{p} = a_2\hat{r}$. Suppose there is, and that the interval starts at t_1. It is seen from (5.30) that, from t_1 on, the $\hat{\gamma}_3$ of country 1 starts increasing. Therefore, from t_1 on, the first economy is not exploiting whereas the second economy is. Before t_1, $\hat{p} - a_1\hat{r}$ is positive, and, from (5.30)

$$(\dot{\hat{p}} - a_1\dot{\hat{r}})/(\hat{p} - a_1\hat{r}) = \hat{r} > 0. \tag{5.32}$$

But for the second economy we have for $t \leq t_1$: $\hat{p} - a_2\hat{r} < 0$. Since $\hat{p}$ and $\hat{r}$ are continuous, the second economy's $\hat{\gamma}_3$ is decreasing before t_1.

This implies that for $t < t_2$

$$(\dot{\hat{p}} - a_2\dot{\hat{r}})/(\hat{p} - a_2\hat{r}) > \hat{r}.$$

But then $\hat{p}$ has decreased before t_1 and $\hat{r}$ has increased, contradicting (5.32). We conclude that, for $\hat{r} > 0$ and $\hat{p} > 0$, there is no non-degenerate interval of time along which the equilibrium prices are constant. The argument given here a fortiori holds when it is assumed, to start with, that $\hat{r}$ is increasing during some interval of time.

ad 3. Suppose $\hat{r}$ approaches a positive constant. Then, from (5.30), there will not be exploitation eventually. Hence, no non-resource production takes place eventually and demand for capital is zero. Then the value of excess demand is not equal to zero, a contradiction. □

It would be interesting to elaborate on some comparative dynamic results. This will not be done here formally. It is clear from theorems 7 and 8 that a large sum of initial stocks of capital necessitates a small initial interest rate, relative to the initial price of resource commodities. The opposite holds for a large sum of initial resource reserves. The larger the smallest rate of time preference, the smaller is the initial resource price. Of course these results hold ceteris paribus.

Finally, there is the problem of the existence of a general competitive equilibrium. The commodity space in which we work is of an infinite dimension. Therefore, the standard techniques to establish general equilibrium cannot be invoked. However, the example given above strongly suggests that equilibria will in general exist under the assumptions made. In addition, Elbers and Withagen (1984) have shown existence of general equilibria in a model of trade in exhaustible resources. Without going into details, one may safely assume that, for the model presented here, the same type of argument can be pursued.

5.5. *Conclusions*

In the preceding sections we have analysed a simple two country world model of general competitive equilibrium. Under the assumption of differing technologies across countries, the main results are:

- there is never simultaneous exploitation,
- there is never simultaneous non-resource production,
- the cheaper resource is exhausted before the more expensive resource starts being exploited,
- at any price constellation the country with the cheaper non-resource technology is producing the non-resource goods,
- the rental rate is non-increasing, the resource price is non-decreasing,
- equilibrium prices are continuous.

As always, these outcomes are dependent on the type of functions involved and on the equilibrium concept used. In this section we shall leave the features of the functions mentioned as they are, since these are customary in international trade models. We shall first compare briefly our results with those obtained in earlier studies by other authors. Second, some remarks will be devoted to the appropriateness of our (and their) equilibrium concept. Finally, suggestions are given for further research.
Most of the earlier studies in this field have been discussed in chapter 2. It is easily seen that the model presented here is in most respects more general than those described there. Kemp and Long (1980c) give a model with rather specific utility functions, there is only one resource-owning country and one non-resource good producing country, there are no extraction costs and no capital is required for production. Chiarella (1980) is more general in that he allows for capital as an input in non-resource production, as well as for technical progress. However, he restricts himself to a Cobb-Douglas technology. In Elbers and Withagen (1984) both countries own an exhaustible resource, which is costly to exploit, but non-resource production is not incorporated in their model. We conclude that Chiarella's model is closest to ours. The two models have several results in common, such as: prices equal marginal products and 'the Solow-Stiglitz efficiency condition,

equating the return on the use of the resource to the marginal product of capital' holds. There is, however, one important exception. In Chiarella's model the resource price and the rental rate monotonically approach positive values, whereas in our model the prices are either constant throughout or approach (p*,0). This difference has to be explained by the fact that we have employed a constant returns to scale exploitation technology, contrary to Chiarella, where exploitation is costless.

One rather peculiar outcome in our model is that the cheaper resource is exhausted before the more expensive resource is taken into exploitation. Peculiar, not because this phenomenon is striking, but because it points at a conceptual problem concerning the equilibrium concept. In chapter 2 the problem of dynamic inconsistency, occurring when one of the participants in trade has an incentive to break the contract made up at the outset of the planning period, has been discussed. There, this feature has been associated with a world where a cartel and a fringe were supplying the resource goods. The phenomenon of dynamic inconsistency could occur in our model as well. Consider figure 5.4 below.

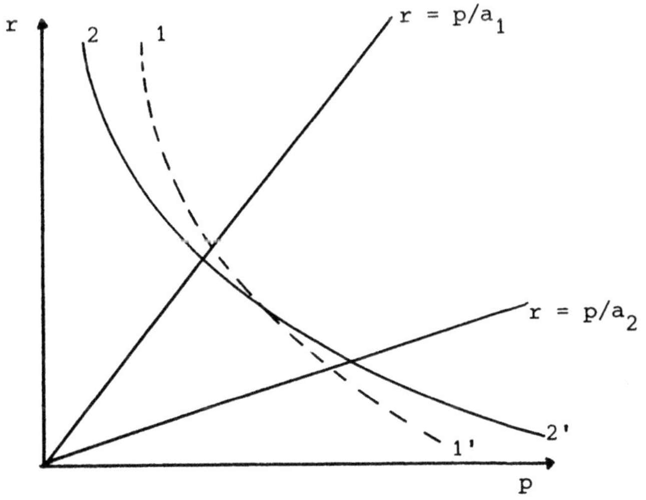

figure 5.4.

Here, if contracts are enforceable, the second country is carrying out both activities from a given instant of time on (at least under the assumptions of theorem 8). It is easily seen that, from that time on, the second country is not motivated to pay the equilibrium rental rate to the capital supplying first country, since country 1 has no reserves left and can therefore not produce on its own. On the other hand, if, at that instant of time, the second country owns no capital, the first country might try to force it to supply the consumer good at an arbitrarily low price.

Evidently this problem is important and deserves a closer examination. First, one would have to find out under which circumstances the problem might arise. Second, and this seems to be more difficult, one wishes to identify the price-path that would constitute a rational expectations general equilibrium. It should be stressed here however, that the problem described is not inherent to trade in exhaustible resources but might occur also in traditional general equilibrium models with dated commodities.

A second line of research would be to generalize the model so as to include increasing and/or decreasing returns to scale, in non-resource production as well as in exploitation technologies.

6. *SUMMARY AND CONCLUSIONS*

6.1. *Introduction*

The present study contains four related essays on the economic theory of exhaustible resources. The common feature of the essays is that they treat the problem of optimal exploitation of exhaustible resources in trading economies. In this final chapter the main results are summarized (6.2). In section 6.3 an attempt is made to indicate the empirical relevance of the results. Section 6.4 gives the conclusions.

6.2. *Summary*

In chapter 2 of this monograph a survey has been given of the literature on trade in exhaustible resources. A broad distinction has been made between *partial equilibrium* models and *general equilibrium* models. Generally speaking, the partial equilibrium approach deals with the problem of optimal exploitation of natural resources when world market prices or world demand schedules are given, whereas in the general equilibrium approach demand is derived within the model. Both branches of research have led to useful insights.
The former line of research is the one pursued most frequently and has covered several issues such as: the impact of extraction costs on optimal exploitation, and the differences in optimal exploitation patterns according to the world market structure, where especially the problem of dynamic inconsistency has received much attention. It has been concluded that two phenomena have been insufficiently studied: first, the problem of simultaneous optimization of exploitation and investment in small price-taking economies and, second, the problem of credit rationing on a world scale. Both issues have been subject to further research, which will be discussed below.
The general equilibrium theory with trade in exhaustible resources, as described in the survey chapter, is very interesting but still lacks

the maturity of the general equilibrium theory developed in 'conventional' models. In chapter 5 we have attempted to offer a contribution in this field.

Chapter 3 deals with the problem of optimal investment and optimal exploitation in a small, price-taking, economy. It is found that there is a strong relationship between capital accumulation and optimal exploitation and that the outcomes are extremely sensitive to variations in the economy's time preference, initial stock of capital, price expectations and balance of payments conditions.

In chapter 4 we have elaborated on the balance of payments conditions and in particular the effect of credit rationing has been studied. It was concluded that in some circumstances no optimal programs exist and that the results concerning sensitivity, found in the preceding chapter, remain valid. In several cases the optimal rates of exploitation are extremal (zero or maximal). When the analysis is extended to a world-wide scale, these cases are unlikely to be candidates for general equilibrium. This observation calls for a general equilibrium approach.

Chapter 5 provides such an analysis. It analyses a model more general than those studied earlier. Equilibrium prices and equilibrium time-paths of commodity flows have been characterized. Under the assumptions usually made in the economic theory of international trade, there is in our model always complete specialization and the Solow/Stiglitz condition for dynamic efficiency is satisfied.

6.3. *Empirical relevance*

Here we tentatively answer the question whether the foregoing analysis is suited to make empirical inferences. This question can be conceived of in different ways. First of all, one can ask for the positive (descriptive) significance of the analysis, in the sense that it may or may not explain actual economic behaviour. Second, there is the possibility of normative implications: can there practical policy recommendations be derived from the models presented? We shall go into both matters, while concentrating on the Dutch situation.

In the design of recent Dutch energy policy an important role is played by *energy scenarios* and the *'plan of sales of natural gas'*.
In 1981 Parliament initiated a large-scale public debate on Dutch energy policy. The results of this debate can be found in the final report of the so-called Stuurgroep (Steering Committee) (1983). In the framework of the debate four energy scenarios have been developed: two on act of the Steering Committee, one by the Ministry of Economic Affairs and one by the Centre for Energy Saving. Energy scenarios describe possible future developments of the economy with special reference to the supply of and demand for the various types of energy. In order to make the outcomes of the scenarios comparable, all four of them depart from some, commonly agreed upon, basic assumptions such as: a given growth rate of international trade over the period under consideration (1982-2000), a steady growth rate of the real world market price of energy, a surplus on the current account amounting to at least 1% of national income and an economic policy directed towards the reduction of inflation and government budget deficit. With respect to the exploitation of natural gas it is assumed that exports from exploitation gradually decline towards zero in 2000 and that the rate of exploitation is given, in accordance with the plans of sales of natural gas, issued by Gasunie in 1980 and 1981 (see below). Basically, each scenario is then the result of alternative policy measures with respect to energy pricing, environmental issues, employment, sectoral structure etc. The final pictures of the scenarios represent a.o. equilibrium supply of and demand for energy per sector of the economy. Whether or not the growth rate of gross national product is an outcome or an assumption in the exercises differs per scenario.
The N.V. Nederlandse Gasunie, a firm partly owned by the Government, annually submits a 'plan of sales of natural gas' to the Minister of Economic Affairs containing proposals concerning purchases, transportation and sales of natural gas. This plan is subject to approval of the Minister who is also responsible for the pricing of natural gas. The plan usually refers to a 25 years period. The 1981 plan is based on an expected average annual growth rate of G.N.P. amounting to 2½%. From this, total demand for energy is derived. Subsequently, it is put forward that, in view of the aim of *conservation* of natural gas, exports should gradually decline and that, since gas is to be

used *efficiently*, deliveries should take place mainly to public utilities (not including electricity plants) and advanced industrial applications. This, and some other considerations, then determine the future exploitation of natural gas.
The relationship between energy scenarios and exploitation plans, described above, poses some problems. First of all, it is highly questionable whether they are mutually compatible. To give one example: none of the scenarios uses (or yields) G.N.P. growth rates as high as 2½% (Gasunie's estimate). But even if compatibility exists, it can be doubted whether the results are optimal. Recall that in each scenario the rate of exploitation was treated as given. But, whatever the objectives of the scenarios are, it might be that more, or less, exploitation of natural gas is beneficial in the light of these objectives. If future Dutch energy policy would be based on one of the four scenarios, then we can say without exaggeration that, irrespective of the ultimate choice of the preferred scenario, this policy is quite partial in nature and will yield suboptimal results. This monograph emphasizes the desirability of a simultaneous design of energy policy and general economic policy. It has been the purpose of chapter 3 to provide a starting point for a more integrated approach (see also Withagen (1981d)). It was concluded that balance of payments conditions and price expectations play a crucial role in this analysis. It may be concluded from chapter 4 on financial world markets that a reconsideration of the Dutch position with respect to current account objectives is in order, whereas chapter 5 may provide an incentive to study models of interrelated economies so as to predict more precisely future price movements of energy-bearers.

Let us now proceed to an analysis of the positive significance of this monograph. In the framework of the public debate there has also been an inquiry into the ideas of many organizations on the exploitation of natural gas. They were confronted with several propositions about the speed of exploitation (although not in quantitative terms), on which they were asked to react. The opinions differ drastically: some of them can be characterized as being extremely conservationist, others support a larger rate of exploitation, provided that the revenues are used to improve the economic structure. These differences can possibly be explained with the aid of the outcomes of chapter 3, saying that an optimal exploitation policy strongly depends on rate of time preference, expected growth rate of energy prices and attitude towards balance of payments conditions. In much the same way could be explained the recent modification in actual energy policy amounting to a reconsideration of export possibilities and the input of natural gas in electricity plants. There is also the recent advice of the Social Economic Council (1983) to embed energy policy in general economic policy. In this context it is appropriate (and perhaps provoking) to mention an early (but not outdated at all) contribution of de Wolff (1964), who offers a long term reflection on the problem of exploitation of Dutch natural gas so as to "maximize the total discounted national economic value of the reserve" (translation by the author).

6.4. *Concluding remarks*

Apart from the issues discussed in the preceding section and the conclusions given per chapter, there are some other general conclusions to be drawn. First, one should be very careful in designing optimal policies for resource extraction. In this context it seems appropriate to cite Koopmans (1965) again: "Ignoring realities in adopting 'principles' may lead one to search for a nonexistent optimum, or to adopt an optimum that is open to unanticipated objections". Second, that especially the design of mechanisms to implement optimal policies in a decentralized way is a challenging field of future research.

APPENDIX A. THE ONE-SECTOR OPTIMAL GROWTH MODEL

In this appendix a brief review is presented of the neoclassical one-sector growth model. Special emphasis will be put on some properties that are relevant for the discussion in chapter 3 of this monograph. The optimal growth model dates back to Ramsey (1928) and has been extended by Cass (1965), Chakravarty (1962), Koopmans (1965 and 1967), Mirrlees (1967), Von Weizsäcker (1965) and many others. For surveys of this literature we refer to Takayama (1974) and Wan (1971). There also one may find discussions about conceptual issues with respect to the horizon, final stocks, rate of time preference etc.

We consider an aggregate model of a closed economy for a *given* period of time. Time is denoted by t and is considered continuous. The initial and final instants of time are 0 and T (possibly infinity). The economy's output is produced by means of capital according to a given production function. Output is devoted to gross investments and consumption. The purpose is to find an allocation which maximizes social welfare over time.

Let K(t) denote the stock of capital at time t, Y(t) the rate of production and C(t) the rate of consumption. A *feasible program* is a set of functions $\{K(t),Y(t),C(t)\}$, defined for $t \in [0,T]$, with K(t) continuous and Y(t) and C(t) piece-wise continuous (see appendix B for a definition) such that

$$Y(t) \leqq F(K(t)), \tag{A1}$$

$$\dot{K}(t) + \mu K(t) + C(t) \leqq Y(t), \tag{A2}$$

$$K(0) \leqq K_0, \quad K(T) \geqq K_T, \tag{A3}$$

$$K(t) \geqq 0, \quad C(t) \geqq 0. \tag{A4}$$

Here, F is a given neoclassical production function. The assumptions about F are:

$$F'(K) > 0, \quad F''(K) < 0, \quad \text{for all } \infty > K \geqq 0,$$

$$F(0) = 0, \quad F'(0) = \infty, \quad F'(\infty) = 0.$$

μ denotes the rate of depreciation and is constant. K_0 is the given initial stock of capital; K_T is the minimal final stock of capital required. $\dot{K}(t) := dK(t)/dt$. A feasible program is called optimal if it maximizes

$$J_T := \int_0^T e^{-\rho t} U(C(t))dt, \qquad \text{(A5)}$$

where ρ (> 0) is the constant rate of time preference and U is the instantaneous utility function, fulfilling:

$$U'(C) > 0, \quad U''(C) < 0, \quad \text{for all } C \geqq 0,$$

$$U'(0) = \infty.$$

Before proceeding to the characterization of an optimal program, we make some remarks. First, in view of the assumptions with respect to F and U, it is straightforward to see that along an optimal program (A1), (A2) and (A3) will hold with equality and that (A4) will hold with strict inequality. Second, the restriction to continuous functions K(t) is natural. A downward jump in the stock would mean that capital is thrown away, which, in view of the perfect malleability of investments and consumption, cannot be optimal. An upward jump in the stock of capital would indicate that, before the instant of time, where the jump occurs, the existing stock of capital has not been fully used, which cannot be optimal, or that capital as a stock has been newly created at an instant of time, which in the closed system under consideration is impossible.

The Hamiltonian of the problem is (upon substitution of (A1) into (A2)):

$$H(K,C,\phi) = e^{-\rho t} U(C) + \phi(F(K) - \mu K - C).$$

Let $\{\hat{K}(t),\hat{C}(t)\}$ be an optimal program. Then, according to Pontryagin's maximum principle (see appendix B), there exists a continuous $\hat{\phi}(t)$, such that

$$\partial H/\partial C = 0 \qquad : \quad e^{-\rho t}\, U'(\hat{C}(t)) = \hat{\phi}(t), \tag{A6}$$

$$\partial H/\partial K = -\dot{\hat{\phi}}(t) \; : \quad \hat{\phi}(t)(F'(\hat{K}(t)) - \mu) = -\dot{\hat{\phi}}(t). \tag{A7}$$

To see how the optimal program looks like, define $K_{\rho+\mu}$ as the solution of

$$F'(K) = \rho + \mu,$$

and $C_{\rho+\mu}$ as

$$C_{\rho+\mu} = F(K_{\rho+\mu}) - \mu K_{\rho+\mu}.$$

$(K_{\rho+\mu}, C_{\rho+\mu})$ will be referred to as the modified golden rule. Consider the locus $\dot{K} = 0$. This is given by $C = F(K) - \mu K$. $\dot{C} = 0$ for $K = K_{\rho+\mu}$, from (A6) and (A7). Both loci are displayed in figure A1.

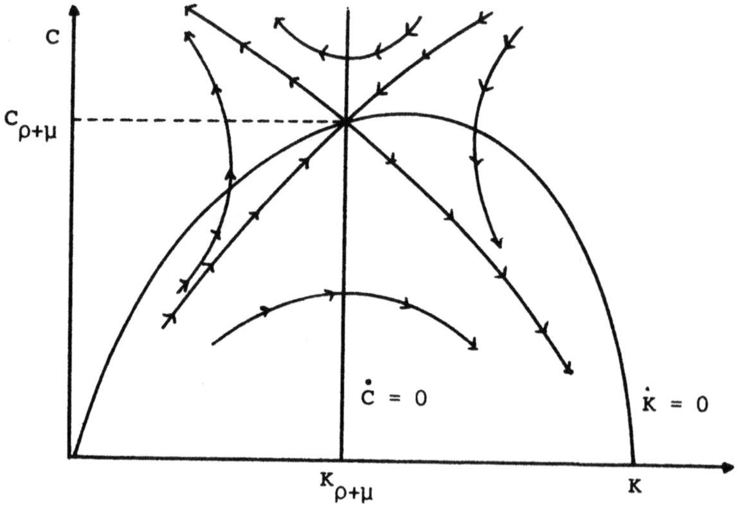

figure A1.

It is clearly seen from (A6) and (A7) that to the left of the line $K = K_{\rho+\mu}$, $\dot{C} > 0$, and to the right of this line, $\dot{C} < 0$. For points above the locus $\dot{K} = 0$, $\dot{K} < 0$, for points under this locus, $\dot{K} > 0$. The arrows in figure A1 represent these findings.

In order to have, in general, a solution of the problem posed, it is necessary that the planning period is large enough to enable the economy to reach at least K_T. When the initial stock of capital is small relative to the required final stock and when the planning period is short, there may not exist a feasible program. Henceforth we shall restrict ourselves to (K_T,T)-tuples such that feasible programs exist.

In view of the strict concavity of the instantaneous utility function and the production function, a program fulfilling (A1)-(A4) and the necessary conditions (A6) and (A7) is optimal. Furthermore, it is the unique optimal program. It has been shown by Cass (1965) that optimal programs exist.

Now consider first the optimal growth problem for $T = \infty$. In this case the constraint $K(T) \geqq K_T$ is omitted. It can been seen from figure A1, that there are three types of programs fulfilling the necessary conditions (A1)-(A3), (A6) and (A7) (see also Takayama (1974)):

Type 1: $\exists_{\bar{t}>0} \ \forall_{t>\bar{t}} \quad K(t) > K_{\rho+\mu}$,

Type 2: $K(t) \to K_{\rho+\mu}$, $C(t) \to C_{\rho+\mu}$ for $t \to \infty$,

Type 3: $\exists_{\bar{t}>0} \ \forall_{t>\bar{t}} \quad K(t) < K_{\rho+\mu}$.

The type 1 programs cannot be optimal for the following reason. From some time on, $K(t) > K_{\rho+\mu}$ and $C(t) < C_{\rho+\mu}$. Therefore, a type 1 program can be improved upon by desinvesting to reduce capital to $K_{\rho+\mu}$, as soon as capital exceeds $K_{\rho+\mu}$. This will give a higher rate of consumption and a larger value of the target function.

Along the type 3 programs, the stock of capital is decreasing eventually, but the rate of consumption is increasing. Hence the stock of capital will eventually become negative, thereby violating feasibility condition (A4).

We conclude that, for an infinite planning period, only the type 2 program is a candidate to be optimal. Such a program exists. Therefore, one should choose the initial rate of consumption on the unique branch leading to the modified golden rule. The modified golden rule is asymptotically approached in a monotonic way.

We turn now to the case of a finite horizon. See figure A2.

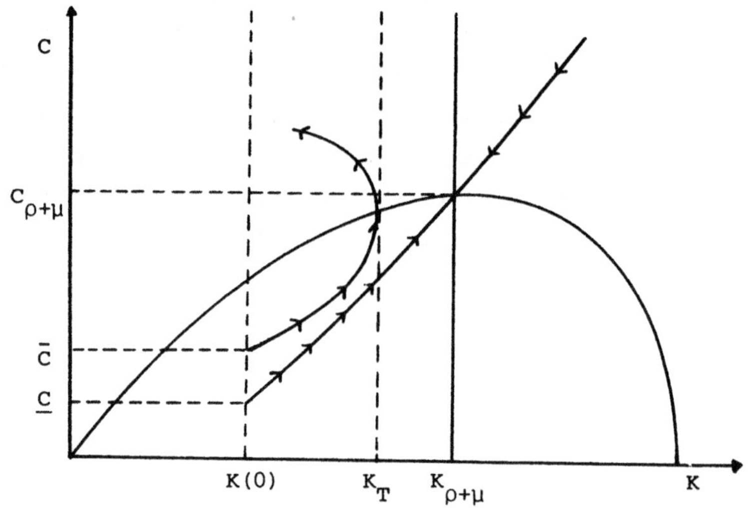

figure A2.

It has been assumed that $K_0 < K_T < K_{\rho+\mu}$. It follows from (A1) and (A2), and (A6) and (A7) that along an optimal program:

$$\dot{K} = F(K) - \mu K - C, \quad \text{(A8)}$$

$$\eta(C)\dot{C}/C = - F'(K) + \rho + \mu, \quad \text{(A9)}$$

where $\eta(C)$ is the elasticity of marginal utility $(U''C/U')$. K(0) is given. Hence, due to the assumptions with respect to U and F, the choice of the initial rate of consumption (C(0)) uniquely determines the paths $\{K(t),C(t)\}$ satisfying (A8) and (A9). Now $\underline{C}$ and $\bar{C}$ are defined as follows. If $C(0) = \underline{C}$, $(K(t),C(t)) \to (K_{\rho+\mu},C_{\rho+\mu})$. If $C(0) = \bar{C}$, there exists b > 0 such that $\dot{K}(b) = 0$, $K(b) = K_T$, where K_T is the number given in figure A2. This means that, if the required final stock were K_T and the final time, (T), were b, the optimal initial rate of consumption would be $\bar{C}$.

In the sequel K_T will be kept fixed. We shall carry out a comparative dynamic analysis on the initial rate of consumption. It has been proved by Cass (1966) that, for a large final time T, the stock of capital along the optimal program is 'close' to the modified golden rule K, except for an initial and a final interval of time. The initial rate of consumption is 'close' to $\underline{C}$. In view of our previous remarks, we can say that, if C(0) is 'close' to $\underline{C}$, there exists a 'large' number c such that the corresponding solution K(t) of (A8) and (A9) satisfies $K(c) = K_T$, $\dot{K}(c) \leqq 0$. On the other hand, if $C(0) = \bar{C}$, there exists $b < c$, such that the corresponding solution satisfies $K(b) = K_T$, $\dot{K}(b) = 0$. This is illustrated in figure A3.

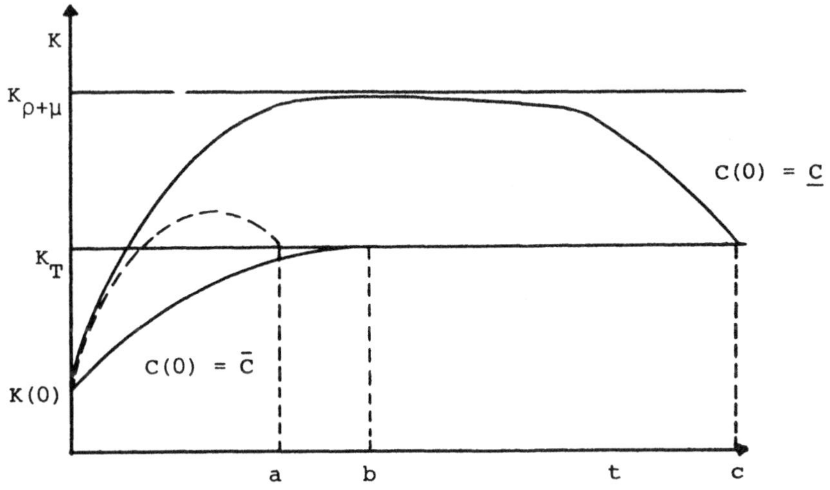

figure A3.

Since the solutions of (A8) and (A9) are unique, it is easily seen that for all $C(0) \in (\underline{C},\bar{C})$ the corresponding K will equal K_T at some instant of time and at that instant of time $\dot{K} < 0$. What we wish to show here, and this is relevant for the discussion in chapter 3, is the following. The closer the initial rate of consumption is to $\underline{C}$, the longer it takes the corresponding K trajectory to reach K_T from above. To see this, suppose first that the dotted K-trajectory in figure A3 corresponds to a $C(0) \in (\underline{C},\bar{C})$. Let hats refer to the dotted trajectory and stars to the trajectory corresponding to $C(0) = \bar{C}$. For $t \leqq a$,

$\hat{K} > K^*$ and therefore

$$-F'(\hat{K}) + \mu + \rho > -F'(K^*) + \mu + \rho,$$

implying that $\eta(\hat{C})\dot{\hat{C}}/\hat{C} > \eta(C^*)\dot{C}^*/C^*$. Furthermore

$$\dot{\hat{K}}(a) = F(\hat{K}(a)) - \mu\hat{K}(a) - \hat{C}(a) \leq 0,$$

$$\dot{K}^*(a) = F(K^*(a)) - \mu K^*(a) - C^*(a) > 0,$$

and therefore $\hat{C}(a) > C^*(a)$. Since $\hat{C}(0) < C^*(0)$, there must have been an instant of time, say v, where both rates of consumption were equal and, at that instant of time, $\hat{C}$ was growing more rapidly that C^*. It follows from (A9) that

$$\eta(C^*(v))(\dot{\hat{C}}(v)/\hat{C}(v) - \dot{C}^*(v)/C^*(v)) = F'(K^*(v)) - F'(\hat{K}(v)) > 0.$$

But this contradicts $\eta(\hat{C})\dot{\hat{C}}/\hat{C} > \eta(C^*)\dot{C}^*/C^*$.
We conclude that, for $C(0) \in (\underline{C},\bar{C})$, the K trajectory reaches K_T after instant of time b. Since the uniqueness of the solutions rules out that K-trajectories intersect, the statement is proved.

The relevance for chapter 3 is now immediate. Look at figure A2. If the objective is to reach K_T from the right within some given period of time, then, if this period is long, the initial rate of consumption should be chosen close to $\underline{C}$. The fastest way to reach K_T from the right is to choose the initial rate of consumption equal to $\bar{C}$.
For different constellations of K_0, K_T and $K_{\rho+\mu}$ similar conclusions hold. The formal argument will not be given here.

APPENDIX B. OPTIMAL CONTROL THEOREMS

In this monograph frequent use is made of optimal control theory. This appendix provides a non-rigorous treatment of the major theorems invoked in the preceding chapters. No proofs will be given. For a neat and advanced approach we refer to Hestenes (1966), Kirsch et al. (1978), Lee and Markus (1967), Luenberger (1969) and Pontryagin et al. (1962).

We study a system during a given period of time. The time variable is denoted by t. The initial instant of time is denoted by 0 and the final time is T, which is supposed to be fixed. The state of the system at each instant of time is characterized by n real numbers $x = (x_1, x_2, \ldots, x_n)$. The variables x_i are called the *state variables*. In the problems we consider in this monograph, the system is an economy, which at each instant of time is characterized by its stock of capital, the size of the natural resource and possibly the number of bonds, held or issued. The motion of the system is caused by three factors. Firstly, time itself may be of influence. Here one can think of the autonomous decay of the stock of capital. Also the state variables may have an impact on the motion of the system: bond holdings increase, ceteris paribus, the number of bond holdings in view of the interest earned. Finally, the system can be controlled. The time-path of the resource stock, for example, is affected by the rate of extraction, and the stock of capital is governed (amongst others) by the rate of consumption. Such variables are called *control variables*. In the models discussed these are the rates of consumption and exploitation, non-resource production and the inputs of capital in the sectors of the economy (chapter 5). Let us assume that there are r control variables, denoted by $u = (u_1, u_2, \ldots, u_r)$. Obviously, there are restrictions on the range of u. The rate of extraction, for example, is restricted to nonnegative real numbers. The objective of the economy is to find controls, such that a certain target is maximized, in casu, social welfare. Thereby, it wishes that the state variables are continuous and that the controls are piece-wise continuous. For the sake of clarity we give a formal definition of the concept of piece-wise continuity. An r-vector valued function

$u: [0,T] \to R^r$ is piece-wise continuous if there exists a partition, $0 = t_o < t_1 < t_2 \ldots < t_p = T$, of $[0,T]$ and continuous functions u^i: $[t_{i-1}, t_i] \to R^r$, for $i = 1,2,\ldots,p$, such that $u(t) = u^i(t)$ $(t_{i-1} < t < t_i)$ for $i = 1,2,\ldots,p$. Alternatively, u is piece-wise continuous if u is continuous, except possibly at a finite number of points. At such points τ

$$\lim_{t \downarrow \tau} u(t) \text{ and } \lim_{t \uparrow \tau} u(t)$$

exist.

We can now proceed to formulate a theorem, due to Hestenes, giving necessary conditions for a rather general problem (see Takayama (1974 pp. 656-659)). The problem is to find a continuous function x(t) and a piece-wise continuous function u(t) maximizing

$$J_T: = \int_0^T f_o(x(t),u(t),t)dt, \tag{B.1}$$

subject to

$$\dot{x}_i(t) = f_i(x(t),u(t),t), \qquad i = 1,2,\ldots,n, \tag{B.2}$$

$$g_j(x(t),u(t),t) \geqq 0, \qquad j = 1,2,\ldots,m', \tag{B.3}$$

$$g_j(x(t),u(t),t) = 0, \qquad j = m'+1,\ m'+2,\ \ldots,m, \tag{B.4}$$

$$\int_0^T h_k(x(t),u(t),t)dt \geqq 0, \qquad k = 1,2,\ldots,l', \tag{B.5}$$

$$\int_0^T h_k(x(t),u(t),t)dt = 0, \qquad k = l'+1,\ l'+2,\ \ldots,l, \tag{B.6}$$

$$x_i(0) = x_i^o, \text{ given}, \qquad i = 1,2,\ldots,n, \tag{B.7}$$

$$x_i(T) = x_i^T, \text{ given}, \qquad i = 1,2,\ldots,n, \tag{B.8}$$

where f_o, f_i $(i = 1,2,\ldots,n)$, g_j $(j = 1,2,\ldots,m)$ and h_k $(k = 1,2,\ldots,l)$ are continuously differentiable in an open set of points, containing the (x,u,t) which satisfy (B.3) and (B.4). The set of points (x,u,t) satisfying (B.3) and (B.4), is denoted by X_o and will be called the set of admissible elements. It is furthermore assumed that the matrix

$$\begin{bmatrix} \frac{\partial g_1}{\partial u_1} & \frac{\partial g_1}{\partial u_2} & \cdots & \frac{\partial g_1}{\partial u_r} & g_1 & 0 & 0 & \cdots & 0 \\ \frac{\partial g_2}{\partial u_1} & \frac{\partial g_2}{\partial u_2} & \cdots & \frac{\partial g_2}{\partial u_r} & 0 & g_2 & 0 & \cdots & 0 \\ \vdots & \vdots & & \vdots & & & & & \\ \frac{\partial g_m}{\partial u_1} & \frac{\partial g_m}{\partial u_2} & \cdots & \frac{\partial g_m}{\partial u_r} & 0 & 0 & 0 & \cdots & g_m \end{bmatrix}$$

häs rank m for all admissible elements. Here we can remark that in the cases, dealt with in this monograph, this condition is always satisfied: our g functions are of very simple forms such as $u_1 \geqq 0$, $\bar{u} - u_1 \geqq 0$, where $\bar{u}$ is a given constant.

The theorem of Hestenes reads:

<u>Theorem B.1</u>

Suppose $\hat{z}(t) := \{\hat{x}(t), \hat{u}(t)\}$ is a solution of the problem posed above. Then there exist multipliers

$$\hat{p}_o,\ \hat{p}(t) = (\hat{p}_1(t), \hat{p}_2(t), \ldots, \hat{p}_n(t)),$$

$$\hat{q}(t) = (q_1(t), q_2(t), \ldots, \hat{q}_m(t))$$

$$\hat{\lambda} = (\hat{\lambda}_1, \hat{\lambda}_2, \ldots, \hat{\lambda}_k),$$

not vanishing simultaneously on $[0,T]$, and functions L and H defined as

$$H(x,u,t,p_o,p,\lambda) = p_o\, f_o(x,u,t) + \sum_{i=1}^{n} p_i\, f_i(x,u,t)$$

$$+ \sum_{k=1}^{l} \lambda_k\, h_k(x,u,t)\ ,$$

$$L(x,u,t,p_o,p,\lambda,q) = H(x,u,t,p_o,p,\lambda) + \sum_{j=1}^{m} q_j\, g_j(x,u,t),$$

such that the following holds:

i) $\hat{p}_o$, $\hat{\lambda}_k$, $k = 1,2,\ldots,l$, are constants. $\lambda_k \geq 0$, $k = 1,2,\ldots,l'$ and

$$\hat{\lambda}_k \int_0^T h_k(\hat{x}(t),\hat{u}(t),t)dt = 0, \qquad k = 1,2,\ldots,l.$$

ii) $\hat{p}_i(t)$, $i = 1,2,\ldots,n$, is continuous and is piece-wise smooth (meaning that $p_i(t)$ can be written as

$$p_i(t) = A + \int_0^t y(\tau)\, d\tau,$$

where $y(t)$ is piece-wise continuous and A is a constant).

iii) $\hat{q}_j(t)$, $j = 1,2,\ldots,m$, is continuous, except possibly at points of discontinuity of $\hat{u}(t)$. For each j, $1 \leq j \leq m'$, we have

$$\hat{q}_j(t) \geq 0, \quad \hat{q}_j(t)\ g_j(\hat{x}(t),\hat{u}(t),t) = 0,$$

iv) $\dot{\hat{x}}_i(t) = \partial\hat{L}/\partial p_i$, $\dot{\hat{p}}_i(t) = -\partial\hat{L}/\partial x_i$, $i = 1,2,\ldots,n$.

$$\partial\hat{L}/\partial u_i = 0, \quad i = 1,2,\ldots,r,$$

where $\partial\hat{L}/\partial p_i$ is the derivative of L with respect to p_i, evaluated at $(\hat{x}, \hat{u}, \hat{p}_o, \hat{p}, \hat{\lambda}, \hat{q})$ and the meaning of $-\partial\hat{L}/\partial x_i$ and $\partial\hat{L}/\partial u_i$ is analogous. Moreover, $\hat{L}$ is continuous on $[0,T]$, and

$$d\hat{L}/dt = \partial\hat{L}/\partial t$$

on each interval of continuity of $\hat{u}$,

v) $H(\hat{x}(t),\hat{u}(t),t, \hat{p}_o,\hat{p}(t),\hat{\lambda}) \geq H(\hat{x}(t),u(t),t,\hat{p}_o,\hat{p}(t),\hat{\lambda})$,

for all admissible $u(t)$. □

Some remarks are in order.

1) L is called the Lagrangean, H is called the Hamiltonian.

2) The nature of the problems we consider is such that $\hat{p}_o$ is necessarily a positive constant. The proof of this statement is not

given here. We refer to Takayama (1974, p. 618). In the main text $\hat{p}_o$ is given the value 1.

3) In the text of chapters 3, 4 and 5 we shall not always explicitly mention conditions such as

$$\hat{\lambda}_k \int_0^T h_k \, (\hat{x}(t), \hat{u}(t), t)dt = 0.$$

4) If L is a concave function of u, then $\partial\hat{L}/\partial u = 0$ implies condition v. In the problems we encounter, L is indeed concave in u, so condition v will not be referred to.

5) The necessary condition $d\hat{L}/dt = \partial\hat{L}/\partial t$ is trivially satisfied in our models.

6) In the main text we are concerned with control problems with an infinite horizon ($T = \infty$). It has been shown by Halkin (1974) that in that case the necessary conditions given still apply for the optimality criterion used in the main text. For $T = \infty$, obviously, no terminal conditions are imposed.

Theorem B.1 is sufficient to deal with the problems we encounter in chapters 3 and 5. In chapter 4 we face a constraint of the type $x(t) \geqq 0$. Then theorem B.1 cannot be used, since there it is assumed that the g-constraints contain u. There is however a theorem by Guinn (1965), dealing with bounded state variables, which can be invoked. We paraphrase Long and Vousden (1977, pp. 20-23) for the case $x_1(t) \geqq 0$. We introduce $g_{m+1}(x(t),u(t),t) := f_1(x(t),u(t),t)$. Suppose $\hat{x}_1(t) > 0$ for $t_o \leqq t < \tau$, for some t_o and τ, and $\hat{x}_1(t) = 0$ for $\tau \leqq t \leqq t_1$ for some t_1, then τ is called a junction time. In this simple case the rank conditions are satisfied. Then, necessary conditions for optimality can be stated as follows.

<u>Theorem B.2</u>

Suppose $\hat{z}(t) := \{\hat{x}(t), \hat{u}(t)\}$ is a solution of the problem posed above. Define the Hamiltonian as in theorem B.1. Define the Lagrangean also as in theorem B.1, with one term added, namely

$$q_{m+1} \, f_1 \, (x,u,t) \, .$$

Then the conditions i) - v) of theorem B.1 hold with the following modifications.

ii) $\hat{p}_i(t)$, $i = 1,2,\ldots,n$, is continuous except possibly at junction times τ, where discontinuities in $\hat{p}_i(t)$ are of the form

$$\hat{p}_i(\tau+) = \hat{p}_i(\tau-) - w ,$$

where w is a constant.

iii) $\hat{q}_j(t)$, $j = 1,2,\ldots,m+1$, is continuous, except possibly at points of discontinuity of $\hat{u}(t)$ and at junction times. For each j, $1 \leqq j \leqq m'$, we have

$$\hat{q}_j(t) \geqq 0, \; \hat{q}_j(t)\; g_j(\hat{x}(t),\hat{u}(t),t) = 0,$$

$$\hat{q}_{m+1}(t) = 0 \text{ when } \hat{x}_1(t) > 0 ,$$

$\dot{\hat{q}}_{m+1}(t)$ is a non-positive function with the same continuity properties as $\hat{u}(t)$.

iv) $\hat{H}$ may not be continuous at junction times. □

Finally, there is the problem of existence of optimal programs. For this we refer to Cesari (1966). For the models we use, existence proofs are given on an ad hoc basis.

In chapter 4, section 4, the following model is analysed. Maximize

$$J := \int_0^\infty e^{-\rho t}\, U(C(t))dt \tag{C.1}$$

subject to

$$\int_0^\infty E(t)dt \leqq S_o , \tag{C.2}$$

$$E(t) \geqq 0 , \tag{C.3}$$

$$\bar{E} - E(t) \geqq 0 , \tag{C.4}$$

$$C(t) \geqq 0 , \tag{C.5}$$

$$\int_0^\infty e^{-rt}\, p_c(t)\, C(t)dt \leqq \int_0^\infty e^{-rt}\, p_e(t)\, E(t)dt + \int_0^\infty e^{-rt}\, r\, B_o dt, \tag{C.6}$$

$$\dot{B}(t) = r\, B(t) + p_e(t)\, E(t) - p_c(t)\, C(t),\; B(0) = B_o , \tag{C.7}$$

$$B(t) \geqq \bar{B} , \tag{C.8}$$

where $p_c(t) = p_c(0)\, e^{\pi t}$, $p_e(t) = p_e(0)\, e^{\gamma t}$. ρ, r, π and γ are given positive constants, S_o, $p_c(0)$, $p_e(0)$ and $\bar{E}$ are given positive constants. $\bar{B}$ is a given negative constant, B_o is given and $B_o > \bar{B}$. The function U is of the type $U(C) = \frac{1}{1+\eta}\, C^{1+\eta}$ with η a negative constant. In this appendix we derive the necessary conditions for optimality given in chapter 4 and we show that a transition from the so-called regime II to the so-called regime I is ruled out for the case $\gamma > r$. When deriving the necessary conditions for optimality, we must use theorem B.2, since (C.8) indicates that here we have a problem with a bounded state variable. It is convenient to write the model in the standard format (B.1) - (B.8). Therefore, we define: $x(t) := B(t) - \bar{B}$, $u_1(t) := C(t)$, $u_2(t) := E(t)$,

$$f_o(x(t),u(t),t) := e^{-\rho t}\, U(u_1(t)),$$

$$f_1(x(t),u(t),t) := r\,x(t) + p_e(t)\,u_2(t) - p_c(t)\,u_1(t) + r\,\bar{B},$$

$$g_1(x(t),u(t),t) := u_2(t),$$

$$g_2(x(t),u(t),t) := \bar{E} - u_2(t),$$

$$g_3(x(t),u(t),t) := u_1(t),$$

$$g_4(x(t),u(t),t) := r\,x(t) + p_e(t)\,u_2(t) - p_c(t)\,u_1(t) + r\bar{B},$$

$$h_1(x(t),u(t),t) := b\,S_o\,e^{-bt} - u_2(t),$$

$$h_2(x(t),u(t),t) := e^{-rt}\,(p_e(t)\,u_2(t) + r\,B_o - p_c(t)\,u_1(t)),$$

$$x(0) := B_o - \bar{B}\,,$$

where b is a positive constant.
The Hamiltonian of the problem is

$$H(x,u,t,p_1,\lambda_1,\lambda_2) = f_o(x,u,t) + p_1 f_1(x,u,t) +$$

$$\lambda_1\,h_1(x,u,t) + \lambda_2\,h_2(x,u,t)\;.$$

The Lagrangean is

$$L(x,u,t,p_1,\lambda_1,\lambda_2,q_1,q_2,q_3,q_4) = H(x,u,t,p_1,\lambda_1,\lambda_2) +$$

$$\sum_{j=1}^{4} q_j\,g_j(x,u,t)\;.$$

Let $\{\hat{x}(t),\ \hat{u}_1(t),\ \hat{u}_2(t)\}$ be the solution of the problem posed. Then, according to theorem B.2, there exist multipliers $\hat{p}_1(t)$, $\hat{q}_1(t)$, $\hat{q}_2(t)$, $\hat{q}_3(t)$, $\hat{q}_4(t)$, $\hat{\lambda}_1$, $\hat{\lambda}_2$, such that:

i) $\hat{\lambda}_1$ and $\hat{\lambda}_2$ are non-negative constants and

$$\hat{\lambda}_1 \int_0^{\infty} (b\,e^{-bt}\,S_o - u_2(t))dt = 0\;, \qquad (C.9)$$

$$\hat{\lambda}_2 \int_0^\infty e^{-rt} (p_e(t)\ \hat{u}_2(t) + r\ B_o - p_c(t)\ \hat{u}_1(t))dt = 0\ . \qquad (C.10)$$

ii) $\hat{p}_1(t)$ is continuous, except possibly at junction times, and is piece-wise smooth,

$$-\dot{\hat{p}}_1(t) = \partial\hat{L}/\partial x: \ -\dot{\hat{p}}_1(t) = r(\hat{p}_1(t) + \hat{q}_4(t)).$$

iii) $\hat{q}_1(t)$, $\hat{q}_2(t)$, $\hat{q}_3(t)$ and $\hat{q}_4(t)$ are continuous, except possibly at points of discontinuity of $\hat{u}(t)$ and at junction times. Furthermore

$$\hat{q}_1(t)\ \hat{u}_2(t) = 0,\ \hat{q}_1(t) \geqq 0,$$

$$\hat{q}_2(t)\ (\bar{E} - \hat{u}_2(t)) = 0,\ \hat{q}_2(t) \geqq 0,$$

$$\hat{q}_3(t)\hat{u}_1(t) = 0,\ \hat{q}_3(t) \geqq 0,$$

$$\hat{q}_4(t) = 0 \text{ when } \hat{x}(t) > 0.$$

$$\dot{\hat{q}}_4(t) \leqq 0.$$

iv) $$\partial\hat{L}/\partial u_1 = 0 : e^{-\rho t}\ U'(\hat{u}_1(t)) - \hat{p}_1(t)\ p_c(t) - \hat{q}_4(t)\ p_c(t) - \hat{\lambda}_2\ e^{-rt}\ p_c(t) + \hat{q}_3(t) = 0\ ,$$

$$\partial\hat{L}/\partial u_2 = 0 : \hat{p}_1(t)\ p_e(t) + \hat{q}_1(t) - \hat{q}_2(t) + \hat{q}_4(t)\ p_e(t) - \hat{\lambda}_1 + \hat{\lambda}_2\ e^{-rt}\ p_e(t) = 0\ .$$

Since $U'(0) = \infty$, $\hat{C}(t) > 0$ for all t; hence $\hat{q}_3(t) = 0$ for all t. Define $\hat{\phi}(t) := \hat{p}_1(t) + \hat{q}_4(t)$, $\hat{\alpha}(t) := \hat{q}_1(t)$, $\hat{\beta}(t) := \hat{q}_2(t)$, $\hat{\lambda} := \hat{\lambda}_1$, $\hat{\mu} := \hat{\lambda}_2$ and $\hat{\kappa}(t) := -\dot{\hat{q}}_4$. Then we have

$$e^{-\rho t}\ U'(\hat{C}(t)) = \hat{\phi}(t)\ p_c(t) + \hat{\mu}\ p_c(t)\ e^{-rt}\ , \qquad (C.11)$$

$$\hat{\mu}\ p_e(t)\ e^{-rt} + \hat{\phi}(t)\ p_e(t) + \hat{\alpha}(t) - \hat{\beta}(t) = \hat{\lambda}\ , \qquad (C.12)$$

$$-\dot{\hat{\phi}}(t) = r\hat{\phi}(t) + \hat{\kappa}(t)\ , \qquad (C.13)$$

$$\hat{\alpha}(t)\ \hat{E}(t) = 0,\ \hat{\alpha}(t) \geqq 0\ , \tag{C.14}$$

$$\hat{\beta}(t)\ (\bar{E} - \hat{E}(t)) = 0,\ \hat{\beta}(t) \geqq 0\ , \tag{C.15}$$

$$\hat{\kappa}(t)\ (\hat{B}(t) - \bar{B}) = 0\ ,\quad \hat{\kappa}(t) \geqq 0\ , \tag{C.16}$$

$$\hat{\mu}[\int_0^\infty e^{-rt}\ (P_e(t)\ \hat{E}(t) + rB_o - p_c(t)\ \hat{C}(t))dt] = 0\ , \tag{C.17}$$

where $\hat{\alpha}(t)$, $\hat{\beta}(t)$, $\hat{\phi}(t)$ and $\hat{\kappa}(t)$ are continuous, except possibly at points of discontinuity of $\hat{C}(t)$ and $\hat{E}(t)$, and at junction times. (C.11) - (C.17) is the set of necessary conditions we work with in chapter 4, section 4.

The second purpose of this appendix is to show that a transition from a regime with $\hat{B} > \bar{B}$ and $\hat{E} = \bar{E}$ to a regime with $\hat{B} > \bar{B}$ and $\hat{E} = 0$ is ruled out. Suppose the contrary and assume that, for $a \leqq t < b$, we have $\hat{B}(t) > \bar{B}$ and $\hat{E}(t) = \bar{E}$, and, for $b \leqq t \leqq c$, $\hat{B}(t) > \bar{B}$ and $\hat{E}(t) = 0$. It follows from (C.16) that $\hat{\kappa}(t) = 0$ for $a \leqq t \leqq c$. Hence along this interval $\dot{\hat{\phi}}/\hat{\phi} = -r$. For $a \leqq t < b$, $\hat{\alpha}(t) = 0$ (C.14) and $\hat{\beta}(t)$ is increasing. At time b the rate of exploitation jumps downwards. Hence $\hat{\beta}(t)$ jumps downwards and in view of (C.12), $\hat{\phi}(t)$ jumps downwards, implying that $\hat{C}(t)$ jumps upwards. Hence a typical $\hat{C}$ trajectory looks as in figure C.1.

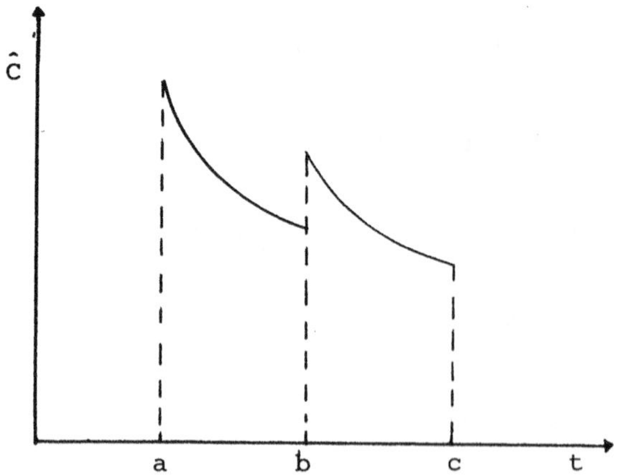

figure C1.

We shall now construct a program with the following properties: the rate of consumption equals the "optimal" rate of consumption; it uses the same amount of the resource and the amount of bonds the economy holds at time c is larger than in the optimal program. Therefore, the alternative program is to be preferred to the optimal program and a contradiction is obtained.

The construction is as follows. Firstly, take the intervals [a,b] and [b,c] of equal length. Let starred variables refer to the alternative program. $E^*(t) = 0$, $C^*(t) = \hat{C}(t)$, for $a \leqq t < b$, and $E^*(t) = \bar{E}$, $C^*(t) = \hat{C}(t)$ for $b \leqq t \leqq c$. For $\hat{B} > \bar{B}$ we have $\dot{\hat{C}}/\hat{C} + \dot{p}_c/p_c = \psi + r$, where $\psi = (\rho - (r-\pi)(1+\eta))/\eta$. This can be seen from (C.12) - (C.17). Hence for $a \leqq t \leqq b$:

$$\dot{\hat{B}}(t) = r\hat{B}(t) + p_e(0)\ \bar{E}\ e^{\gamma t} - p_c(a)\ \hat{C}(a+)\ e^{(\psi+r)(t-a)}.$$

Solving this differential equation yields

$$\hat{B}(t) = e^{rt}[V\ e^{(\gamma-r)a}\{e^{(\gamma-r)(t-a)}-1\} - \frac{p_c(a)\ \hat{C}(a+)}{\psi}\ e^{-ra}\{e^{\psi(t-a)}-1\}$$

$$+ e^{-ra}B_a]\ ,\quad a \leqq t \leqq b\ , \tag{C.18}$$

where $V := p_e(0)\ \bar{E}/(\gamma-r)$.

For $B^*(t)$ we obtain in an analogous way:

$$B^*(t) = e^{rt}[-\frac{p_c(a)\ \hat{C}(a+)}{\psi}\ e^{-ra}\{e^{\psi(t-a)}-1\} + e^{-ra}\ B_a]\ ,$$

$$a \leqq t \leqq b\ .$$

Hence

$$\hat{B}(b) - B^*(b) = e^{rb}[V\ e^{(\gamma-r)a}\{e^{(\gamma-r)(b-a)}-1\}]\ . \tag{C.19}$$

For $b \leqq t \leqq c$ we have:

$$\hat{B}(t) = e^{rt}[-\frac{p_c(b)\ \hat{C}(b+)}{\psi}\ e^{-rb}\{e^{\psi(t-b)}-1\} + e^{-rb}\ \hat{B}(b)]\ ,$$

$$B^*(t) = e^{rt}[V\ e^{(\gamma-r)b}\{e^{(\gamma-r)(t-b)}-1\} - \frac{p_c(b)\ \hat{C}(b+)}{\psi}\ e^{-rb}\{e^{\psi(t-b)}-1\}$$

$$+ e^{-rb}\ B^*(b)]\ .$$

Hence

$$\hat{B}(c) - B^*(c) = e^{rc}[-V\, e^{(\gamma-r)b}\{e^{(\gamma-r)(c-b)}-1\} + e^{-rb}(\hat{B}(b)-B^*(b))]$$

$$= e^{rc}\, V\, \{-e^{(\gamma-r)c} + e^{(\gamma-r)b} + e^{(\gamma-r)b} - e^{(\gamma-r)a}\}$$

$$< 0 ,$$

since $\gamma - r > 0$. Now it has to be proved that $B^*(t) > \bar{B}$ for $a \leqq t \leqq c$. In order to see this, first remark that, since $\hat{B}(b) > \bar{B}$, we can, by a proper choice of (b-a), take care that $B^*(b) > \bar{B}$. It then follows that for $a \leqq t \leqq b$, $B^*(t) > \bar{B}$. Suppose this were not the case. Then $B^*(t)$ would be increasing for some interval of time, where $B^*(t) < 0$. This contradicts

$$\dot{B}^*(t) = rB^*(t) - p_c(t)\,\hat{C}(t) ,$$

which is negative for $B^*(t) < 0$. Next it is shown that, also by a proper choice of (c-b) (and hence b-a), the condition that $B^*(t) > \bar{B}$ for $b \leqq t \leqq c$, is satisfied.
For $b \leqq t \leqq c$ we have:

$$g(t) := \hat{B}(t) - B^*(t) = e^{rt}[e^{-rb}(\hat{B}(b)-B^*(b)) - V(e^{(\gamma-r)t}-e^{(\gamma-r)b})]$$

$$= e^{rt}[V(e^{(\gamma-r)b}-e^{(\gamma-r)a}) - V(e^{(\gamma-r)t}-e^{(\gamma-r)b})]$$

$$= e^{rt}\, V\, e^{(\gamma-r)b}[1-e^{(\gamma-r)(a-b)} - e^{(\gamma-r)(t-b)} + 1] ,$$

hence

$$\dot{g}(t) := \dot{\hat{B}}(t)-\dot{B}^*(t) = r\, e^{rt}\, V\, e^{(\gamma-r)b}[1-e^{(\gamma-r)(a-b)}-e^{(\gamma-r)(t-b)}+1]$$

$$+ e^{rt}\, V\, e^{(\gamma-r)b}\, [(\gamma-r)\, e^{(\gamma-r)(t-b)}]$$

$$= e^{rt}\, V\, e^{(\gamma-r)b}[r-re^{(\gamma-r)(a-b)}-re^{(\gamma-r)(t-b)}$$

$$+ r - \gamma e^{(\gamma-r)(t-b)} + re^{(\gamma-r)(t-b)}]$$

$$= r\, e^{rt}\, V\, e^{(\gamma-r)b}[1-e^{(\gamma-r)(a-b)}- \frac{\gamma}{r}\, e^{(\gamma-r)(t-b)}+1].$$

Since $\gamma > r$, we can choose b-a (and therefore c-b) such that $g'(t) < 0$ for $b \leqq t \leqq c$. Then also $g''(t) < 0$ in that interval. Now, see figure C.2.

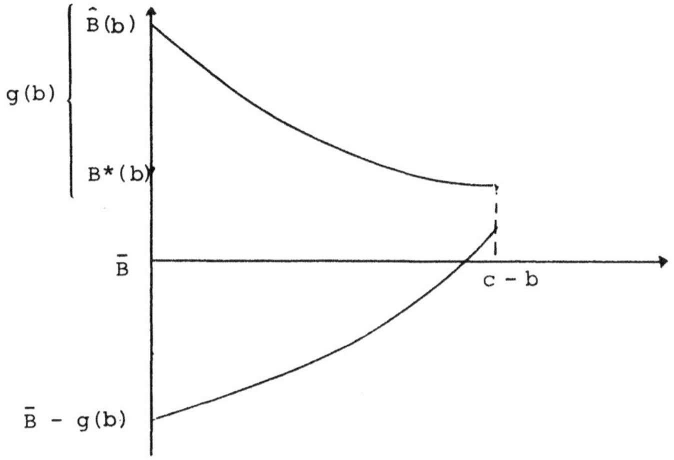

figure C2.

The time path of $\hat{B}(t)$ for $t \geqq b$ is given. By taking c-b small enough, we can take care that $B^*(t) > \bar{B}$, for $b \leqq t \leqq c$.

REFERENCES

Aarrestad, J. (1978): "Optimal savings and exhaustible resource extraction in an open economy," Journal of Economic Theory, vol. 19, pp. 163-179.

Aarrestad, J. (1979): "Resource extraction, financial transactions and consumption in an open economy," Skandinavian Journal of Economics, vol. 81, pp. 552-565.

Arrow, K.J. (1968): "Applications of control theory to economic growth," in Mathematics of the decision sciences, G.D. Dantzig and A.F. Keinott (eds.), Providence R.I., American Mathematical Society, pp. 85-120.

Arrow, K.J. and Kurz, M. (1968): Public investment, the rate of return and optimal fiscal policy, Baltimore, John Hopkins.

Cass, D. (1965): "Optimum growth in an aggregate model of capital accumulation," Review of Economic Studies, vol. 32, pp. 233-240.

Cass, D. (1966): "Optimum growth in an aggregative model of capital accumulation: a turnpike theorem," Econometrica, vol. 34, pp 833-850.

Cesari, L. (1966): "Existence theorems for weak and usual optimal solutions in Lagrange problems with unilateral constraints - I," American Mathematical Society, Transactions 124, pp. 369-412.

Chakravarty, S. (1962): "The existence of an optimum savings program," Econometrica, vol. 30, pp. 178-187.

Chiarella, C. (1980): "Trade between resource-poor and resource-rich economies as a differential game," in Exhaustible Resources, Optimality and Trade, M.C. Kemp and N.V. Long (eds.), Amsterdam, North-Holland, pp. 219-246.

Chichilnisky, G. (1982): "Resources and North-South trade; a macro-analysis in open economies," paper presented at the European Meeting of the Econometric Society, Dublin, 1982.

Crabbé, P.J. (1982): "Resources and types of uncertainty; information and controling in stochastic economic models of non-renewable resources," in Optimal Control Theory and Economic Applications, G. Feichtinger (ed.), Amsterdam, North-Holland, pp. 189-208.

Cremer, J. and Weitzman, N. (1976): "Opec and the monopoly price of world oil," European Economic Review, vol. 8, pp. 155-164.

Dasgupta, P. and Heal, G. (1979): Economic theory and exhaustible resources, Welwyn, James Nisbet and Co ltd.
Dasgupta, P., Eastwood, R. and Heal, G. (1978): "Resource management in a trading economy," Quarterly Journal of Economics, vol. 92, pp. 297-306.
Diewert, W., (1982 a): "Duality approaches to microeconomic theory," in Handbook of mathematical economics, K. Arrow and M. Intriligator (eds), Amsterdam, North-Holland, pp. 535-599.
Diewert, W.E. (1982b): Duality theory in economics, Amsterdam, North-Holland.
Elbers, C. and Withagen, C. (1982): "The optimal exploitation of natural resources when conversion is necessary," Report AE 12/82, Faculty of Actuarial Science and Econometrics, University of Amsterdam, Amsterdam.
Elbers, C. and Withagen, C. (1984): "Trading in exhaustible resources in the presence of conversion costs, a general equilibrium approach," Journal of Economic Dynamics and Control, vol. 8, pp. 197-209.
Forrester, J.W. (1971): World Dynamics, Cambridge, Wright Allen Press.
N.V. Nederlandse Gasunie (1984): Plan of sales of natural gas (in Dutch), Groningen, N.V. Nederlandse Gasunie.
Gilbert, R.J. (1978): "Dominant firm pricing policy in a market for an exhaustible resource," Bell Journal of Economics, vol. 9, pp. 384-395.
Gray, L.C. (1914): "Rent under the assumption of exhaustibility," Quarterly Journal of Economics, vol. 28 , pp. 466-489.
Guinn, T. (1965): "The problem of bounded space coordinates as a problem of Hestenes," Journal of S.I.A.M. Control, vol. 3, pp. 181-190.
Halkin, H. (1974): "Necessary conditions for optimal control problems with infinite horizons," Econometrica, vol. 42, pp. 267-272.
Harris, H. (1978): "Trade and depletable resources: the small open economy," Discussion Paper 289, Dept. of Economics, Queen's University, Kingston, Canada.
Harris, H. (1981): "Trade and depletable resources: the small open economy," Canadian Journal of Economics, vol. 14, pp. 649-664.
Heal, G. (1976): "The relation between price and extraction cost for

a resource with a backstop technology," Bell Journal of Economics, vol. 7, p. 371-378.

Herfindahl, O.C. (1955): "Some fundamentals of mineral economics," Land Economics, vol. 31, pp. 131-138.

Hestenes, M.R. (1966): Calculus of variations and optimal control theory, New York, Wiley.

Hotelling, H. (1931): "The economics of exhaustible resources," Journal of Political Economy, vol. 39, pp. 137-175.

Inada, K. (1964): "On a two-sector model of economic growth: comments and a generalization," Review of Economic Studies, vol 30, pp. 119-127.

Jevons, W.S. (1865): The coal question, London, MacMillan.

Kay, J.A. and Mirrlees, J.A. (1975): "The desirability of natural resource depletion," in The economics of natural resource depletion, D.W. Pearce and J. Rose (eds.), London, The MacMillan Press. pp. 140-176.

Kemp, M.C. and Long, N.V. (1979): "International trade with an exhaustible resource: a theorem of Rybczinsky type," International Economic Review, vol. 20, pp. 671-677.

Kemp, M.C. and Long, N.V. (1980 a): "Exhaustible resources and the Stolper-Samuelson-Rybczinsky theorems," in Exhaustible Resources, Optimality and Trade, M.C. Kemp and N.V. Long (eds.), Amsterdam, North-Holland, pp. 179-182.

Kemp, M.C. and Long, N.V. (1980 b): "Exhaustible resources and the Heckscher-Ohlin theorem," in Exhaustible Resources, Optimality and Trade, M.C. Kemp and N.V. Long (eds.), Amsterdam, North-Holland, pp. 183-186.

Kemp, M.C. and Long, N.V. (1980 c): "The interaction of resource-rich and resource-poor economies," in Exhaustible Resources, Optimality and Trade, M.C. Kemp and N.V. Long (eds.), Amsterdam, North-Holland, pp. 197-210.

Kemp, M.C. and Ohyama, M. (1978): "On the sharing of trade gains by resource-poor and resource-rich countries," Journal of International Economics, vol. 8, pp. 93-115.

Kemp, M.C. and Suzuki, H. (1975): "International trade with a wasting but possibly replenishable resource," International Economic Review, vol. 16, pp. 712-728.

Kirsch, A., Warth, W. and Werner, J. (1978): Notwendige

optimalitätsbedingungen und ihre Anwendung, Berlin, Springer.
Koopmans, T.C. (1957): Three essays on the state of economic science, New York, McGraw-Hill.
Koopmans, T.C. (1965): "On the concept of optimal economic growth," The econometric approach to development planning, Pontificiae Academiae Scientiarium Scriptum Varia, Amsterdam, North-Holland, pp. 225-287.
Koopmans, T.C. (1967): "Objectives, constraints and outcomes in optimal growth models," Econometrica, vol. 35, pp. 1-15.
Lawrence, C. and Levy, V. (1980): "On sharing the gains from international trade: an asymmetrical model with mobility of capital and natural resources," Research Report 133, Dept. of Economics, The Hebrew University, Jerusalem.
Lee, E.B. and Markus, L. (1967): Foundations of optimal control theory, New York, Wiley.
Lewis, T.R. and Schmalensee, R. (1980 a): "Cartel and oligopoly pricing of non-replenishable natural resources," in Dynamic optimization and applications to economics, P.T. Liu (ed.), New York, Plenum Press, pp. 133-156.
Lewis, T.R. and Schmalensee, R. (1980 b): "On oligopolistic markets for non-renewable natural resources," Quarterly Journal of Economics, vol. 95, pp. 475-491.
Long, N.V. (1974): "International borrowing for resource extraction," International Economic Review, vol. 15, pp. 168-183.
Long, N.V. (1977): "Optimal exploitation and replenishment of a natural resource," in Applications of control theory to economic analysis, J.D. Pitchford and S.J. Turnovsky (eds.), Amsterdam, North-Holland, pp. 81-106.
Long, N.V. and Vousden, N. (1977): "Optimal control theorems," in Applications of control theory to economic analysis, J.D. Pitchford and S.J. Turnovsky (eds.), Amsterdam, North-Holland, pp. 11-34.
Luenberger, D.G. (1969): Optimization by vector space methods, New York, Wiley.
Mirrlees, J. (1967): "Optimal growth when technology is changing," Review of Economic Studies, vol. 34, pp. 25-50.
Newbery, D. (1981): "Oil prices, cartels, and the problem of dynamic inconsistency," Economic Journal, vol. 91, pp. 617-646.
Nordhaus, W. (1975): "The demand for energy: an international

perspective," in Proceedings of the IIASA Workshop on Energy Demand, W. Nordhaus (ed.), IIASA, Laxenburg, pp. 511-587.

Peterson, F.D. and Fisher, A.C. (1977): "The exploitation of extractive resources, a survey," The Economic Journal, vol. 87, pp. 681-721.

Pindyck, R.S. (1978): "Gains to producers from cartelization of exhaustible resources," Review of Economics and Statistics, vol. 60, pp. 238-251.

Pontryagin, L.S. et al. (1962): The mathematical theory of optimal processes, New York, Interscience.

Prebish, R. (1959): "Commercial policy in underdeveloped countries," American Economic Review, vol. 49, pp. 251-264.

Ramsey, F.P. (1928): "A mathematical theory of saving," Economic Journal, vol. 38, pp. 543-559.

Ruys, P. (1974): Public goods and decentralization, Rotterdam, Tilburg University Press.

Salant, W.S. (1976): "Exhaustible resources and industrial structure: a Nash-Cournot approach to the world oil market," Journal of Political Economy, vol. 84, pp. 1079-1093.

Shell, K. (1967): "Optimal programs of capital accumulation for an economy in which there is exogenous technical change," in Essays on the theory of optimal economic growth, K. Shell (ed.), Cambridge Mass., M.I.T. Press, pp. 1-30.

Singer, H.W. (1950): "The distribution of gains between investing and borrowing countries," American Economic Review, vol. 40, pp. 473-489.

Sociaal-Economische Raad (1983): Advice on natural gas policy (in Dutch), 's-Gravenhage, Sociaal-Economische Raad.

Solow, R.M. and Wan, F.Y. (1976): "Extraction costs in the theory of exhaustible resources," Bell Journal of Economics, vol. 7, pp. 359-370.

Stiglitz, J. (1976): "Monopoly and the rate of extraction of exhaustible resources," American Economic Review, vol. 66, pp. 655-661.

Stuurgroep Maatschappelijke Discussie Energiebeleid (1983): Final report on the public debate (in Dutch), Leiden, Stenfert Kroese B.V.

Suzuki, H. and Ogawa, M. (1979): "International trade with exhaustible natural resources," Zeitschrift für Nationalökonomie,

vol. 39, pp. 131-142.
Takayama, A. (1974): Mathematical Economics, Hinsdale, Illinois, The Dryden Press.
Ulph, A.M. (1982): "Modeling partially cartelised markets for exhaustible resources," in Economic Theory of Natural Resources, W. Eichhorn et al. (eds.), Würzburg, Physica Verlag, pp. 269-291.
Ulph, A.M. and Folie, G.M. (1977): "A dominant firm model of resource depletion," C.R.E.S. working paper R/W.P. 13, Australian National University, Canberra.
Ulph, A.M. and Folie, G.M. (1980 a): "Exhaustible resources and cartels: an intertemporal Nash-Cournot model," Canadian Journal of Economics, vol. 13, pp. 645-658.
Ulph, A.M. and Folie, G.M. (1980 b): "Dominant firm models of resource depletion," Paper presented to A.U.T.E. conference, Durham.
Uzawa, H. (1961): "On a two-sector model of economic growth," Review of Economic Studies, vol. 29, pp. 40-49.
Vousden, N. (1974): "International trade and exhaustible resources, a theoretical model," International Economic Review, vol. 15, pp. 149-167.
Wan, H.Y. (1971): Economic growth, New York, Harcourt Brace Jovanovich.
Weddepohl, H. (1970): Axiomatic choice models and duality, Rotterdam, Tilburg University Press.
Weizsäcker, C.C. von (1965): "Existence of optimal programs of accumulation for an infinite time horizon," Review of Economic Studies, vol. 32, pp. 85-114.
Withagen, C. (1981 a): "The optimal exploitation of natural resources, a survey," De Economist, vol. 129, pp. 504-531.
Withagen, C. (1981 b): "Optimal foreign borrowing, varying prices and natural resources," Report AE 11/81, Faculty of Actuarial Science and Econometrics, University of Amsterdam, Amsterdam.
Withagen, C. (1981 c): "Note on the optimality of competitive exploitation of natural resources," Report AE 10/81, Faculty of Actuarial Science and Econometrics, University of Amsterdam, Amsterdam.
Withagen, C (1982): "The exploitation of Dutch natural gas, an alternative approach," De Economist, vol. 130, pp. 71-100.
Withagen, C. (1983 a): "Reply to 'The exploitation of our natural

gas'," De Economist, vol. 131, pp. 92-93.
Withagen, C. (1983 b): "The optimal exploitation of a natural resource when there is full complementarity," Journal of Economic Dynamics and Control, vol. 6, pp. 239-252.
Wolff, P. de (1964): "Economic aspects of natural gas," (in Dutch), Reprint 91, The Hague, Central Planning Bureau.
Zimmerman, M. (1977): "Modeling depletion in a mineral industry: the case of coal," Bell Journal of Economics, vol. 8, pp. 41-65.

157: Optimization and Operations Research. Proceedings 1977. ted by R. Henn, B. Korte, and W. Oettli. VI, 270 pages. 1978.

158: L. J. Cherene, Set Valued Dynamical Systems and Economic w. VIII, 83 pages. 1978.

. 159: Some Aspects of the Foundations of General Equilibrium ory: The Posthumous Papers of Peter J. Kalman. Edited by J. Green. 67 pages. 1978.

. 160: Integer Programming and Related Areas. A Classified liography. Edited by D. Hausmann. XIV, 314 pages. 1978.

. 161: M. J. Beckmann, Rank in Organizations. VIII, 164 pages. 1978.

. 162: Recent Developments in Variable Structure Systems, Economics and Biology. Proceedings 1977. Edited by R. R. Mohler and Ruberti. VI, 326 pages. 1978.

163: G. Fandel, Optimale Entscheidungen in Organisationen. 43 Seiten. 1979.

. 164: C. L. Hwang and A. S. M. Masud, Multiple Objective Deion Making – Methods and Applications. A State-of-the-Art Survey. 351 pages. 1979.

. 165: A. Maravall, Identification in Dynamic Shock-Error Models. , 158 pages. 1979.

l. 166: R. Cuninghame-Green, Minimax Algebra. XI, 258 pages. 79.

l. 167: M. Faber, Introduction to Modern Austrian Capital Theory. 196 pages. 1979.

l. 168: Convex Analysis and Mathematical Economics. Proceedings 78. Edited by J. Kriens. V, 136 pages. 1979.

l. 169: A. Rapoport et al., Coalition Formation by Sophisticated ayers. VII, 170 pages. 1979.

l. 170: A. E. Roth, Axiomatic Models of Bargaining. V, 121 pages. 79.

l. 171: G. F. Newell, Approximate Behavior of Tandem Queues. XI, 0 pages. 1979.

ol. 172: K. Neumann and U. Steinhardt, GERT Networks and the me-Oriented Evaluation of Projects. 268 pages. 1979.

ol. 173: S. Erlander, Optimal Spatial Interaction and the Gravity odel. VII, 107 pages. 1980.

ol. 174: Extremal Methods and Systems Analysis. Edited by A. V. acco and K. O. Kortanek. XI, 545 pages. 1980.

ol. 175: S. K. Srinivasan and R. Subramanian, Probabilistic Analysis Redundant Systems. VII, 356 pages. 1980.

ol. 176: R. Färe, Laws of Diminishing Returns. VIII, 97 pages. 1980.

ol. 177: Multiple Criteria Decision Making-Theory and Application. roceedings, 1979. Edited by G. Fandel and T. Gal. XVI, 570 pages 980.

ol. 178: M. N. Bhattacharyya, Comparison of Box-Jenkins and Bonn onetary Model Prediction Performance. VII, 146 pages. 1980.

ol. 179: Recent Results in Stochastic Programming. Proceedings, 979. Edited by P. Kall and A. Prékopa. IX, 237 pages. 1980.

ol. 180: J. F. Brotchie, J. W. Dickey and R. Sharpe, TOPAZ – General lanning Technique and its Applications at the Regional, Urban, nd Facility Planning Levels. VII, 356 pages. 1980.

ol. 181: H. D. Sherali and C. M. Shetty, Optimization with Disjunctive Constraints. VIII, 156 pages. 1980.

ol. 182: J. Wolters, Stochastic Dynamic Properties of Linear Econometric Models. VIII, 154 pages. 1980.

ol. 183: K. Schittkowski, Nonlinear Programming Codes. VIII, 242 ages. 1980.

ol. 184: R. E. Burkard and U. Derigs, Assignment and Matching roblems: Solution Methods with FORTRAN-Programs. VIII, 148 ages. 1980.

Vol. 185: C. C. von Weizsäcker, Barriers to Entry. VI, 220 pages. 1980.

Vol. 186: Ch.-L. Hwang and K. Yoon, Multiple Attribute Decision Making – Methods and Applications. A State-of-the-Art-Survey. XI, 259 pages. 1981.

Vol. 187: W. Hock, K. Schittkowski, Test Examples for Nonlinear Programming Codes. V. 178 pages. 1981.

Vol. 188: D. Bös, Economic Theory of Public Enterprise. VII, 142 pages. 1981.

Vol. 189: A. P. Lüthi, Messung wirtschaftlicher Ungleichheit. IX, 287 pages. 1981.

Vol. 190: J. N. Morse, Organizations: Multiple Agents with Multiple Criteria. Proceedings, 1980. VI, 509 pages. 1981.

Vol. 191: H. R. Sneessens, Theory and Estimation of Macroeconomic Rationing Models. VII, 138 pages. 1981.

Vol. 192: H. J. Bierens: Robust Methods and Asymptotic Theory in Nonlinear Econometrics. IX, 198 pages. 1981.

Vol. 193: J. K. Sengupta, Optimal Decisions under Uncertainty. VII, 156 pages. 1981.

Vol. 194: R. W. Shephard, Cost and Production Functions. XI, 104 pages. 1981.

Vol. 195: H. W. Ursprung, Die elementare Katastrophentheorie. Eine Darstellung aus der Sicht der Ökonomie. VII, 332 pages. 1982.

Vol. 196: M. Nermuth, Information Structures in Economics. VIII, 236 pages. 1982.

Vol. 197: Integer Programming and Related Areas. A Classified Bibliography. 1978 – 1981. Edited by R. von Randow. XIV, 338 pages. 1982.

Vol. 198: P. Zweifel, Ein ökonomisches Modell des Arztverhaltens. XIX, 392 Seiten. 1982.

Vol. 199: Evaluating Mathematical Programming Techniques. Proceedings, 1981. Edited by J.M. Mulvey. XI, 379 pages. 1982.

Vol. 200: The Resource Sector in an Open Economy. Edited by H. Siebert. IX, 161 pages. 1984.

Vol. 201: P. M. C. de Boer, Price Effects in Input-Output-Relations: A Theoretical and Empirical Study for the Netherlands 1949–1967. X, 140 pages. 1982.

Vol. 202: U. Witt, J. Perske, SMS – A Program Package for Simulation and Gaming of Stochastic Market Processes and Learning Behavior. VII, 266 pages. 1982.

Vol. 203: Compilation of Input-Output Tables. Proceedings, 1981. Edited by J. V. Skolka. VII, 307 pages. 1982.

Vol. 204: K.C. Mosler, Entscheidungsregeln bei Risiko: Multivariate stochastische Dominanz. VII, 172 Seiten. 1982.

Vol. 205: R. Ramanathan, Introduction to the Theory of Economic Growth. IX, 347 pages. 1982.

Vol. 206: M.H. Karwan, V. Lotfi, J. Telgen, and S. Zionts, Redundancy in Mathematical Programming. VII, 286 pages. 1983.

Vol. 207: Y. Fujimori, Modern Analysis of Value Theory. X, 165 pages. 1982.

Vol. 208: Econometric Decision Models. Proceedings, 1981. Edited by J. Gruber. VI, 364 pages. 1983.

Vol. 209: Essays and Surveys on Multiple Criteria Decision Making. Proceedings, 1982. Edited by P. Hansen. VII, 441 pages. 1983.

Vol. 210: Technology, Organization and Economic Structure. Edited by R. Sato and M.J. Beckmann. VIII, 195 pages. 1983.

Vol. 211: P. van den Heuvel, The Stability of a Macroeconomic System with Quantity Constraints. VII, 169 pages. 1983.

Vol. 212: R. Sato and T. Nôno, Invariance Principles and the Structure of Technology. V, 94 pages. 1983.

Vol. 213: Aspiration Levels in Bargaining and Economic Decision Making. Proceedings, 1982. Edited by R. Tietz. VIII, 406 pages. 1983.

Vol. 214: M. Faber, H. Niemes und G. Stephan, Entropie, Umweltschutz und Rohstoffverbrauch. IX, 181 Seiten. 1983.

Vol. 215: Semi-Infinite Programming and Applications. Proceedings, 1981. Edited by A. V. Fiacco and K. O. Kortanek. XI, 322 pages. 1983.

Vol. 216: H. H. Müller, Fiscal Policies in a General Equilibrium Model with Persistent Unemployment. VI, 92 pages. 1983.

Vol. 217: Ch. Grootaert, The Relation Between Final Demand and Income Distribution. XIV, 105 pages. 1983.

Vol. 218: P. van Loon, A Dynamic Theory of the Firm: Production, Finance and Investment. VII, 191 pages. 1983.

Vol. 219: E. van Damme, Refinements of the Nash Equilibrium Concept. VI, 151 pages. 1983.

Vol. 220: M. Aoki, Notes on Economic Time Series Analysis: System Theoretic Perspectives. IX, 249 pages. 1983.

Vol. 221: S. Nakamura, An Inter-Industry Translog Model of Prices and Technical Change for the West German Economy. XIV, 290 pages. 1984.

Vol. 222: P. Meier, Energy Systems Analysis for Developing Countries. VI, 344 pages. 1984.

Vol. 223: W. Trockel, Market Demand. VIII, 205 pages. 1984.

Vol. 224: M. Kiy, Ein disaggregiertes Prognosesystem für die Bundesrepublik Deutschland. XVIII, 276 Seiten. 1984.

Vol. 225: T. R. von Ungern-Sternberg, Zur Analyse von Märkten mit unvollständiger Nachfragerinformation. IX, 125 Seiten. 1984

Vol. 226: Selected Topics in Operations Research and Mathematical Economics. Proceedings, 1983. Edited by G. Hammer and D. Pallaschke. IX, 478 pages. 1984.

Vol. 227: Risk and Capital. Proceedings, 1983. Edited by G. Bamberg and K. Spremann. VII, 306 pages. 1984.

Vol. 228: Nonlinear Models of Fluctuating Growth. Proceedings, 1983. Edited by R. M. Goodwin, M. Krüger and A. Vercelli. XVII, 277 pages. 1984.

Vol. 229: Interactive Decision Analysis. Proceedings, 1983. Edited by M. Grauer and A. P. Wierzbicki. VIII, 269 pages. 1984.

Vol. 230: Macro-Economic Planning with Conflicting Goals. Proceedings, 1982. Edited by M. Despontin, P. Nijkamp and J. Spronk. VI, 297 pages. 1984.

Vol. 231: G. F. Newell, The M/M/∞ Service System with Ranked Servers in Heavy Traffic. XI, 126 pages. 1984.

Vol. 232: L. Bauwens, Bayesian Full Information Analysis of Simultaneous Equation Models Using Integration by Monte Carlo. VI, 114 pages. 1984.

Vol. 233: G. Wagenhals, The World Copper Market. XI, 190 pages. 1984.

Vol. 234: B. C. Eaves, A Course in Triangulations for Solving Equations with Deformations. III, 302 pages. 1984.

Vol. 235: Stochastic Models in Reliability Theory. Proceedings, 1984. Edited by S. Osaki and Y. Hatoyama. VII, 212 pages. 1984.

Vol. 236: G. Gandolfo, P. C. Padoan, A Disequilibrium Model of Real and Financial Accumulation in an Open Economy. VI, 172 pages. 1984.

Vol. 237: Misspecification Analysis. Proceedings, 1983. Edited by T. K. Dijkstra. V, 129 pages. 1984.

Vol. 238: W. Domschke, A. Drexl, Location and Layout Planning. IV, 134 pages. 1985.

Vol. 239: Microeconomic Models of Housing Markets. Edit
K. Stahl. VII, 197 pages. 1985.

Vol. 240: Contributions to Operations Research. Proceedings,
Edited by K. Neumann and D. Pallaschke. V, 190 pages. 1985.

Vol. 241: U. Wittmann, Das Konzept rationaler Preiserwartu
XI, 310 Seiten. 1985.

Vol. 242: Decision Making with Multiple Objectives. Procee
1984. Edited by Y. Y. Haimes and V. Chankong. XI, 571 pages.

Vol. 243: Integer Programming and Related Areas. A Class
Bibliography 1981–1984. Edited by R. von Randow. XX, 386 pa
1985.

Vol. 244: Advances in Equilibrium Theory. Proceedings, 1984. E
by C. D. Aliprantis, O. Burkinshaw and N. J. Rothman. II, 235 pa
1985.

Vol. 245: J. E. M. Wilhelm, Arbitrage Theory. VII, 114 pages.

Vol. 246: P. W. Otter, Dynamic Feature Space Modelling, Filt
and Self-Tuning Control of Stochastic Systems. XIV, 177 pages.

Vol. 247: Optimization and Discrete Choice in Urban Syst
Proceedings, 1983. Edited by B. G. Hutchinson, P. Nijkamp
M. Batty. VI, 371 pages. 1985.

Vol. 248: Plural Rationality and Interactive Decision Processes.
ceedings, 1984. Edited by M. Grauer, M. Thompson and
Wierzbicki. VI, 354 pages. 1985.

Vol. 249: Spatial Price Equilibrium: Advances in Theory, Comput
and Application. Proceedings, 1984. Edited by P. T. Harker. VII,
pages. 1985.

Vol. 250: M. Roubens, Ph. Vincke, Preference Modelling.
94 pages. 1985.

Vol. 251: Input-Output Modeling. Proceedings, 1984. Edite
A. Smyshlyaev. VI, 261 pages. 1985.

Vol. 252: A. Birolini, On the Use of Stochastic Processes in Mod
Reliability Problems. VI, 105 pages. 1985.

Vol. 253: C. Withagen, Economic Theory and International Trad
Natural Exhaustible Resources. VI, 172 pages. 1985.

GPSR Compliance

The European Union's (EU) General Product Safety Regulation (GPSR) is a set of rules that requires consumer products to be safe and our obligations to ensure this.

If you have any concerns about our products, you can contact us on ProductSafety@springernature.com

In case Publisher is established outside the EU, the EU authorized representative is:

Springer Nature Customer Service Center GmbH
Europaplatz 3
69115 Heidelberg, Germany

Batch number: 10844829

Printed by Printforce, the Netherlands